SKETCHBOOK

CENTRAL COAST CALIFORNIA

STORIES, JOURNAL/COLORING BOOK
(A book you can make your own)

DEAMER DUNN

The Central Coast is not only one of the most beautiful regions in the world, it is stocked with diverse and interesting beings. From the cliffs and redwoods of Big Sur to the farmlands of Salinas, this is an inspiring and productive land. Join my journey within this special spot of the world by making this book your own.

ISBN-13: 978-1973803867

ISBN-10: 1973803860

Publisher: Createspace
Book Resellers:
https://www.createspace.com/pub/l/createspacedirect.do

Editor: Dani Cyrer

All Art by Deamer

First Addition
Pajaro Street Inc

Thanks, Appreciation & Disclosures

Most of my sketch victims were unaware that my camera, eye and pencil clad fingers had focused upon them. I thank all of them for being interesting and appeal to their forgiveness for the depictions they inspired. Inevitably, not only are my drawings stylized, they rarely are up to the task of showing any individuals finest beauty. Admirers pressed me to create these books more based on the feeling captured by my style than any individual representation. In other words, if you recognize yourself, hopefully you can enjoy the work with humor, especially if you are the subject of one of the accompanying fictional stories. For the most part, the tales I write for this series of sketchbooks are on individuals I know nothing of, beyond what I observed from drawing them. Consider these as bonus material for inspiring you to make this book your own.

All my Omar T novels are matched with a sketchbook. This book corresponds with Omar T in Monterey, A California, Central Coast story. In the tradition of a light-hearted contemporary mystery novel, enter the son of a restaurateur and an artist, Mr. Omar T Black. He is a jack-of-all-trades, master-of-none, with passions for women, food, adult beverages, art and adventure. Part travel book, part mystery, part literary reference, these stories are meant to be fun as well as culturally descriptive. Chef Omar enlightens readers to local cuisine with detailed descriptions and even recipes. Art and literature aficionado Omar is drawn to the mysteries of creativity and thought. Omar T the man falls in love, and/or lust, rather easily. All Omar T novels carry a guarantee of lifting your spirits as well as feeding your appetite for good food and great living! These Mystery "Lite" stories, concentrate on something intriguing, rather than violence. For a fun additional Central Coast Adventure, get yourself a copy of Omar T in Monterey. ENJOY!

Artist/Author Deamer Dunn
Author Web Site: http://artbz.bz
Amazon Author Page: https://www.amazon.com/author/deamerdunn
(Please pass on your impressions; write a review on Amazon and/or other sites)

YouTube Author/Artist Page (music videos of art & book sketches):
https://www.youtube.com/user/deamerdunn

I would love to hear from you: deamer@artbz.bz

As a Journal/Coloring Book:

Not only am I not opposed to you turning this book over to a child or the kid in you, I would find it endearing that these drawings would inspire you to play with adding color. My paintings and even my writing, often start with the black and white of a sketch. In case you haven't heard, coloring books for adults are becoming quite a passion. Perhaps our ever-complicated world and its demands on our attention are fueling this trend. I think that we all wish that we had more time for reading. For many, perhaps a little coloring can still feed a passion for getting into a book and more easily allow the satisfaction of finishing something. Why settle for a computer created coloring book when you can add life to images created as a celebration of human richness? Families could find this book as a source for good conversation. How we all interact with each other is not only interesting, discussing this could be educational.

Not only is this book designed to be fun as a coloring book, it is also laid out in a journal format. By leaving you a blank page with each drawing, the idea is you can add your own thoughts, ideas and images. Why settle for a blank book to keep track of life when you can associate your thoughts with an image—a sketch that you can also add your own color to? The idea is that this is a book that you can make your own.

ENJOY!

Index

IMAGES WITH STORIES:

IMAGES WITH BLANK PAGES FOR YOU:

Big Sur: Theo, The Henry Miller Library Cat

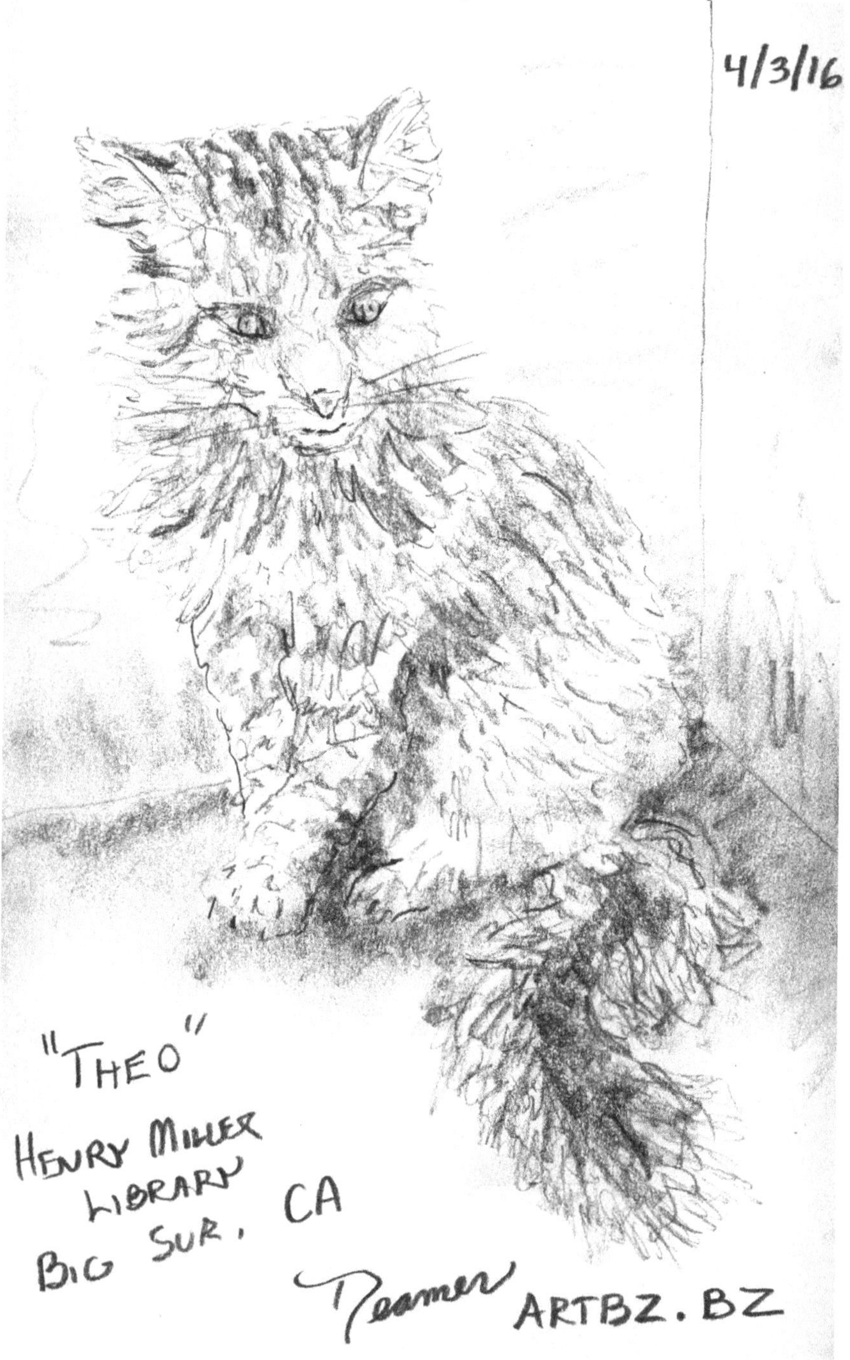

No, I don't know the words you humans use, but you really are not that hard to understand. I've only known the library as my home, so I'm rather used to you all coming and going. Some of you don't notice me, some of you ignore me, some of you try to talk to me, and there are those of you that can't keep your hands off me. I don't mind any which way really, life in the public is all I know. It was strange when the people stopped coming. Sure I have noticed that less people come when it rains, especially when it rains for days on end like it did this winter. Suddenly, there were no people coming to the library. At first, I just enjoyed the extra space, though there were days where I actually missed getting some extra attention. Not understanding people's words, I didn't know what all my people were talking about; I could tell that they were worried. How was I to understand that the heavy winter rains had so damaged a bridge that there was no longer access to or from where most of our visitors came from—and then a landslide... I did start to realize that it was more than just a problem happening with the library, my home. The locals who came by on a regular basis looked as worried as my people. Soon, many of them were no longer coming by. It seems that they had to move away. Then it started to get real personal. Those few who were left began to box up many of the books. I could understand that they were desperate, that they had to get our stuff someplace where people could get to it. But I couldn't understand why. Why was this special place suddenly isolated? Why wasn't anyone coming to visit anymore? Where did all of those regular visitors go, all of the friends of my friends? Will they empty the library? What will I do if it is empty? What will I do if no one comes to visit? What will they do with me? What will happen to me?

Salinas: 3 Women and a Pour House

Salinas is still a farm town. We are the capital of one of the richest counties in all of America. We have a downtown and we have a lot of the good and bad of bigger cities. Yet, our fields of produce, some of the most productive and valuable in the world, still surround the city and keep us with a certain rural quality, even though the city is also a regional center.

It often seems so random how we make friendships. It was very random how Joni, Melanie and I got to know each other. It seems like it was fate that we would not only get acquainted, but also that it was essential that we would become friends. Not that we are clones of each other, it is in fact our differences that seem to give some balance to our friendship. It is not just our hairstyles that are different. We each come from very different types of families and upbringings. Each of our romantic lives has also been quite different. Joni has a cat, I have a dog and Melanie has her hobbies. Some days, I think our furry friends and hobbies are the only things that keep us going. Life can seem complicated. When we were little girls it seemed like our inevitable future was to find a prince and live happy-ever-after. Then, as we got older, it seemed that all we ever heard was that we girls need to find our own way, take charge, find our inner passion, achieve! Under this scenario, love if found, is a byproduct, not the goal. It is all so confusing, but gives us girls plenty to talk about!

I guess you could say that Salinas with its regional importance but still small town feel, suffers from a similar battle with identity. The Farmer's Union Pour House is a great addition to our small town/capital city. You could say that it reflects our dual desires. It is as beautiful as any city bar, but its relaxed staff and country music fill the room with comfort. It is such a pleasure to go to a place that offers the joys of a selection of craft beers and local wines, instead of all the usual generic stuff. This is the kind of place supplies a platform for meeting interesting people, as well as giving us girls a place to laugh, flirt and solve some problems. Yay for us!!!

Santa Cruz and a Local Book Shop

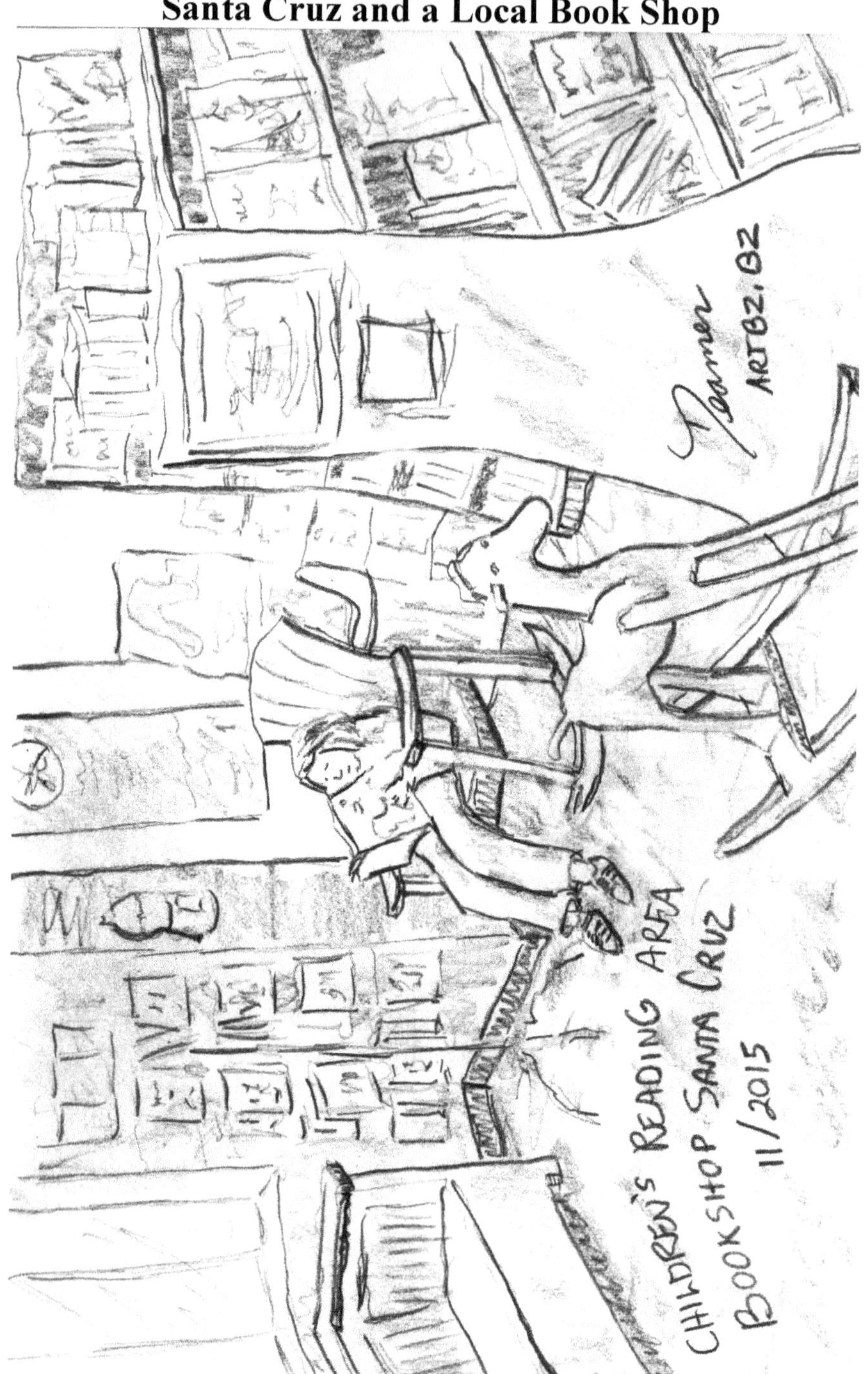

Apparently, my grandmother brought my mother to Bookshop Santa Cruz shortly after the store's opening in 1966. I also have memories of my mother bringing me to the bookstore when I was a little girl. I didn't mind Ma dragging me into town, as long as I was able to cuddle up with all of the children's books. She would leave me for hours while she danced about doing her errands. It is typical of Santa Cruz to be one of the few cities that has been able to retain a local bookshop, especially one that is thriving. Oh, we too had a moment of weakness after the 1989 Loma Prieta earthquake made a mess of our downtown. We put aside our anti-corporate culture long enough to allow some big guys to come in and influx our devastated town and economy with some desperately needed cash. This included bringing in the small business killer at the time, a Borders Books, to be an anchor of our revitalization. In some poetic justice, our Borders is now long gone and our local bookshop lives on. After all, we are still Santa Cruz, home to a plethora of forest forgers and the UC Santa Cruz banana slugs.

I bring my daughter to our bookshop now and put her on the same rocking horse that I played on as a child. In this day and age I don't ever leave her alone like my mother did me, but I feel the same warm friendliness with today's staff that I remember from the past. Apparently much of the country thinks that we our out of touch liberals. They believe that Santa Cruz is the epic center of the "left coast." I smile at such suggestions. I feel a great pride at how my community still fights for local businesses, regional foodstuffs and our environment. Even our homeless probably have more rights and opportunities than ordinary citizens in much the world. I wonder, who are the ones that are really out of touch? My apologies if you find me a bit preachy. I guess that is one of the things that I like about living here. Most folks like to speak and listen openly, even if someone has a different opinion. I don't want to give you the wrong impression; we are pretty laid back. Whether, surfing, sailing, dining out or enjoying a bookstore I think you will find that most people living and visiting Santa Cruz are relaxed, happy.

I can't predict my child's future, but I know that she will grow up in a community filled with diversity in thought and ideas. She is already getting a good taste of both of these, every time we come to downtown Santa Cruz and enjoy all the books in our local, thriving, bookstore.

Carmel: Morning Coffee and the Paper

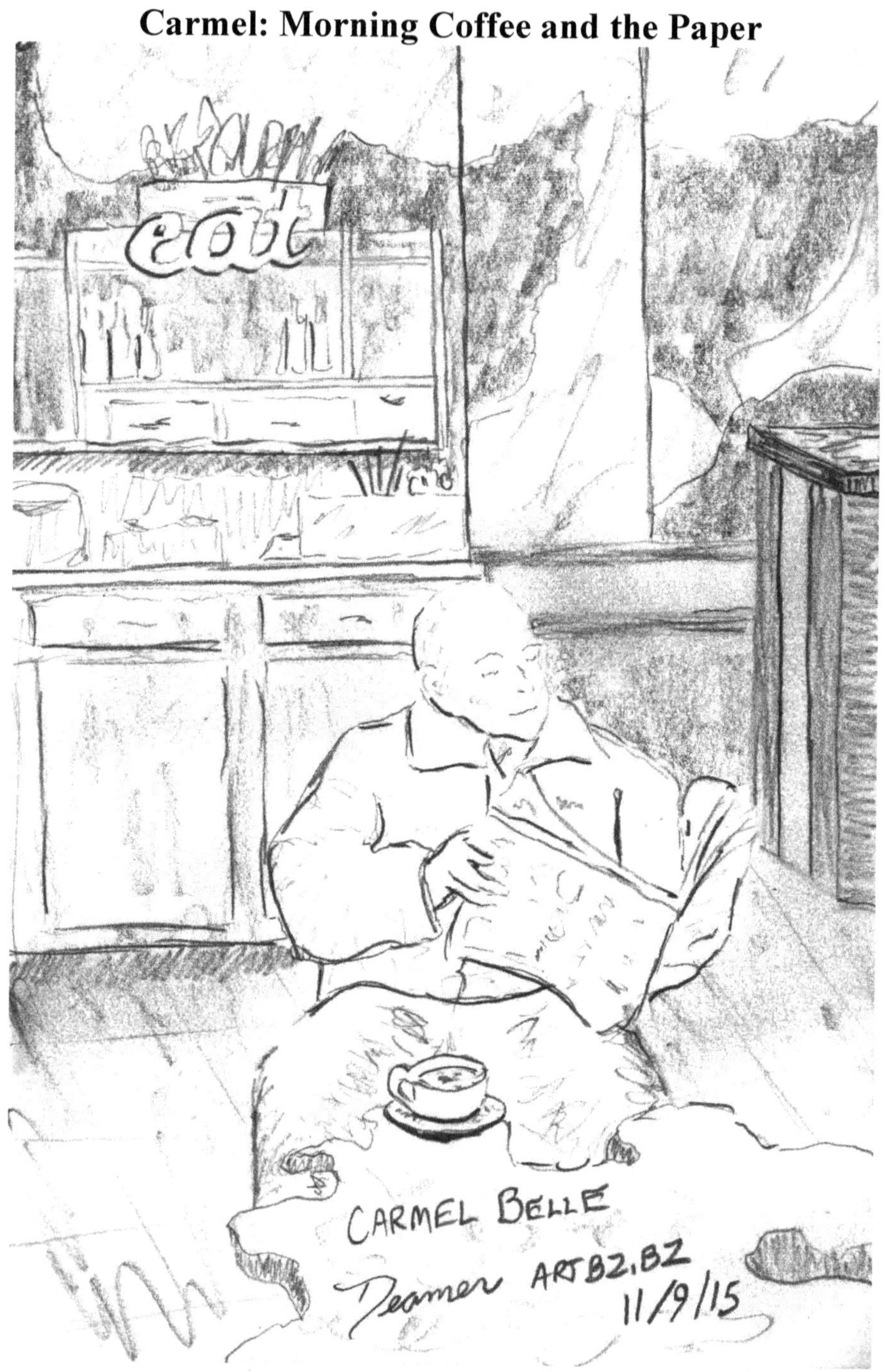

There is nothing like the morning paper and a cup of coffee. Like peas and their pod, a baby and its womb—comfort! I have made it a routine to walk into town for my coffee and paper reading—it's a way of assuring that I get out of the house. Yes, I feel blessed to live in Carmel-by-the-Sea. I'm sure, even if you have never been to the Central Coast of California, if you ever heard Carmel's full name, you would think it would have to be somewhere special. Indeed, we residents are rather the envy of the thousands of tourists who, on a daily basis, make their way to our little piece of paradise. Many are admirers of the European way of life, since we have been called the city most resembling an old European village, on this side of America. I do love walking the streets and hearing all the different languages being spoken by the locals and visitors alike. We do get many travelers who love dogs as well. We are considered one of the most dog friendly towns in the world. The variety of doggy water bowls outside of all of our businesses and all of the doggy treat menus, within our restaurants, are a great source of amusement and endearment. The fact that Clint Eastwood was once our mayor isn't as well known as in his film heyday, but such history of Clint and all of our other movie star residents and visitors is still a draw. Of course none of this compares with the simple staggering beauty that is this coastline and how it magnificently meets the ocean. The plethora of trees, all of the unique cottage style architecture and God's finest sea and land, is a beauty unsurpassed anywhere in the world. Forty years ago, my young wife and I decided that we had to visit this place yearly and that we would make every sacrifice to retire here. We both worked very hard and saved and managed our money so that we could make this simple dream come true. We kept to our yearly visits, hauling the kids with us as our family grew. It all worked out perfectly. First we bought the property; then we built the home. What we didn't plan for was for one of us to get sick. After a lot of thought of selling the home of our dreams, once retired, I decided to move in by myself. I still love Carmel as much as we both did. I guess you could say that I still feel like she is with me in everything I do here. The kids do come and visit but their lives are very complicated. Every time the phone rings, I expect them to be telling me what city or country they are moving to next. I have been thinking about getting a dog. At least, in this town, that guarantees you someone to dine with…

San Jose: I Wonder

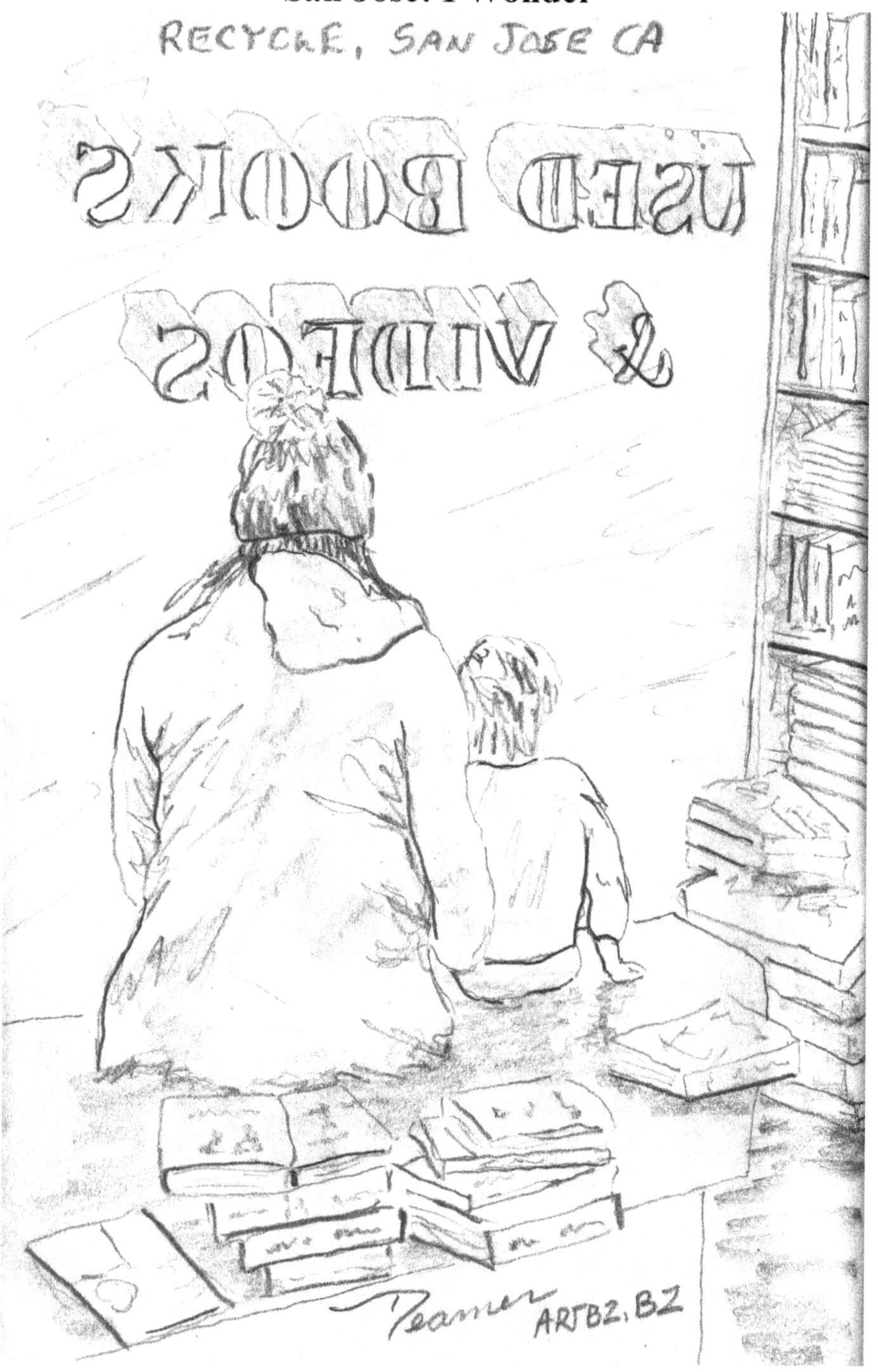

I wonder about just about everything. My mother tells me that I was a quiet child, that I kept most of my thoughts to myself. Lately, she has become vocal about my past because she says that my son Ryan is so much like me. I suppose she is right but I didn't see myself as being all that quiet. I did always love books, which in my case really stood out since neither my father nor mother were into reading. They preferred to have friends and neighbors over for cocktails or they would settle into their regular television shows. This was fine with me because it made it easy to retire to my room and read. I started reading to Ryan before he could really understand what I was reading. Most of all, I think he enjoyed the sound of my voice. Intuitively, I think that he knew that what I was doing was for him. It was also for me. Opening, handling and reading any book still feels special to me. Between my job, husband and Ryan it is hard if not impossible to find any quiet time for reading for myself. Ryan became interactive with me even before he started talking. He would reach out, point, grab a page— usually with a smile on his face. It was an easy transition for us to move from the oversized picture books into stories. The only conflict that we now have is that the stories don't put him to sleep so easily anymore. Instead, he wants me to read more and more. I guess I should start to encourage him to read more on his own. I'm not sure that I want him to do that without me. I've thought of bringing a book of my choice to his bed so that we could read our own books together. For now we have started going out to our local bookstore every Saturday. We, of course, spend most of our time in the children's section. I also take him around and show him books that I have read or would like to read. He seems to enjoy it, when I explain to him the stories that I've read or why I would want to read a particular book. Maybe the transition will be natural.

I miss that time when I had so much time to read. My parents seemed to have more leisure time than my husband and me. Dad worked for the same company all through his whole career. Mom worked too, but on and off, sometimes just part-time. It seems that everything costs too much for that to ever be an option for my husband and me. Not to mention that everything seems so complicated, there is just so much to manage. Oh, it is overwhelming to even think about it. For now, I will make sure that Ryan and I walk down to the bookstore every Saturday morning. Well, at least until that time that my son no longer wants to hang out with his mom…

16

HENRY
MILLER
LIBRARY
BIG SUR
CA
4/2016
ARTBZ. BZ

DEAMER DUNN

"MAGNUS"
HENRY MILLER LIBRARY
BIG SUR, CA
"DAVID"
"CHRIS"
ARTBZ.BZ
DAVID GESSNER "ALL THE WILD THAT REMAINS" 4/3/16
Reamer

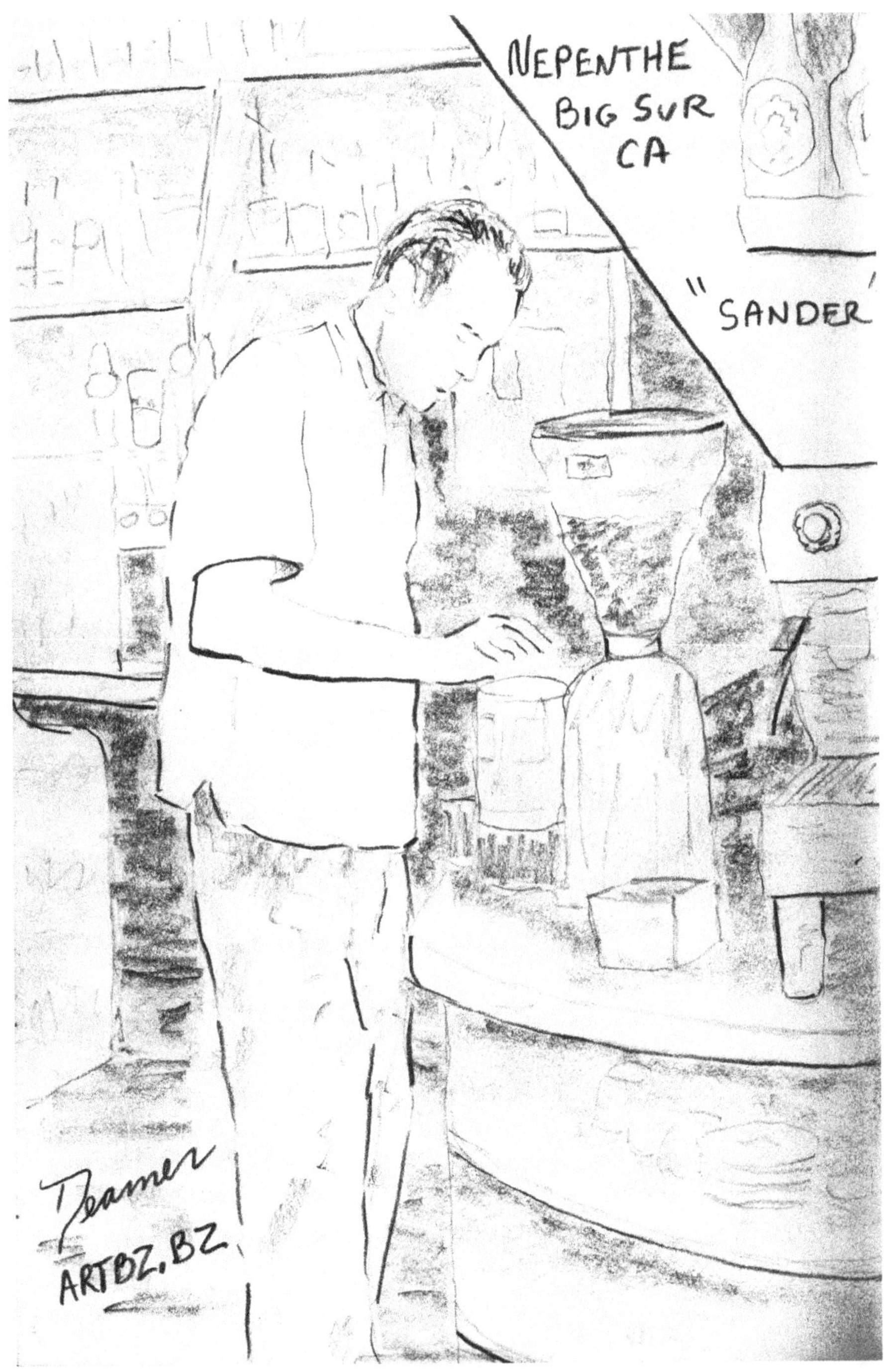

NEPENTHE
BIG SUR
CA
" SANDER
Beamer
ARTBZ.BZ

22

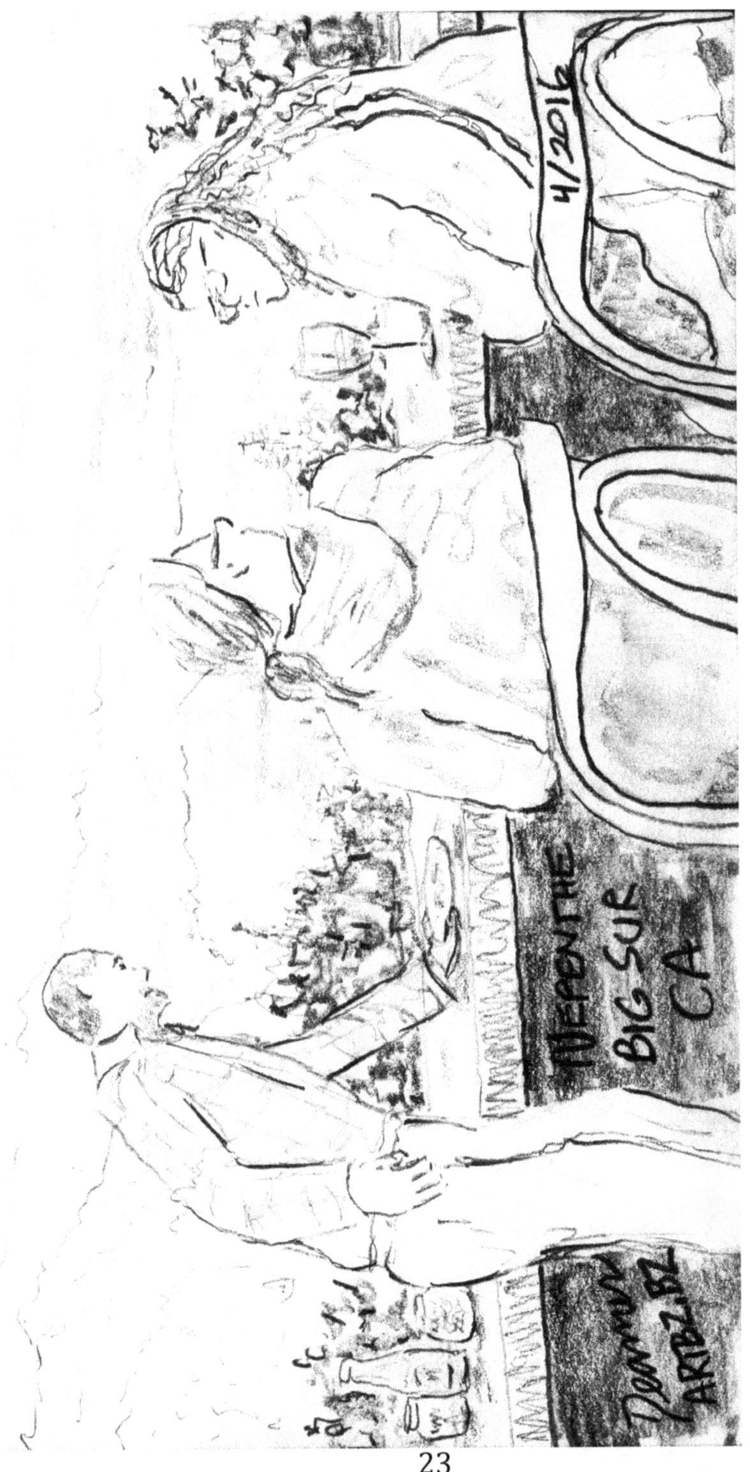

4/2016
BIG SUR
CA

DEAMER DUNN

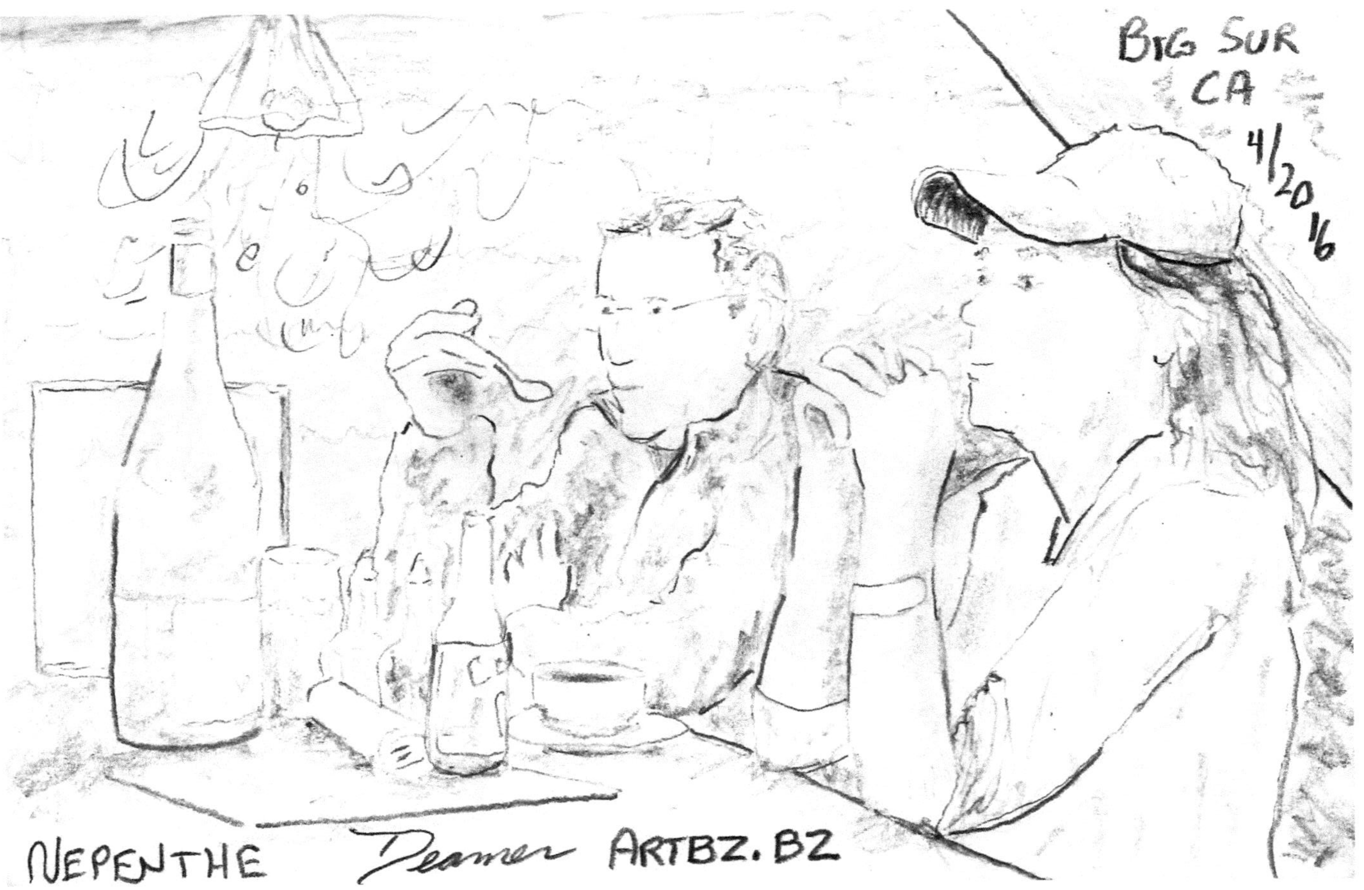

Big Sur
CA
4/20/16
NEPENTHE
Deamer ArtBz.bz

DEAMER DUNN

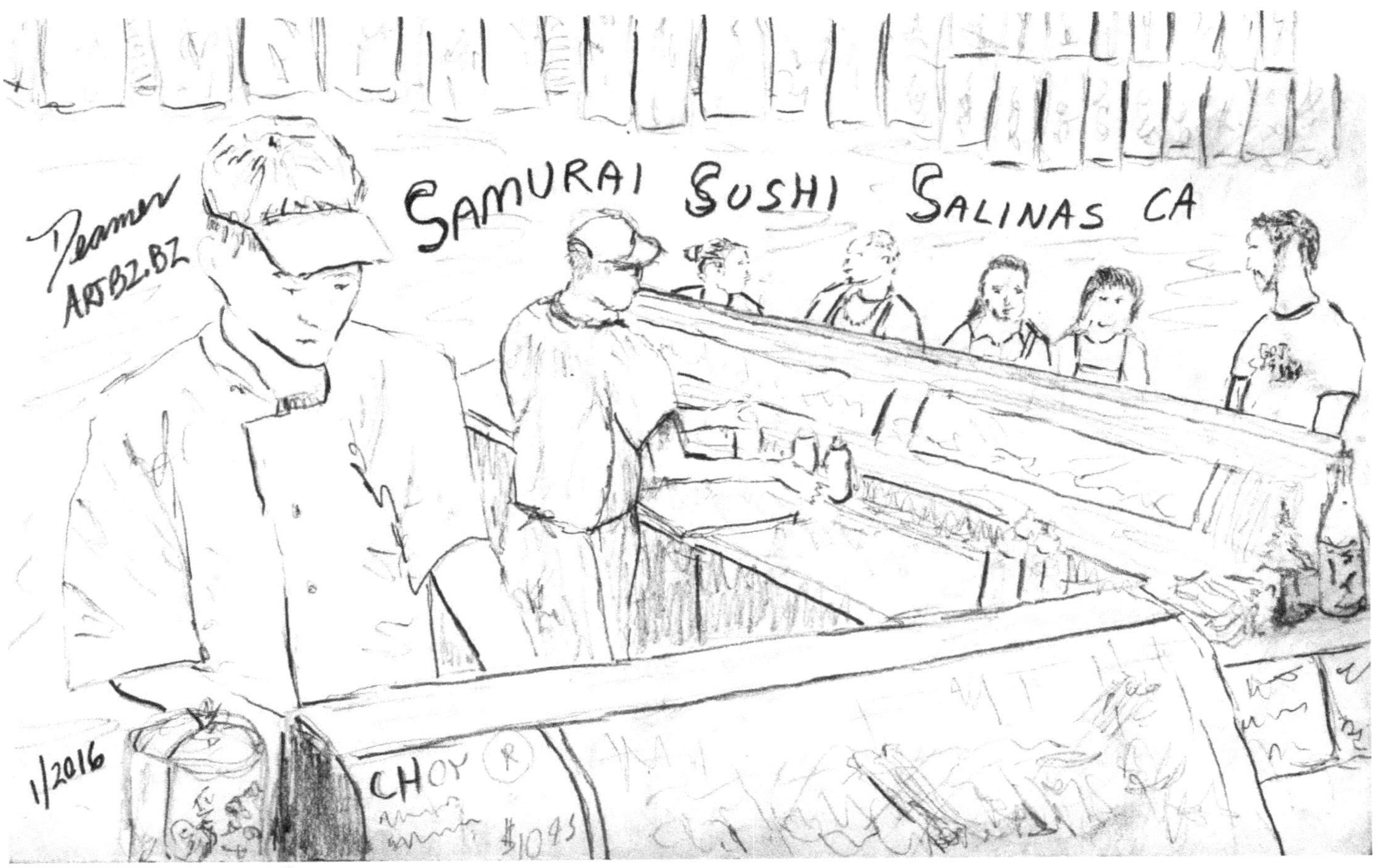
Deamer
ARTBZ.BZ
SAMURAI SUSHI   SALINAS CA
CHOY
$10.95
1/2016

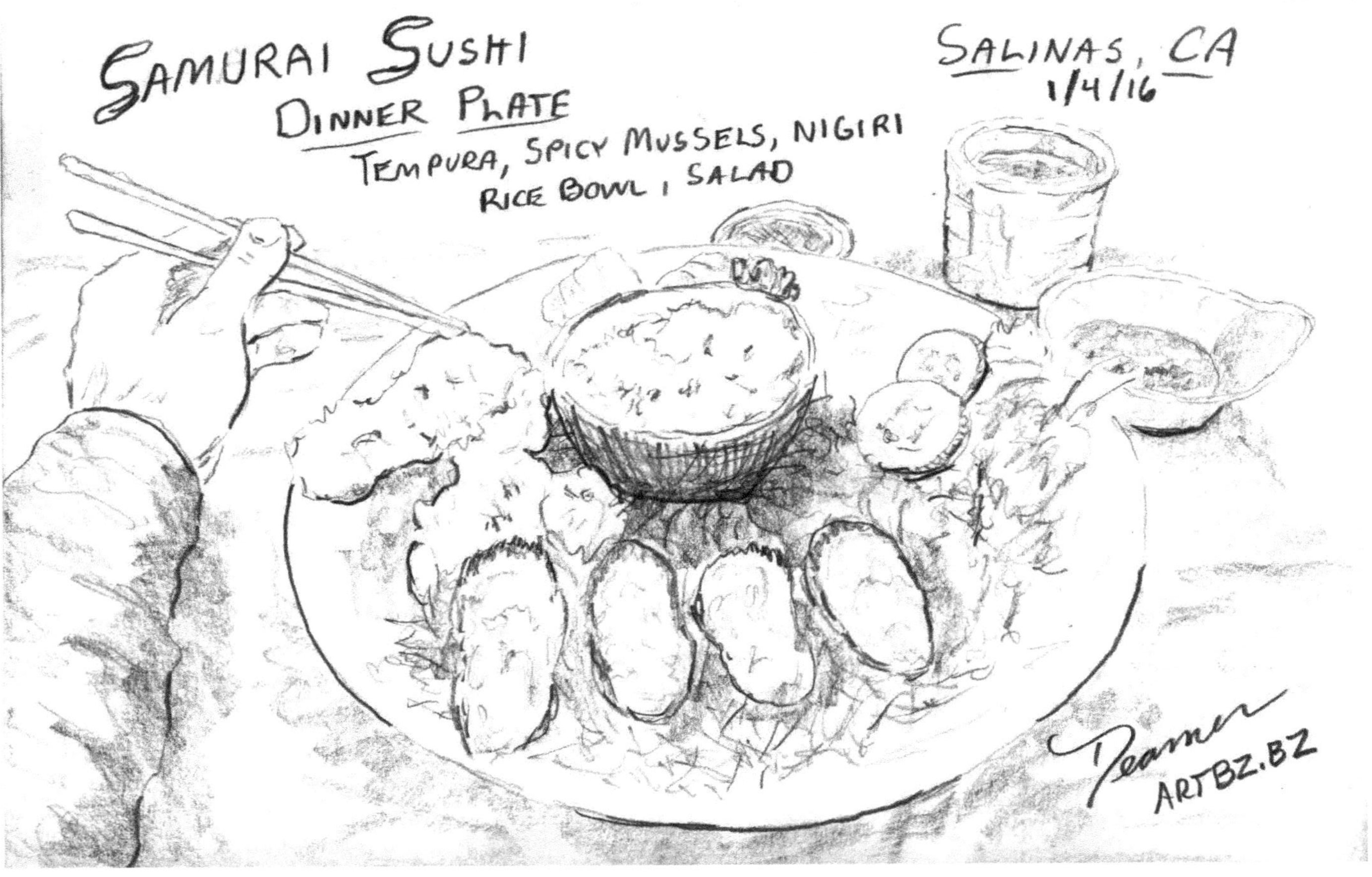
SAMURAI SUSHI
DINNER PLATE
TEMPURA, SPICY MUSSELS, NIGIRI
RICE BOWL, SALAD
SALINAS, CA
1/4/16
ARTBZ.BZ

30

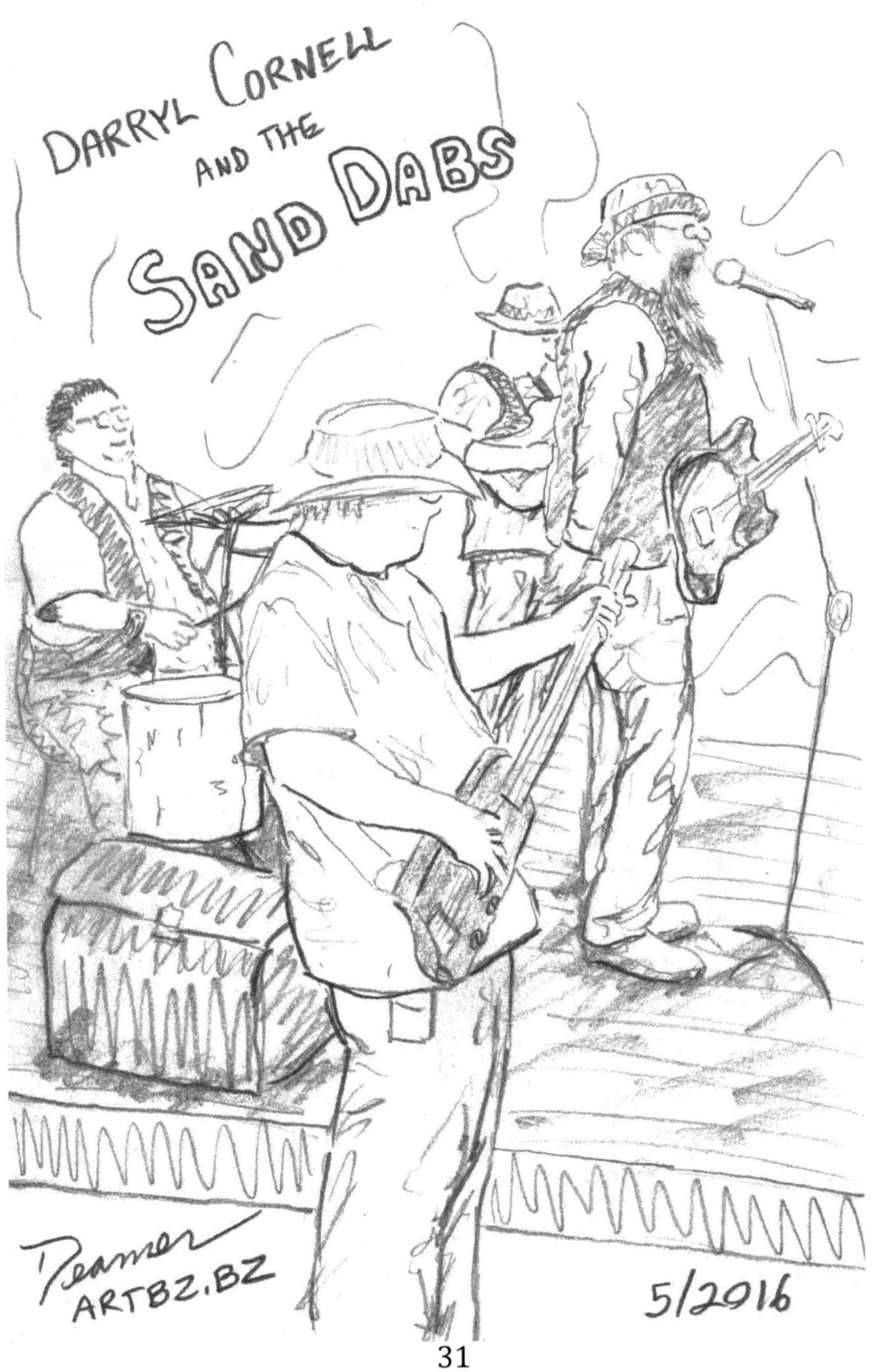
DARRYL CORNELL
AND THE
SAND DABS
ARTBZ.BZ
5/2016

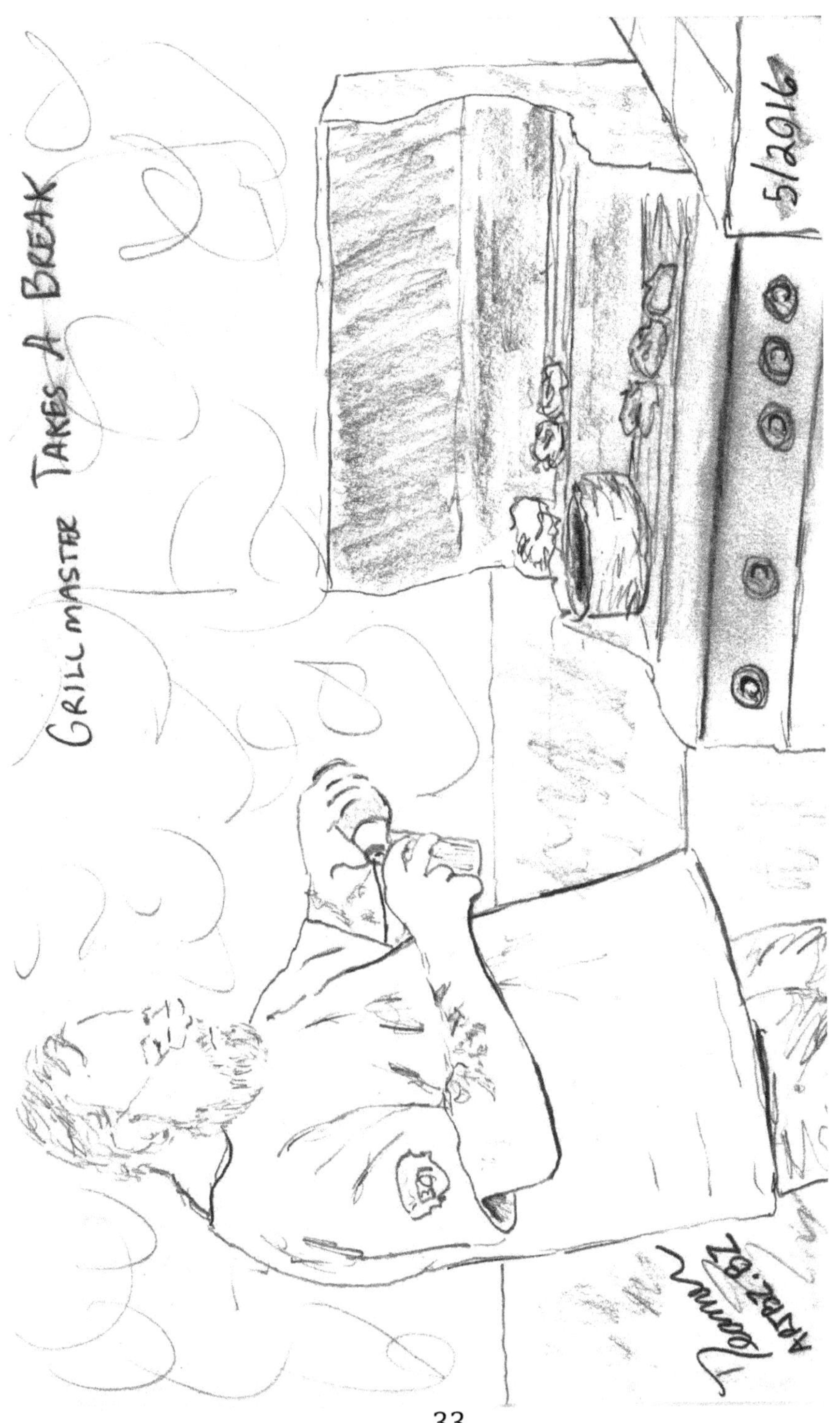
GRILL MASTER TAKES A BREAK
5/2016

DEAMER DUNN

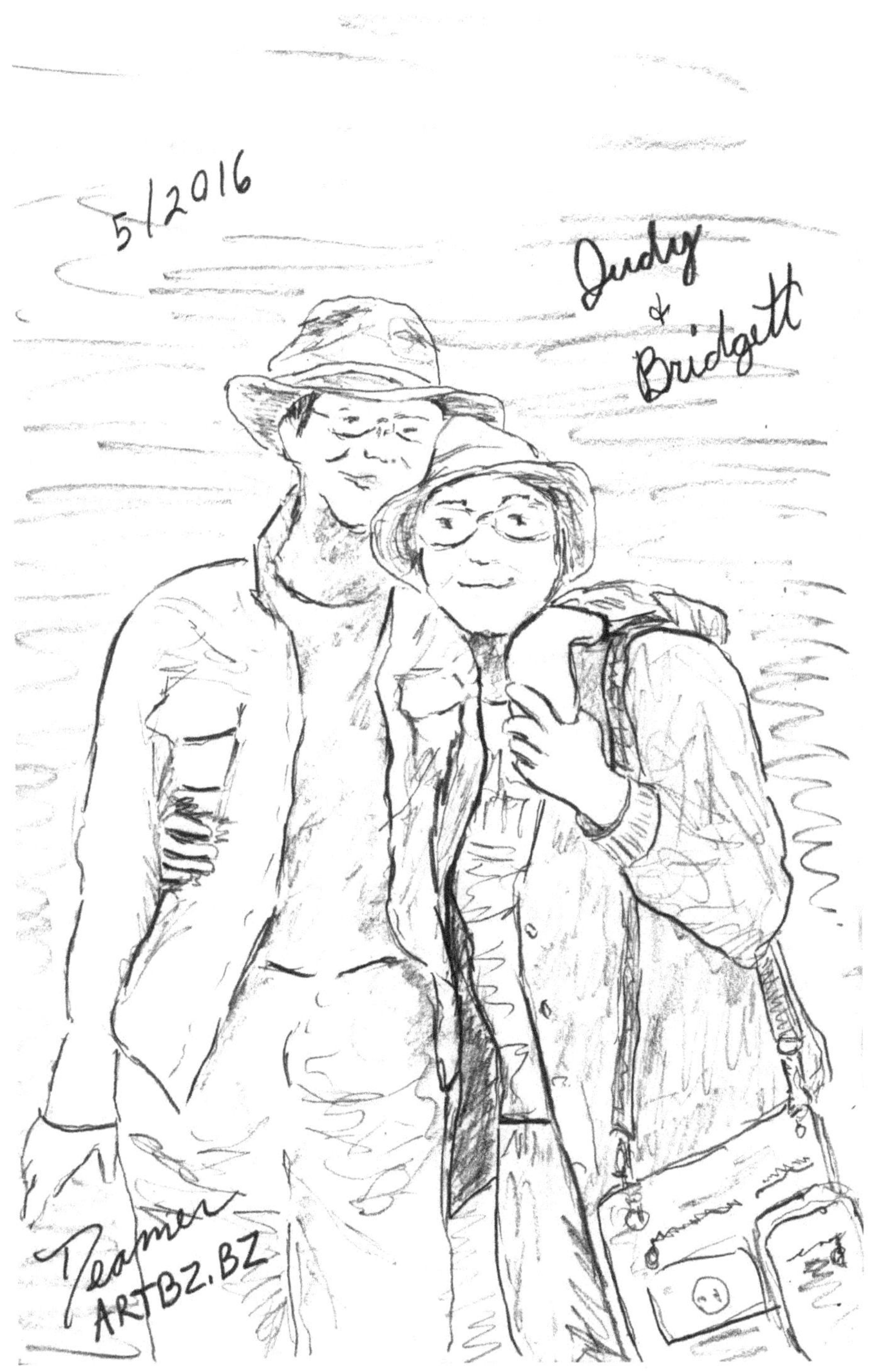
5/2016
Judy
&
Bridgett
Reamer
ARTBZ.BZ

DEAMER DUNN

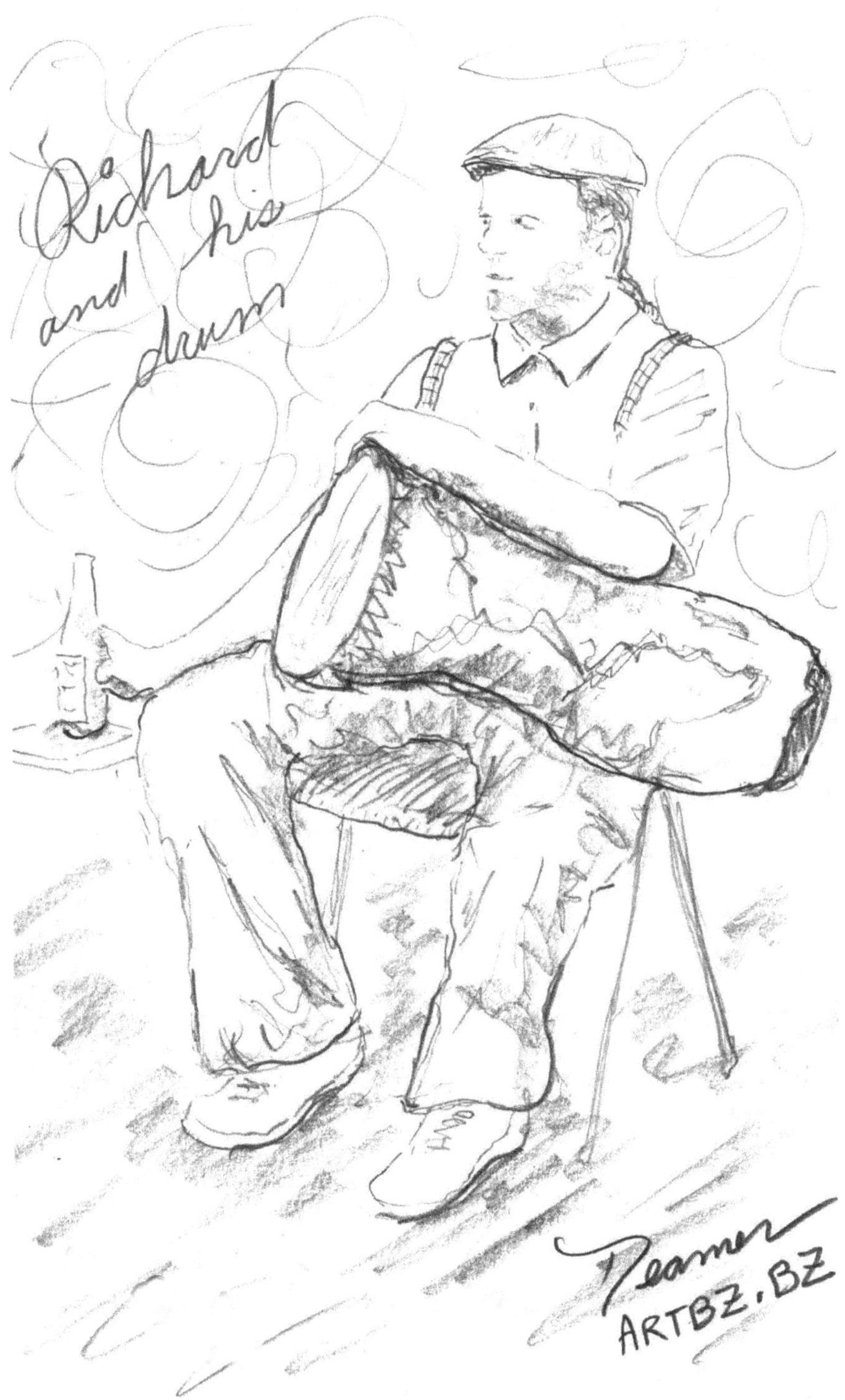
Richard
and his
drum
ARTBZ, BZ

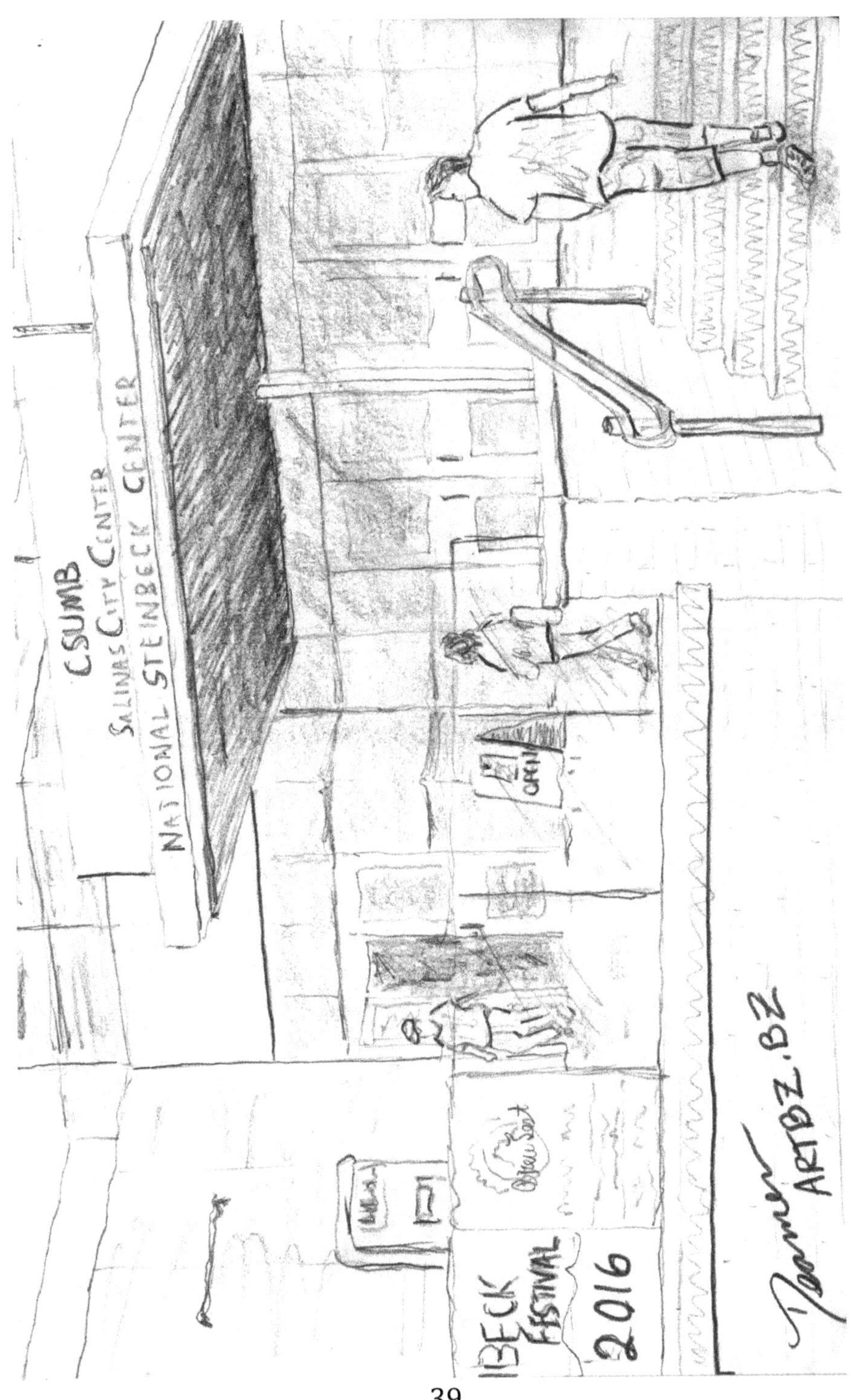
CSUMB
SALINAS CITY CENTER
NATIONAL STEINBECK CENTER
OPEN
BECK FESTIVAL
2016
ARTBZ.BZ

DEAMER DUNN

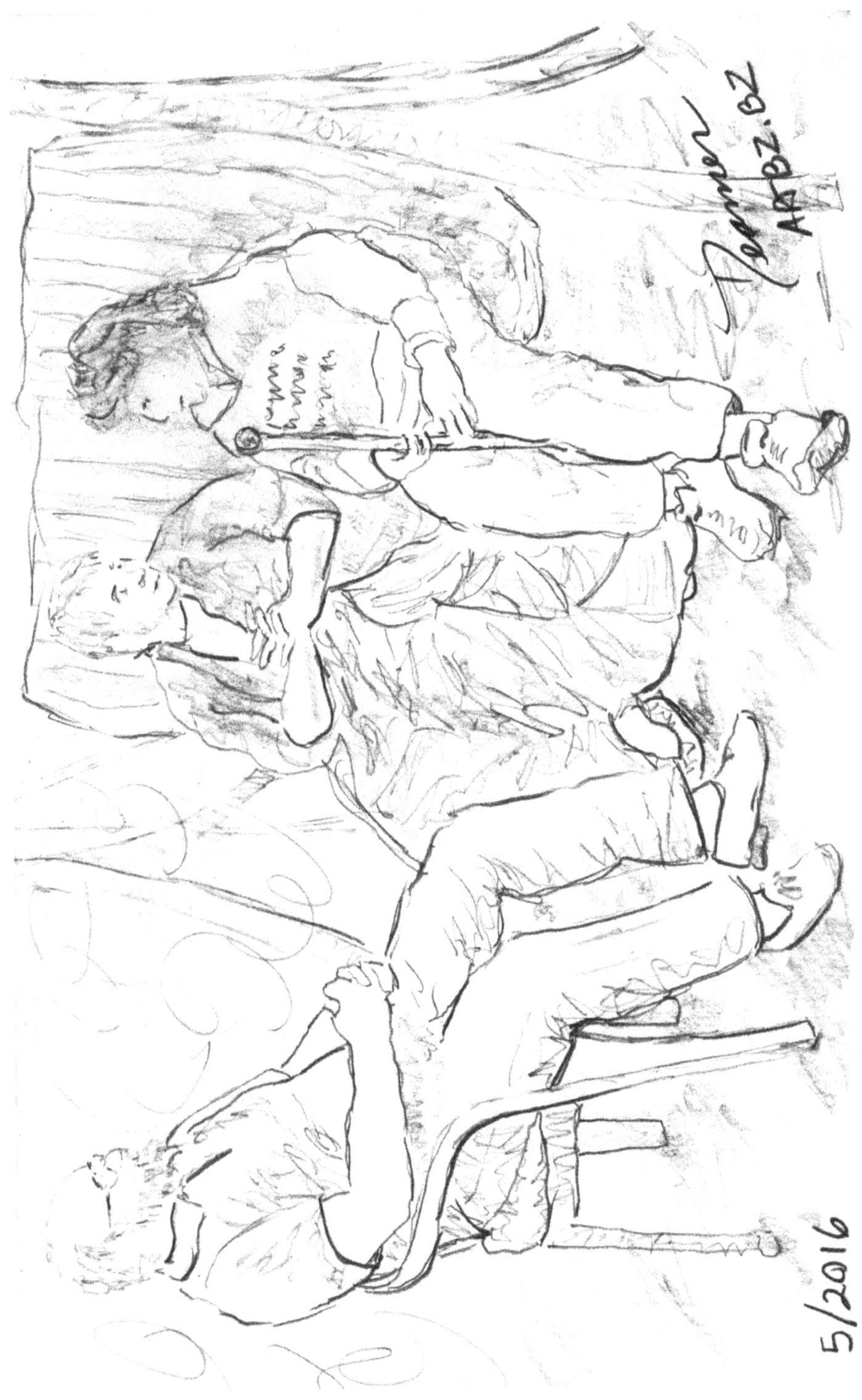

DEAMER DUNN

42

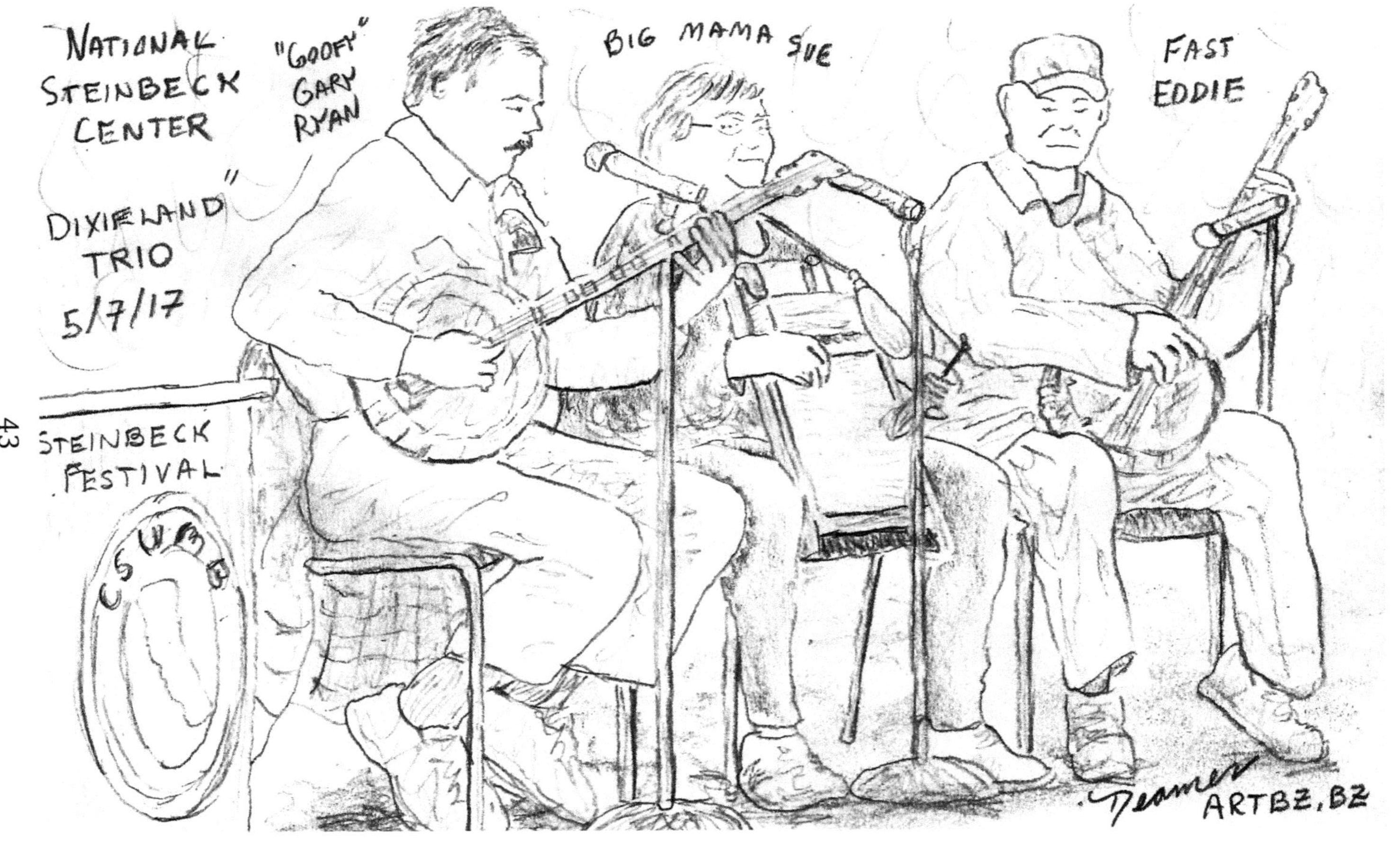
NATIONAL STEINBECK CENTER
"GOOFY" GARY RYAN
BIG MAMA SUE
FAST EDDIE
DIXIELAND TRIO
5/7/17
STEINBECK FESTIVAL
CSUMB
Deamer
ARTBZ.BZ

DEAMER DUNN

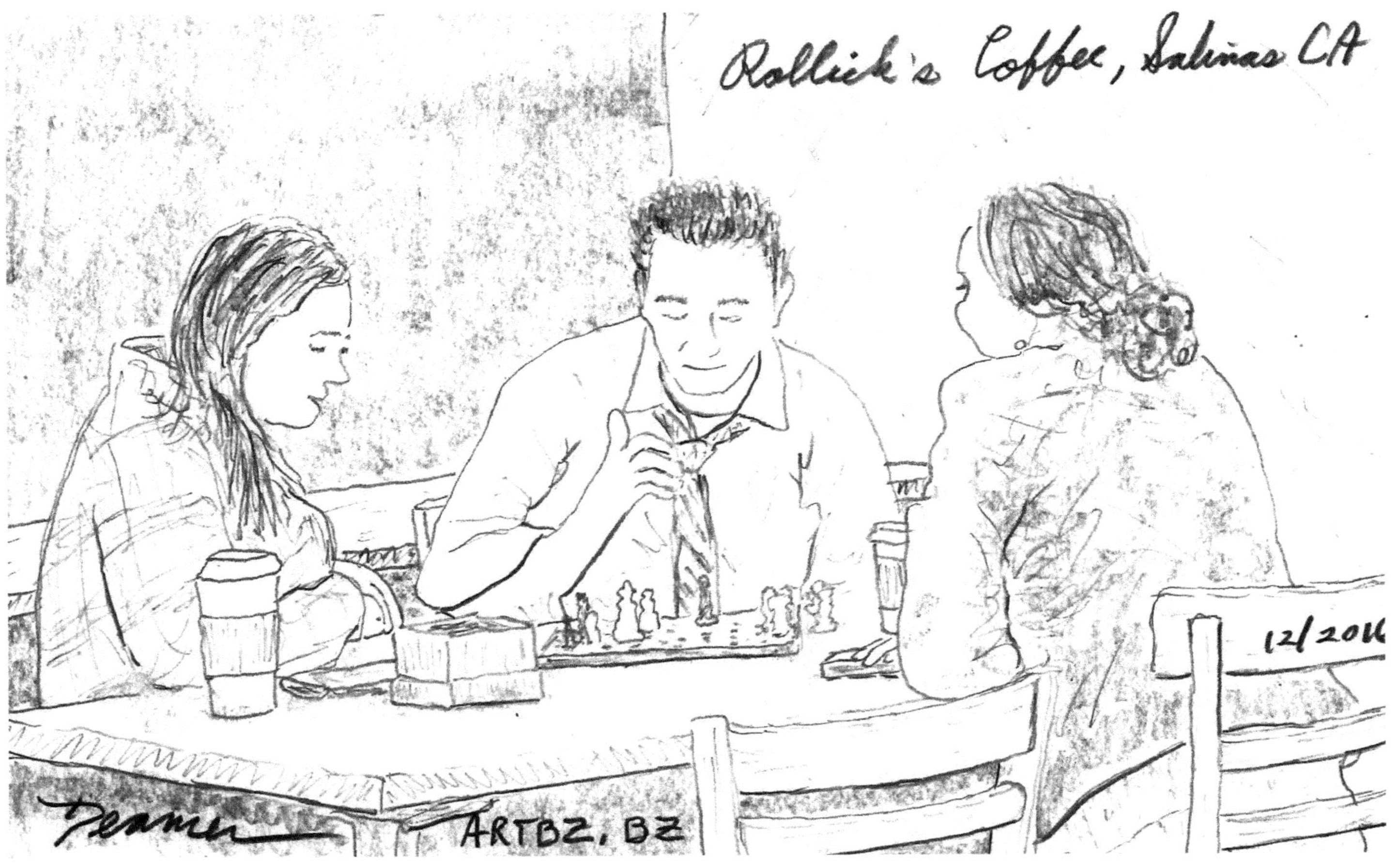
Rollick's Coffee, Salinas CA
12/2014
ARTB2.B2

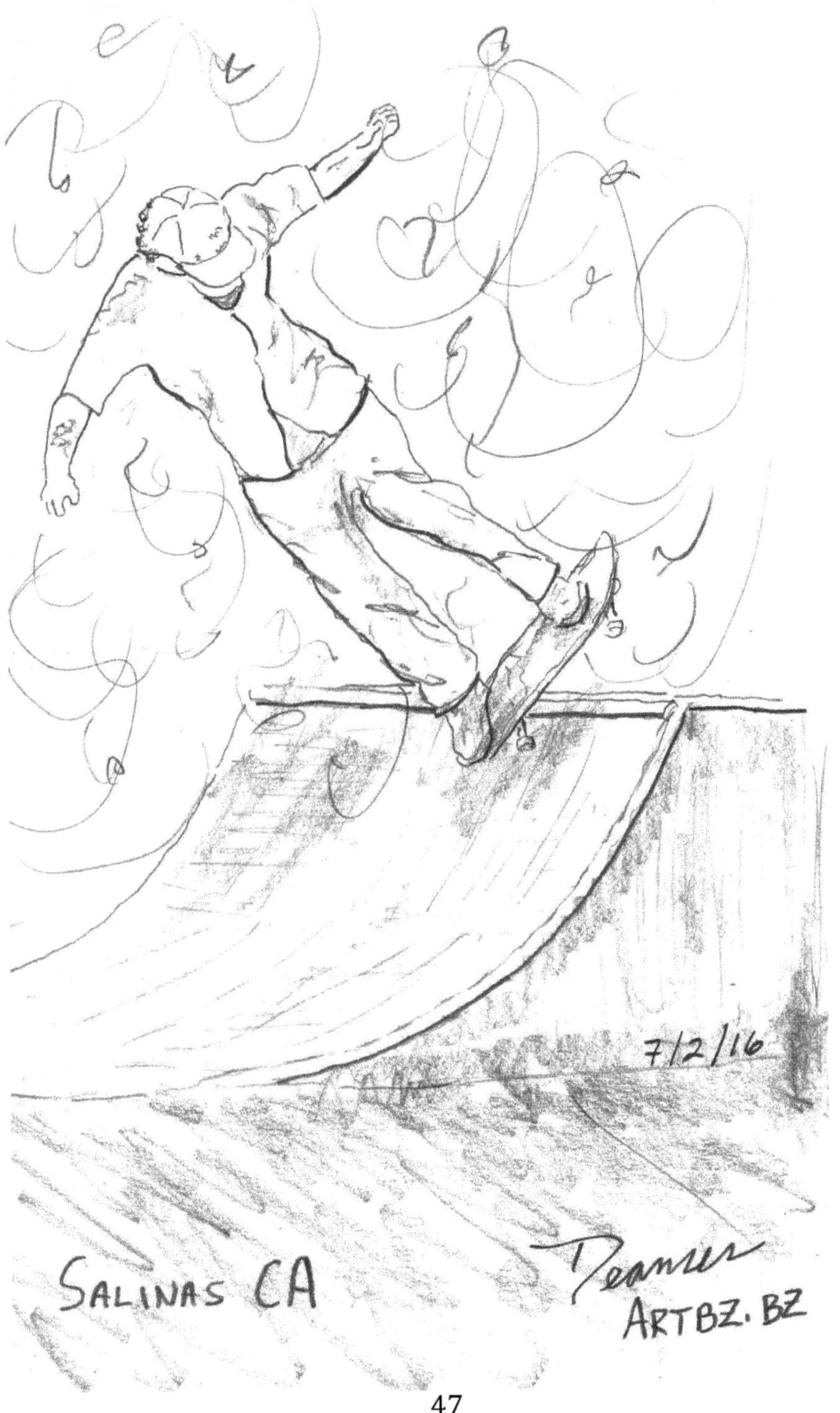

7/2/16
SALINAS CA
ARTBZ. BZ

48

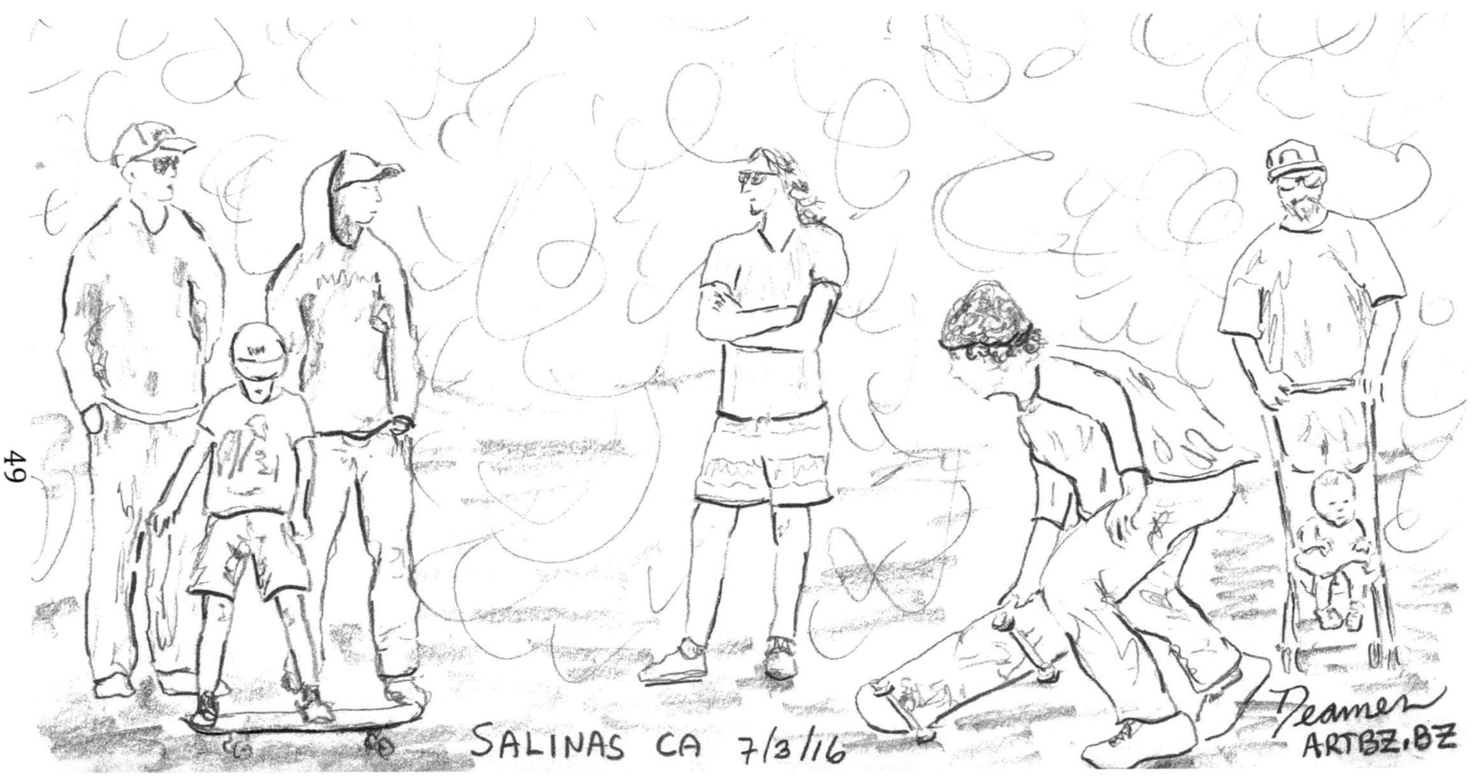
SALINAS CA 7/3/16
Reamer
ARTBZ.BZ

50

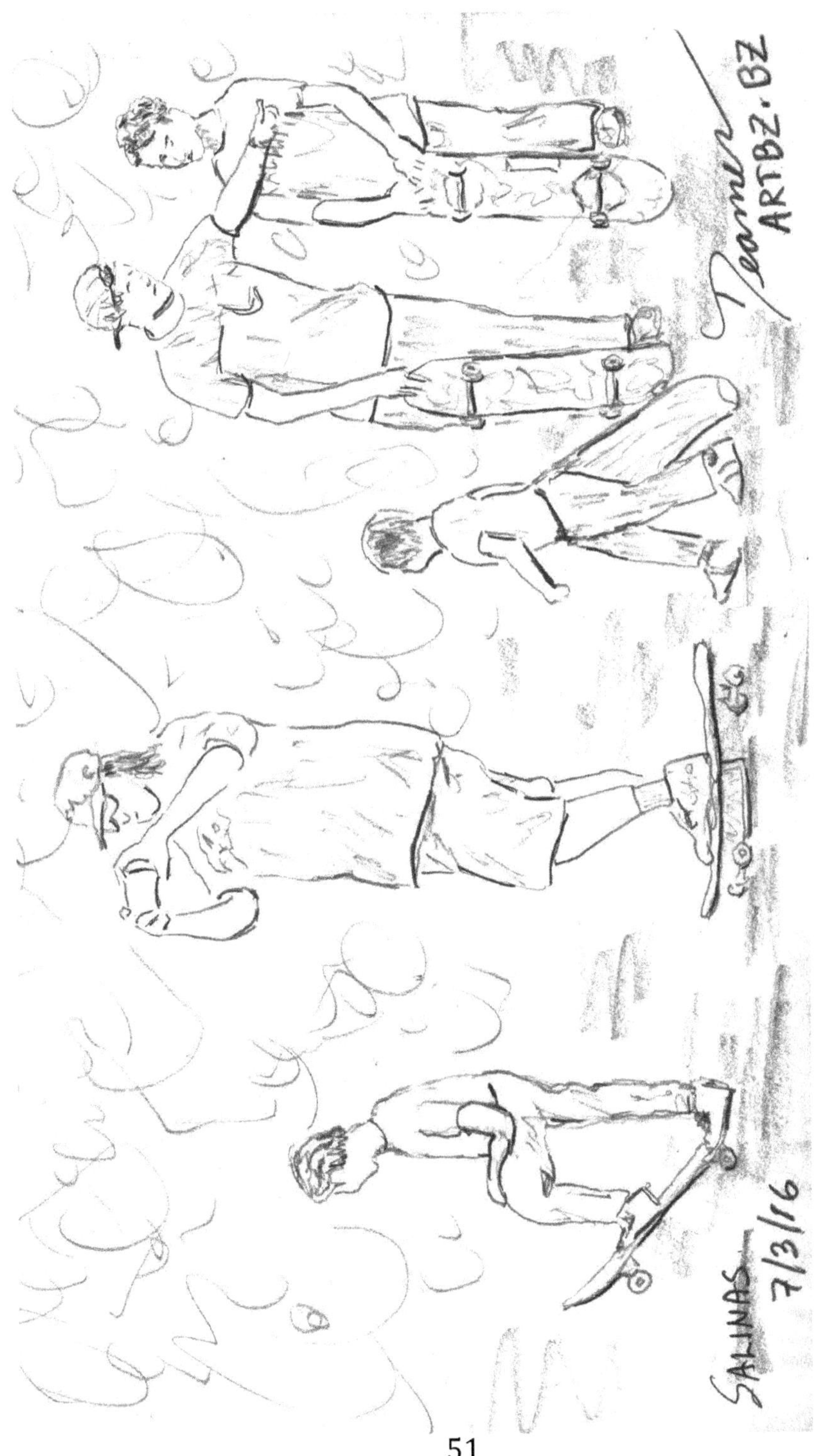
Jeannie
ARTB2.B2
SALINAS
7/3/16

52

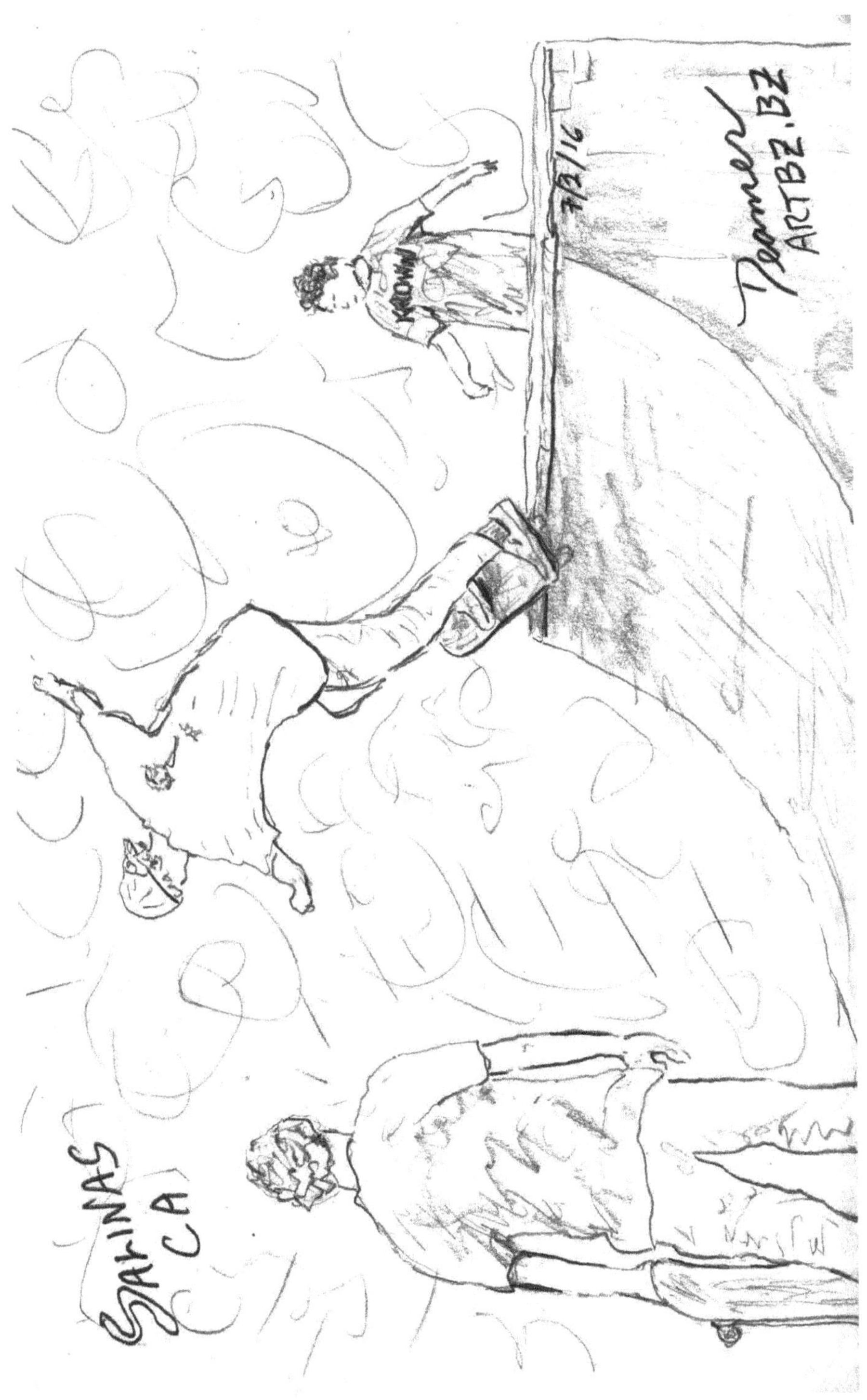

SALINAS
CA
7/2/16
ARTBZ.BZ

54

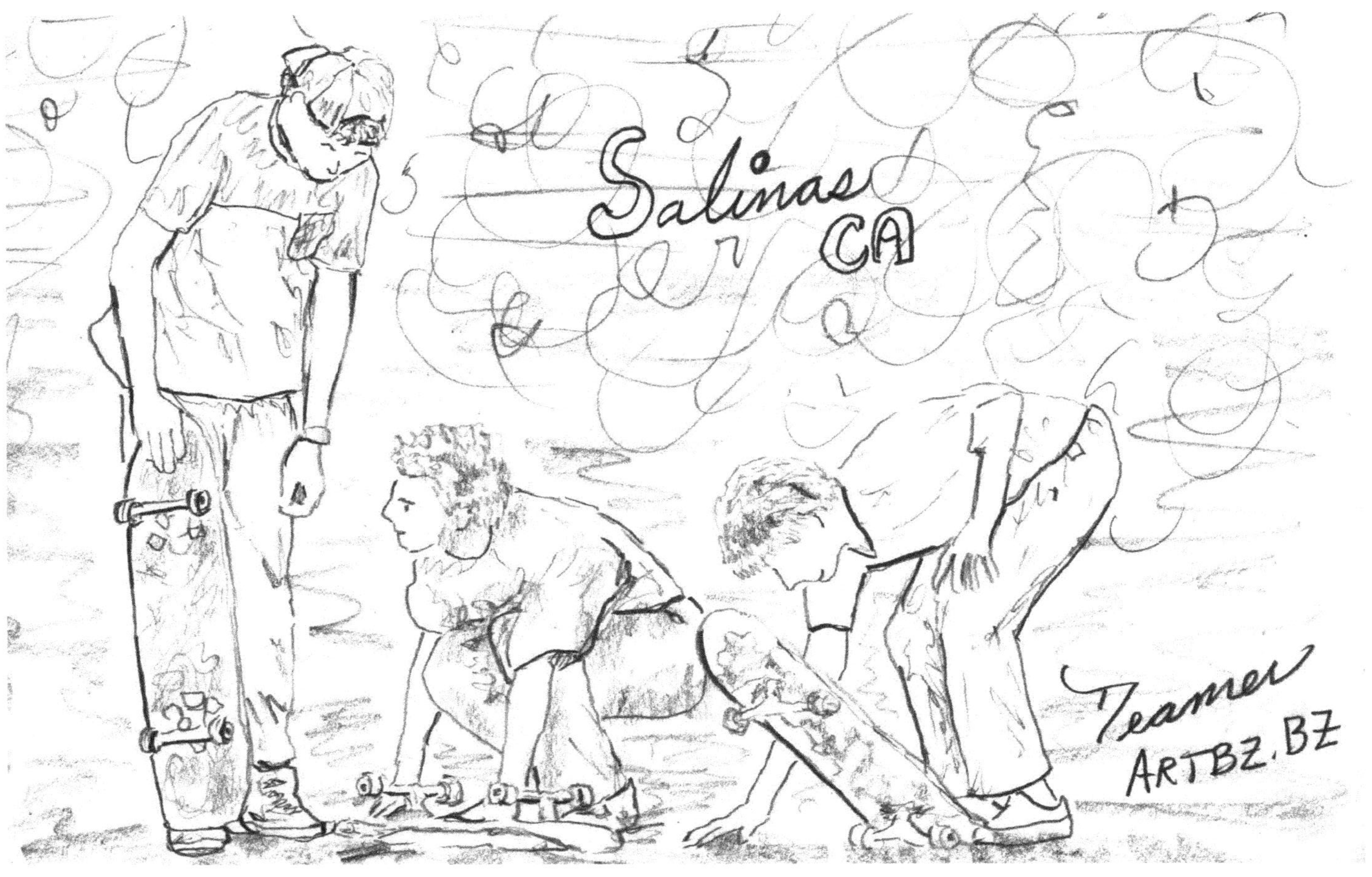

Salinas CA
Teamer
ARTBZ.BZ

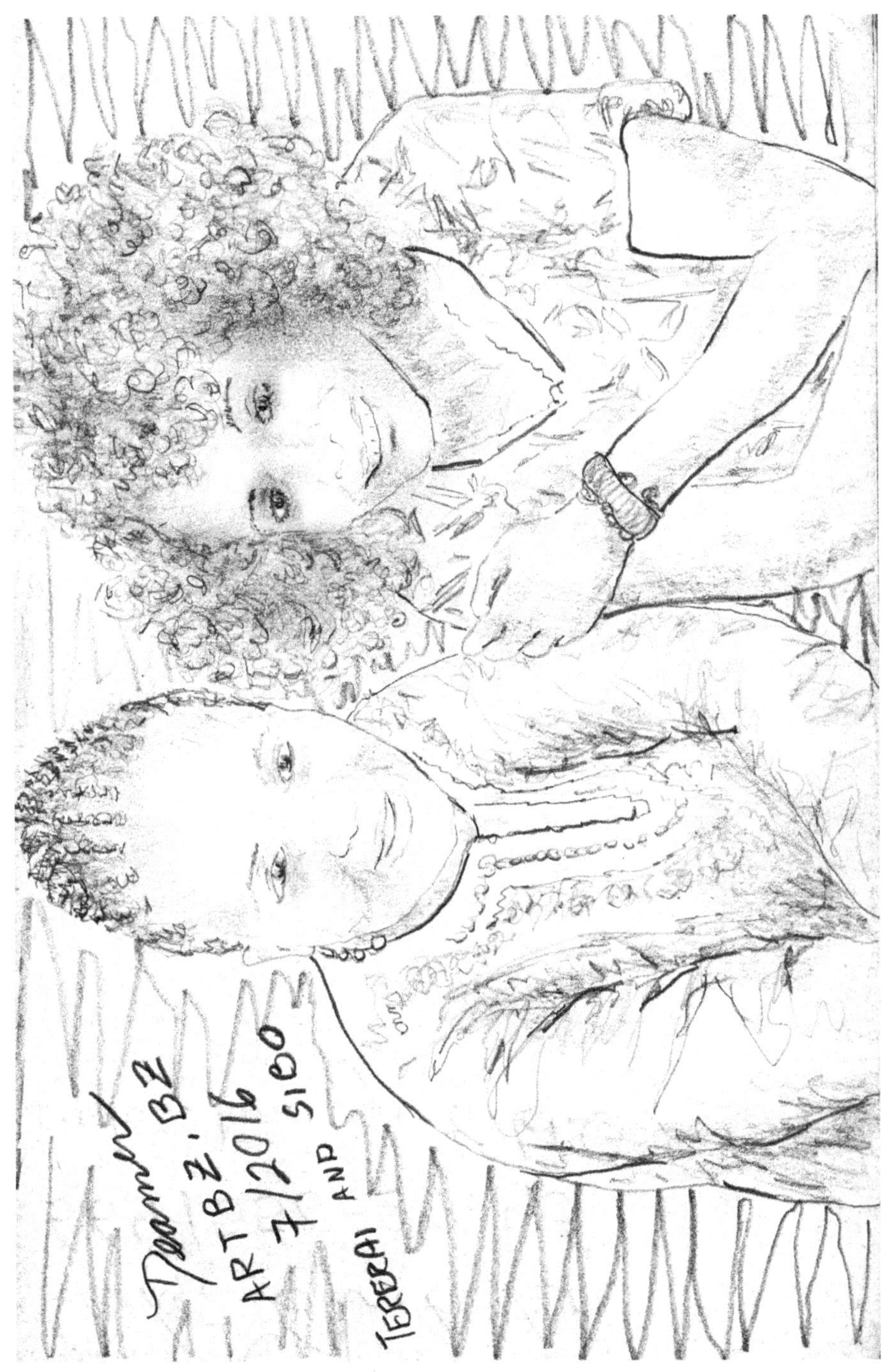
Tsamon BZ
ART BZ 7/2016
5,60
TERERAI AND

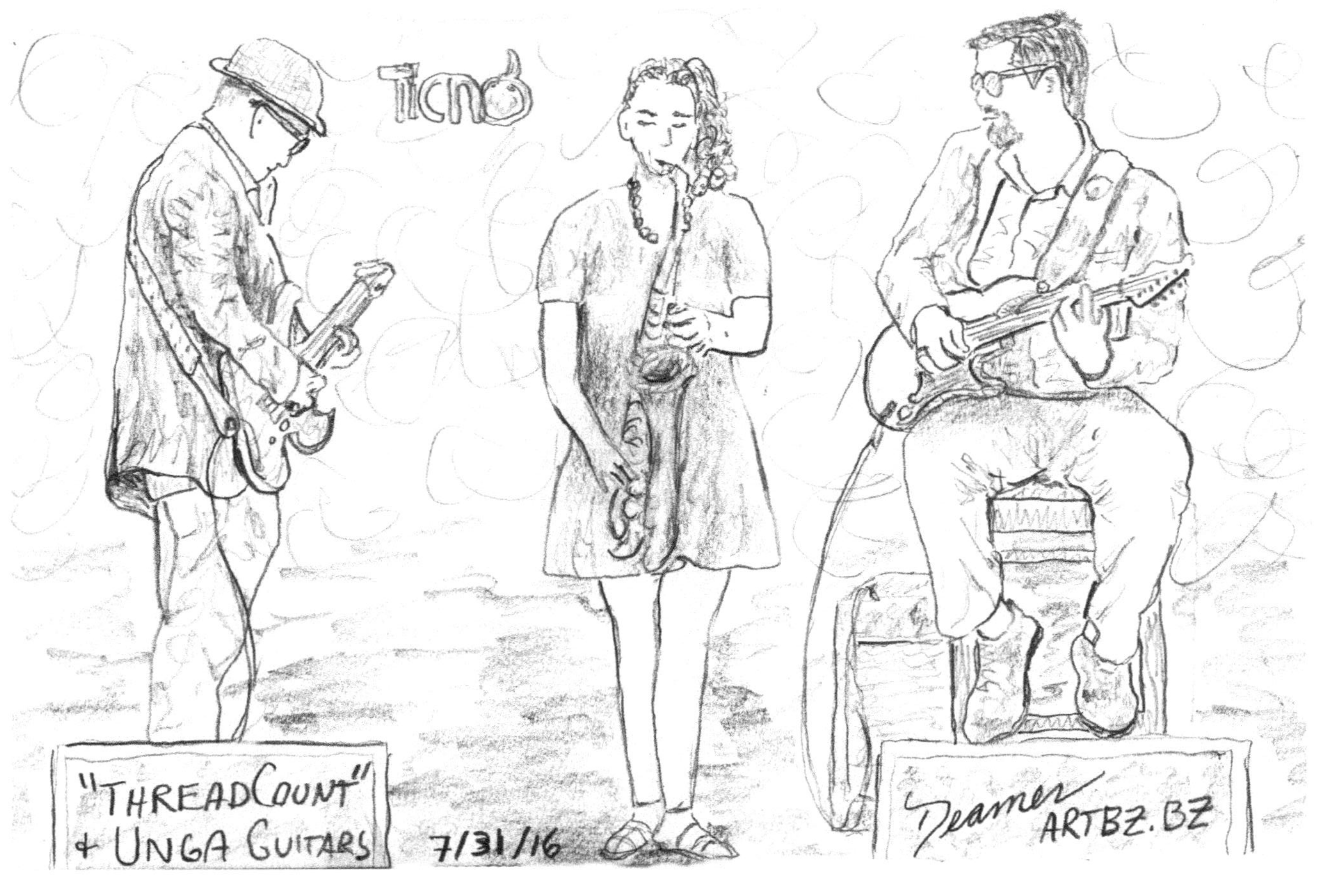
Ticno
"ThreadCount"
+ Unga Guitars
7/31/16
Dreamer
ARTBZ.BZ

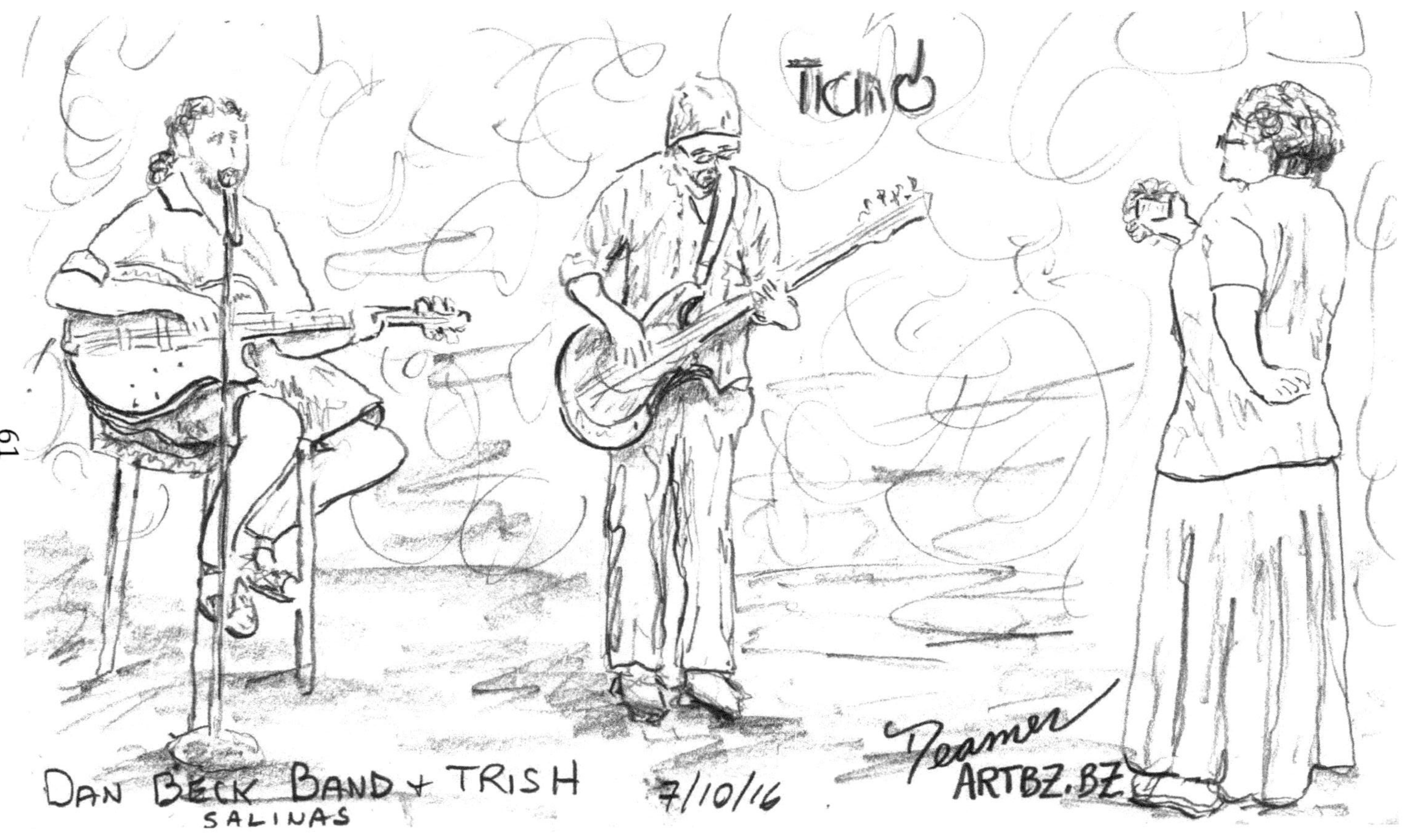
Ticino
Dan Beck Band + Trish
SALINAS
7/10/16
Teamer
ARTBZ.BZ

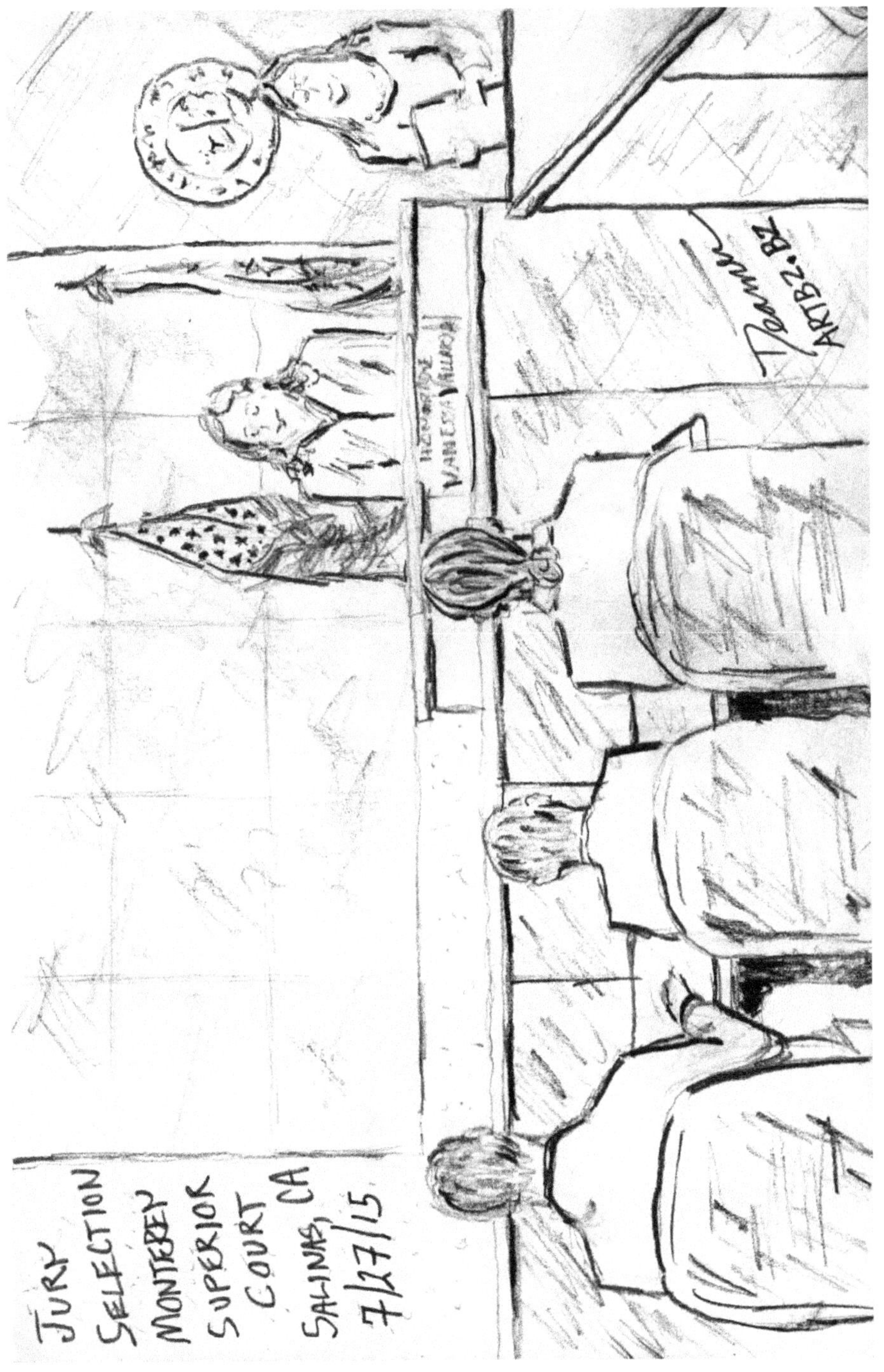
JURY
SELECTION
MONTEREY
SUPERIOR
COURT
SALINAS, CA
7/27/15
HONORABLE
VANESSA VILLAREAL
Joanna
ARTBZ.BZ

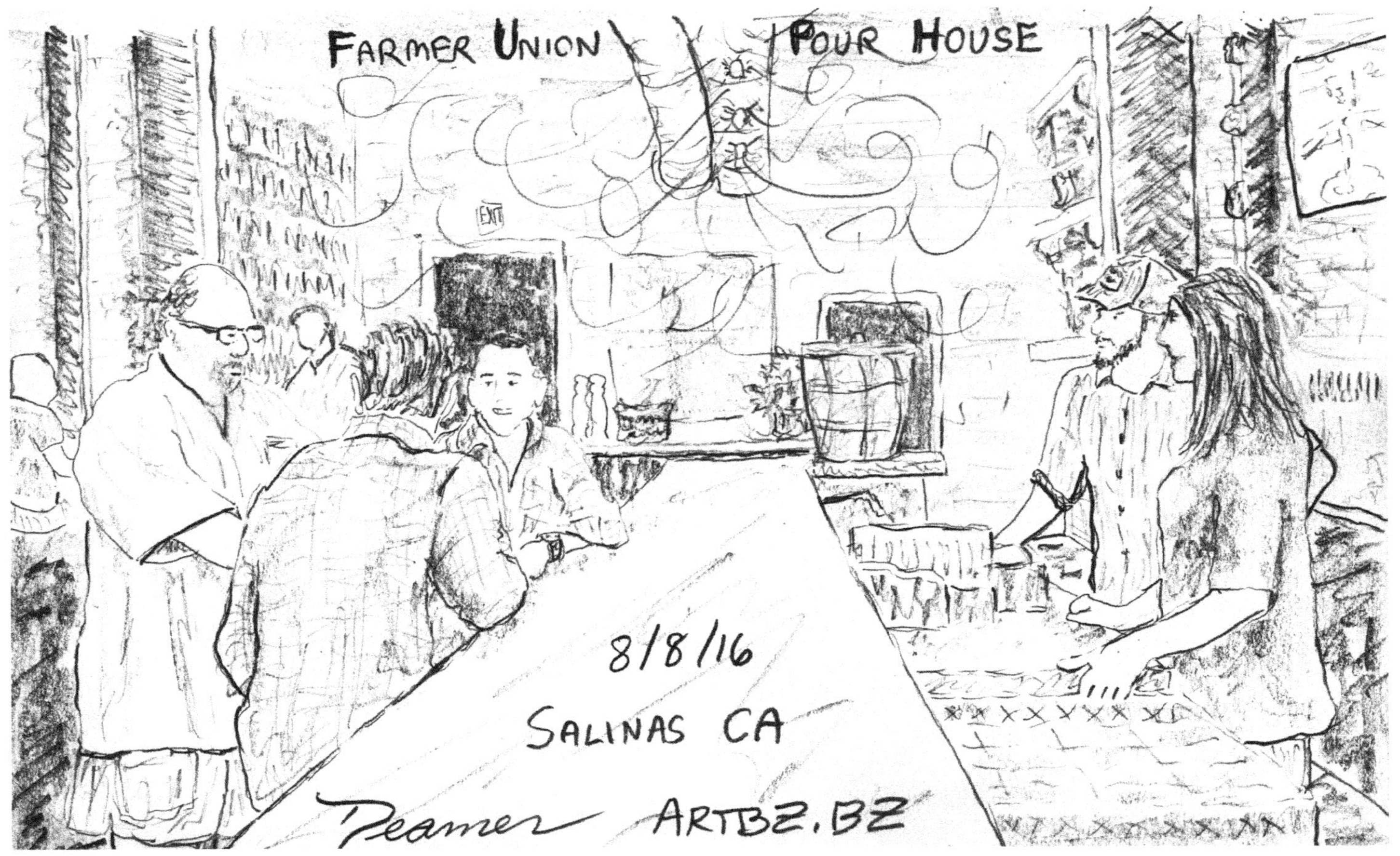
FARMER UNION
POUR HOUSE
EXIT
8/8/16
SALINAS CA
Reamer ARTB2.B2

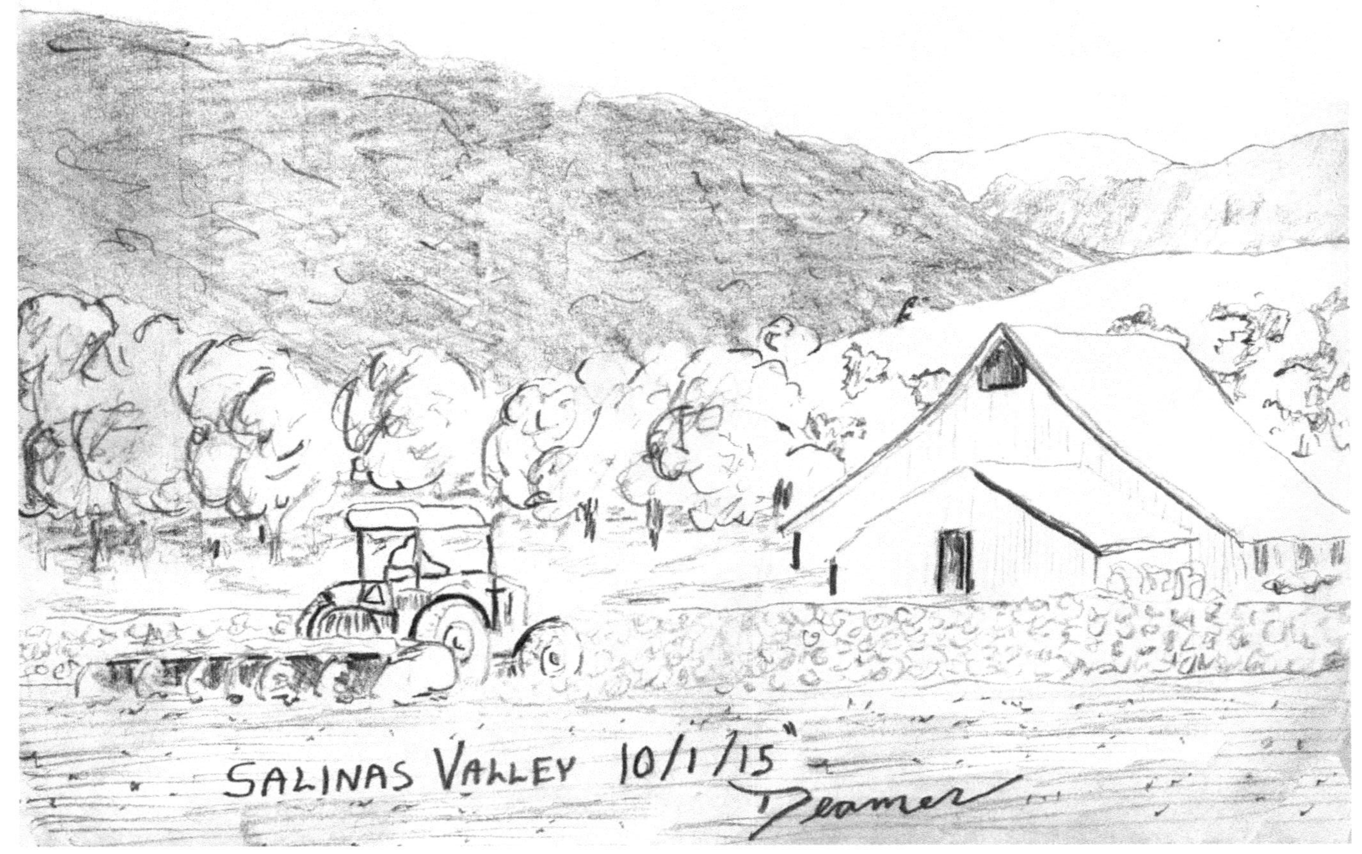
SALINAS VALLEY 10/1/15

68

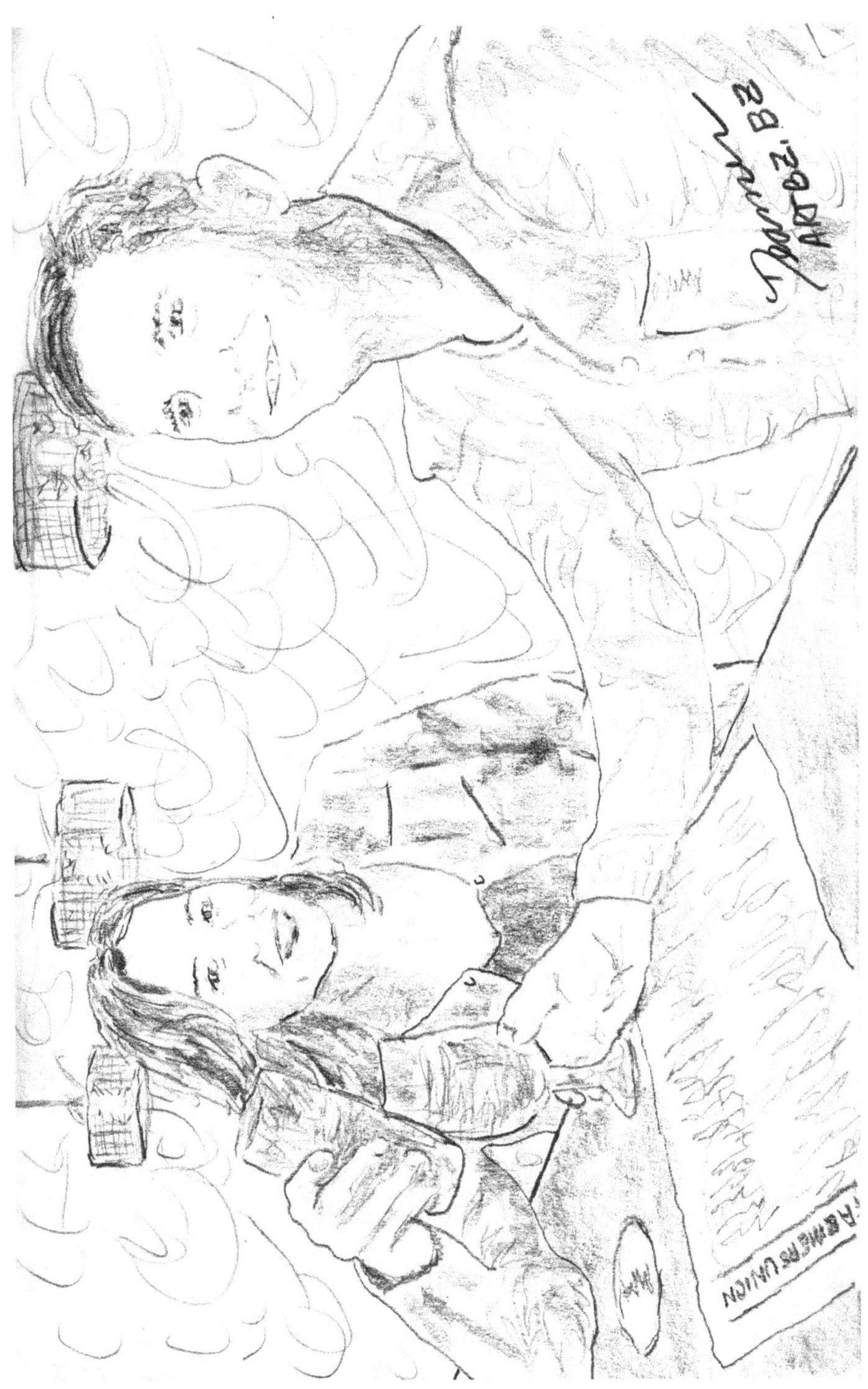

70

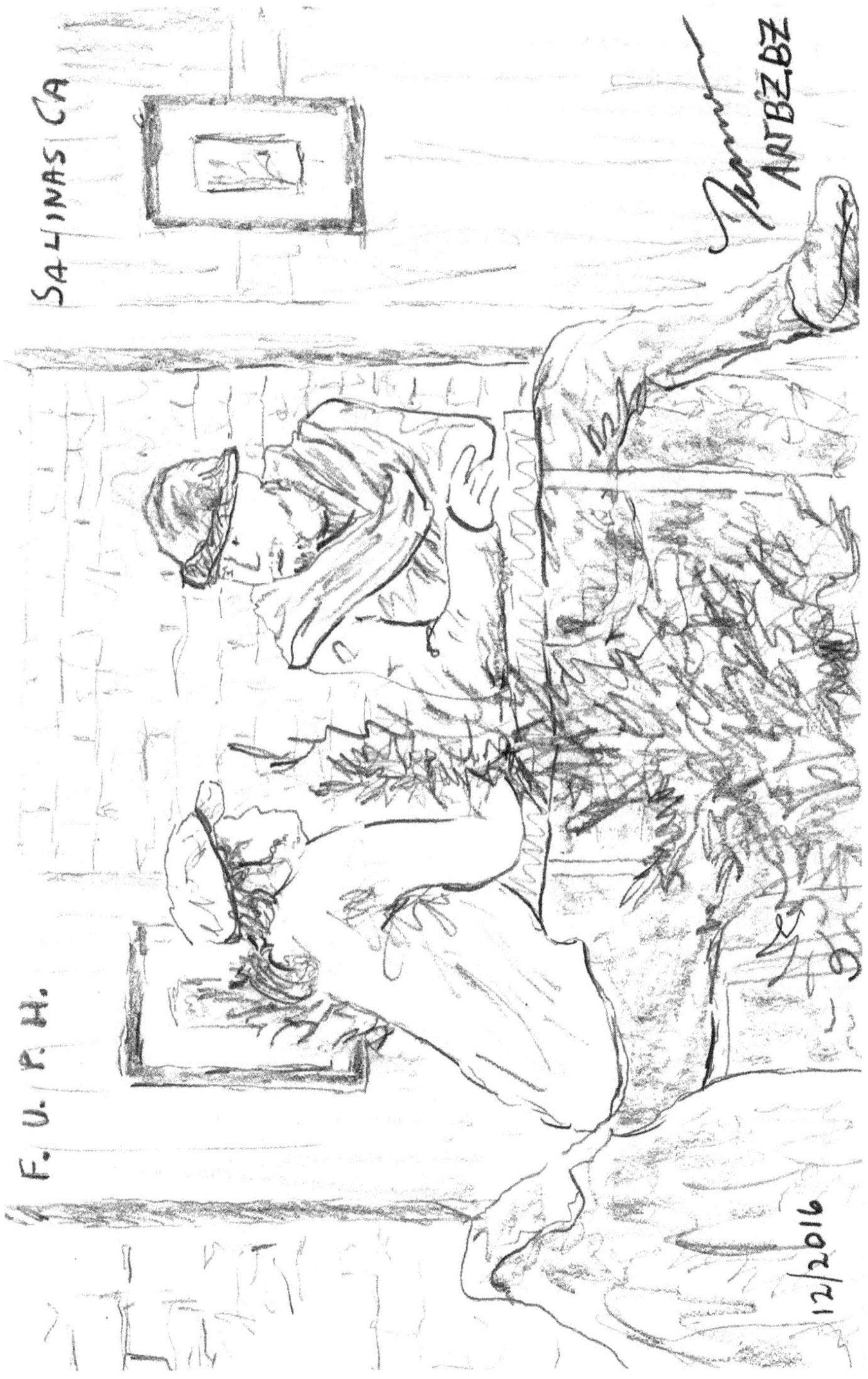

SALINAS CA
F. U. R. H.
ARTBZ.BZ
12/2016

72

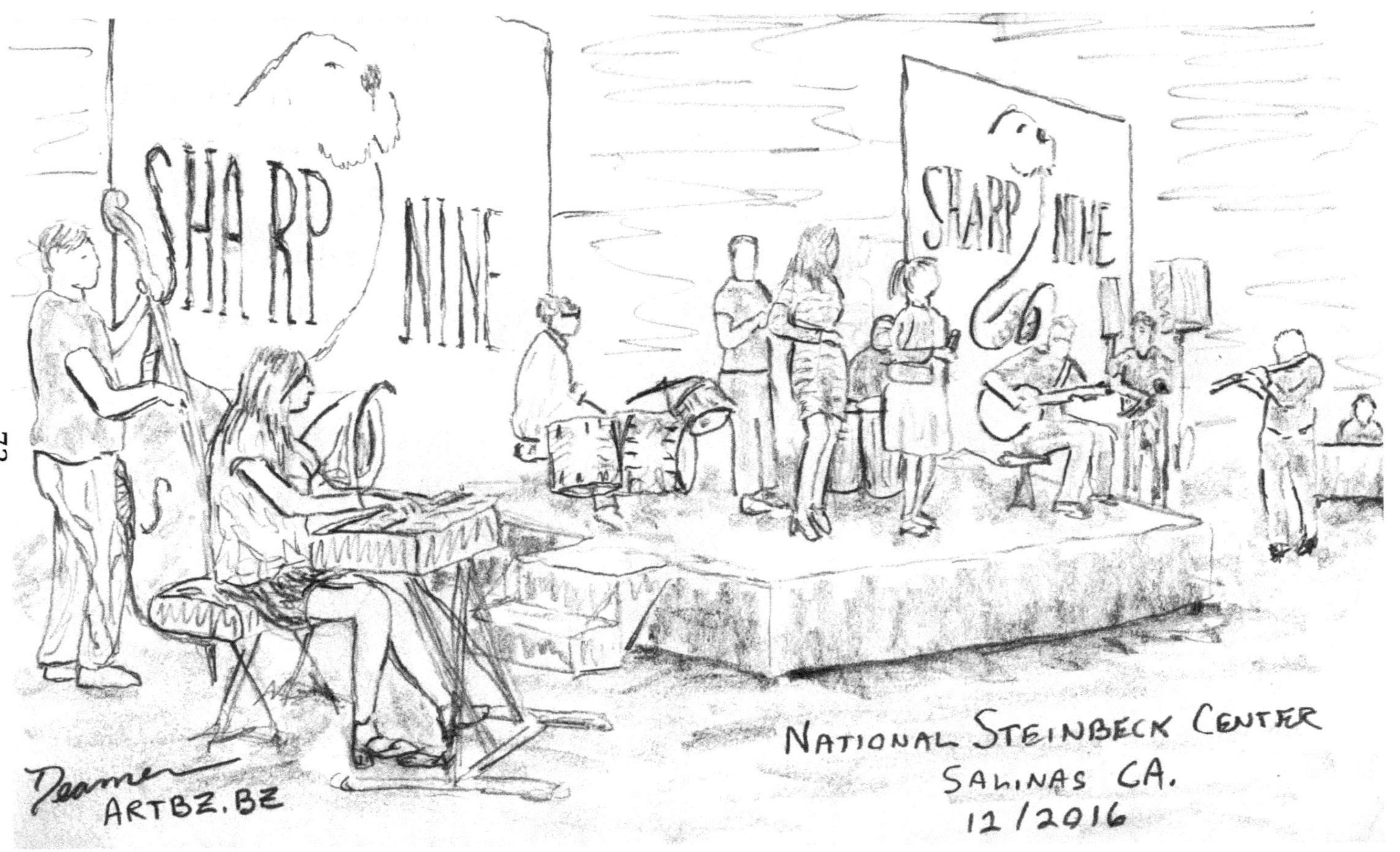
SHARP NINE
SHARP NINE
National Steinbeck Center
Salinas CA.
12/2016
ARTBZ.BZ

DEAMER DUNN

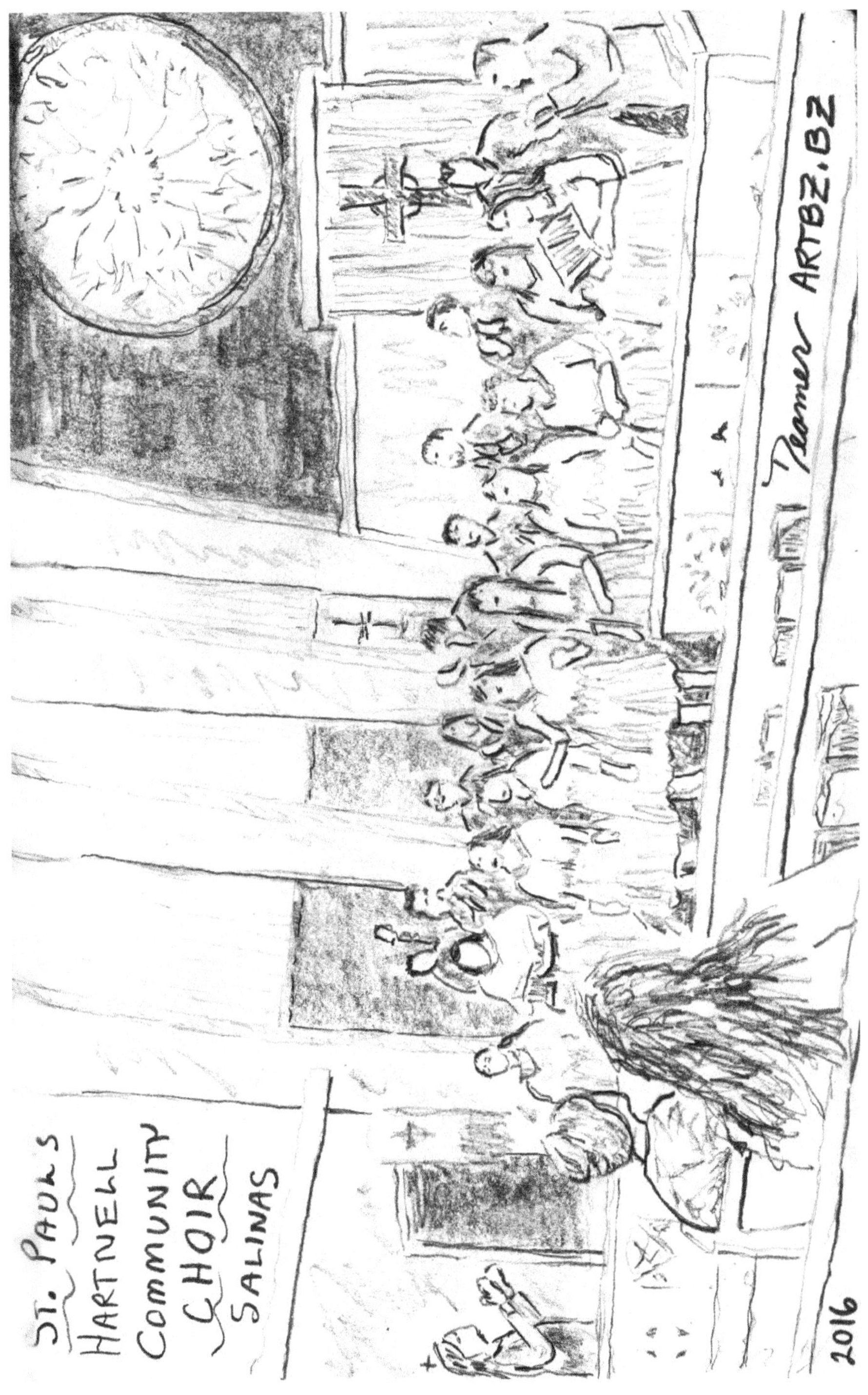

St. Paul's
Hartnell
Community
Choir
Salinas
2016

76

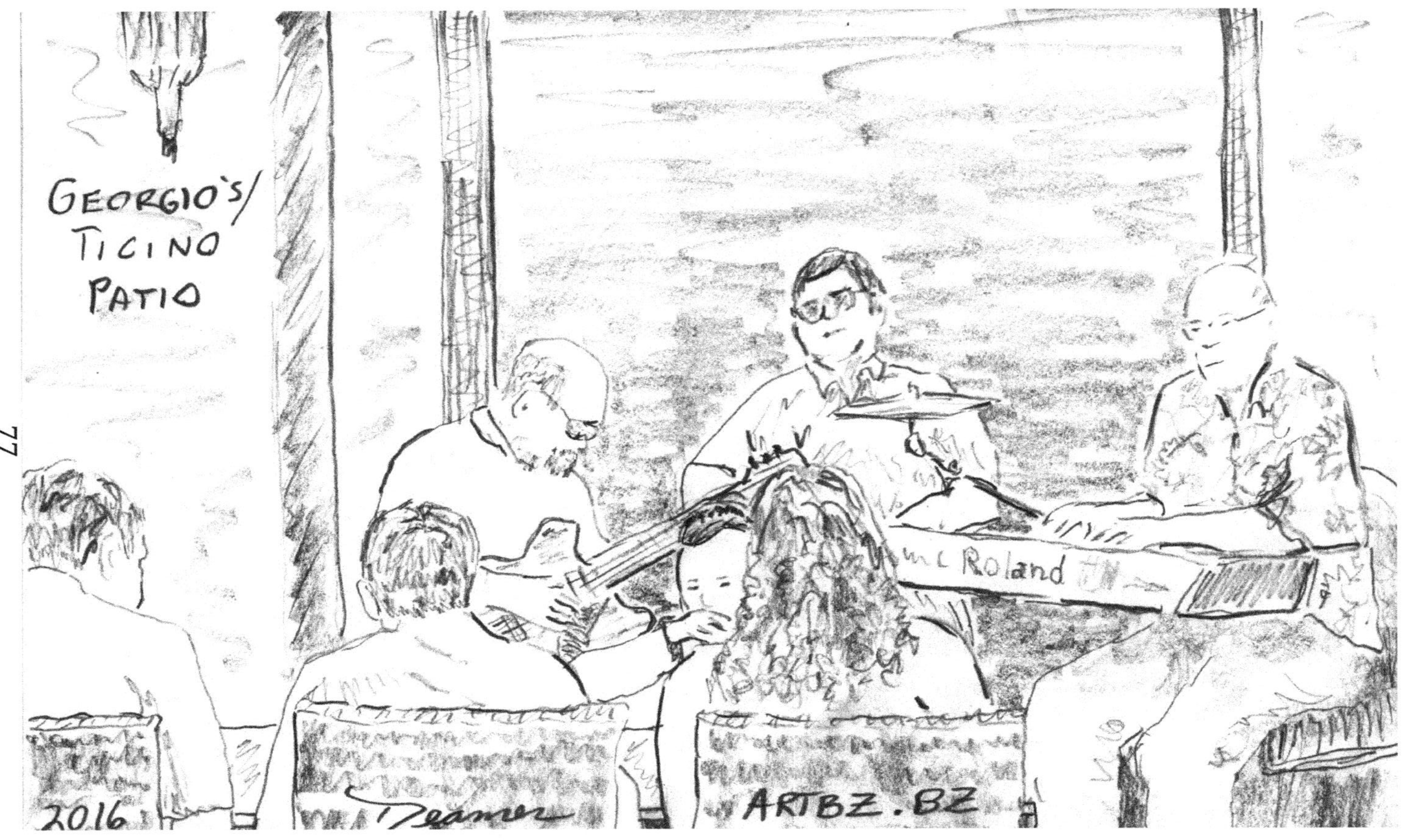
GEORGIO'S/
TICINO
PATIO
Roland
2016
ARTBZ.BZ

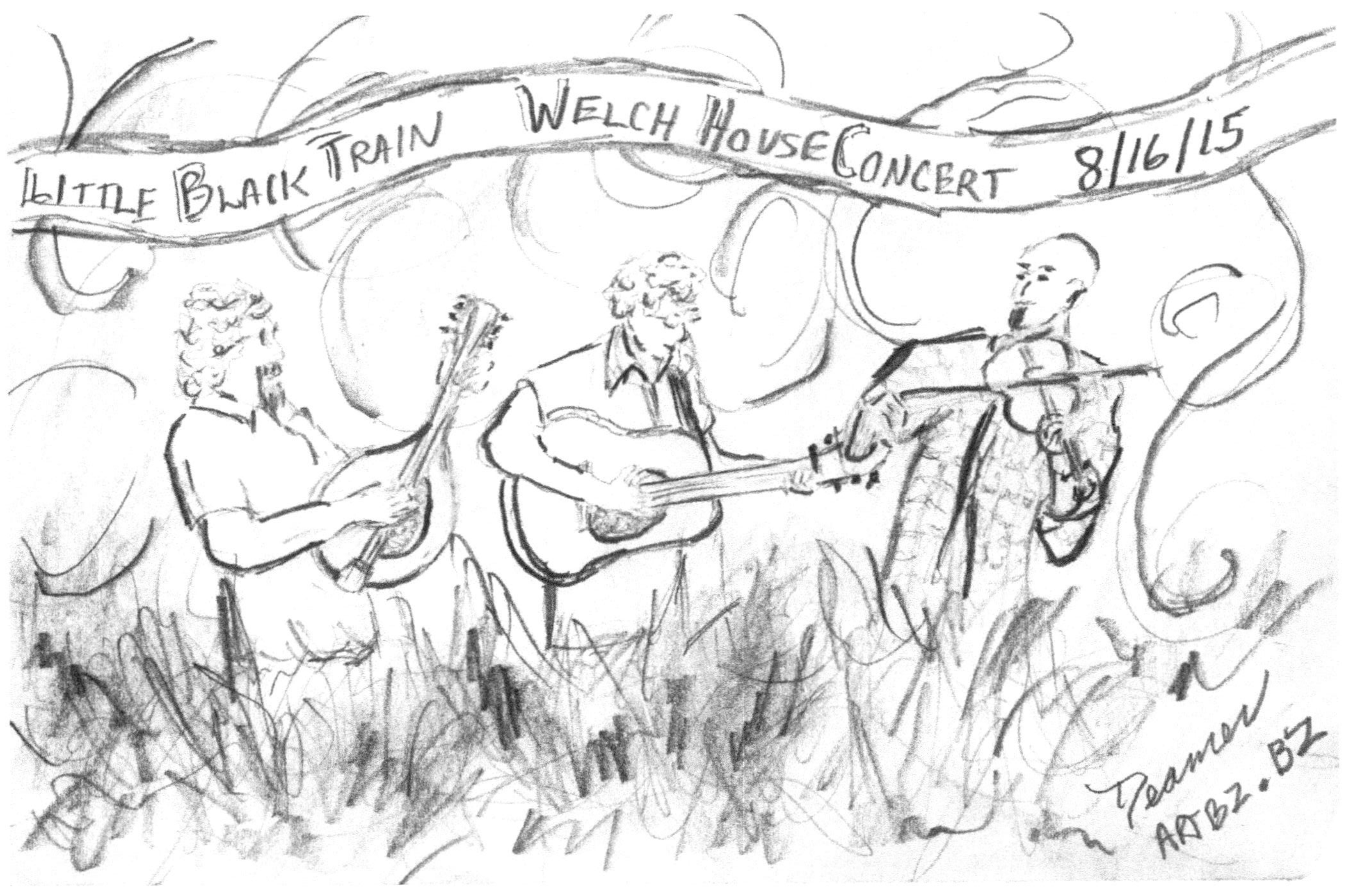
LITTLE BLACK TRAIN   WELCH HOUSE CONCERT   8/16/15

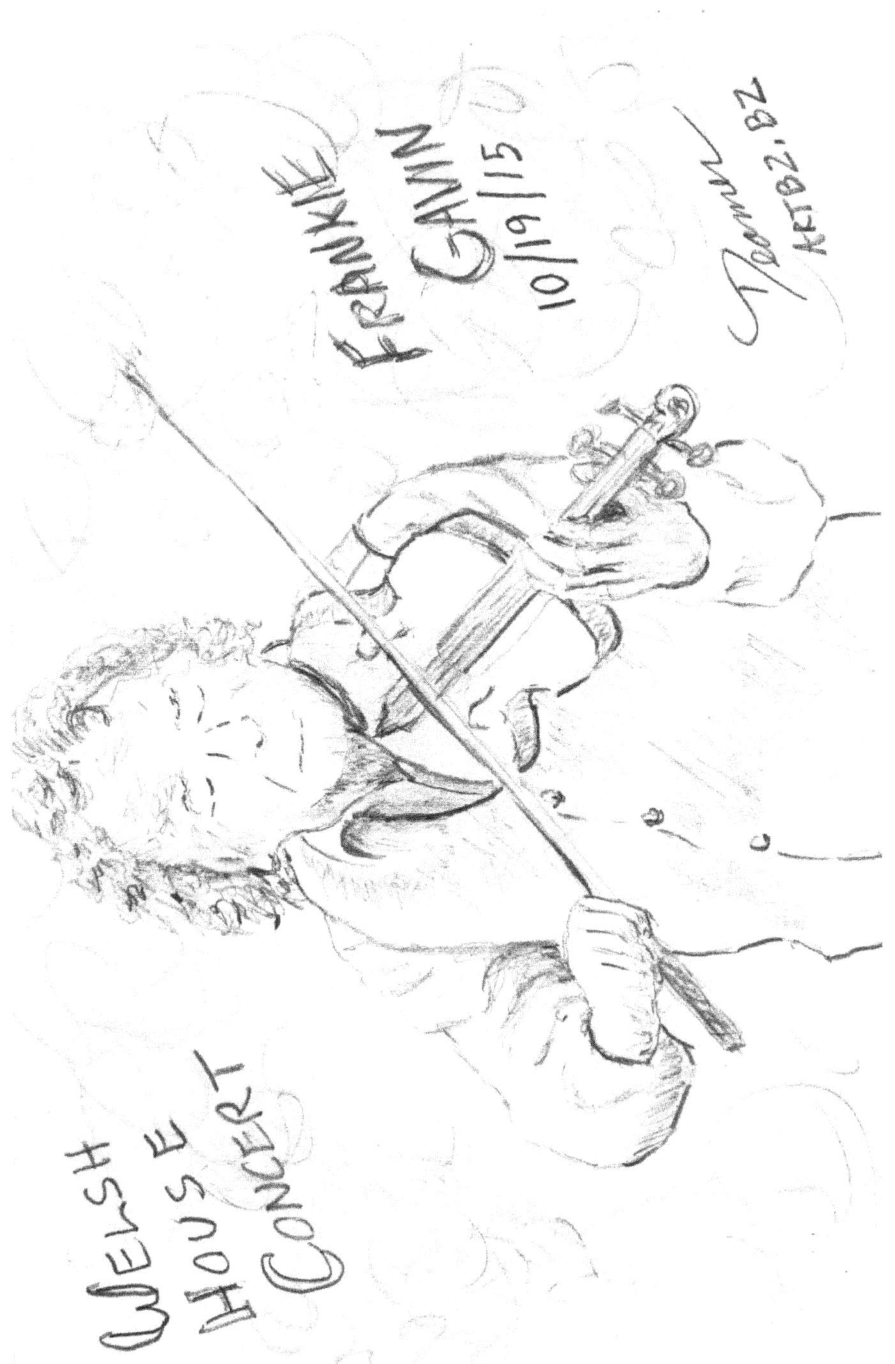
FRANKIE
GAVIN
10/19/15
Toomin
KRTB2, BZ
WELSH
HOUSE
CONCERT

82

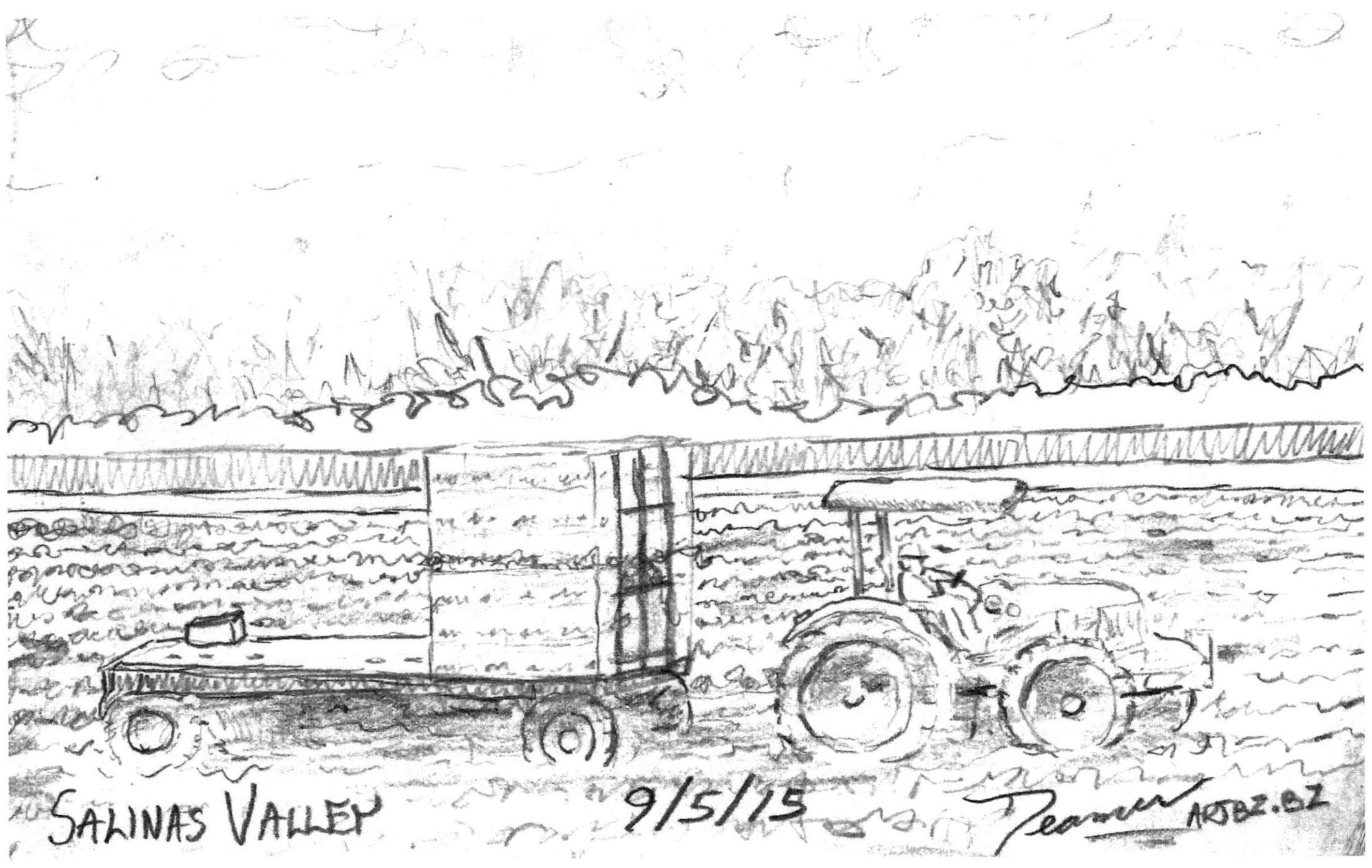

SALINAS VALLEY
9/5/15

84

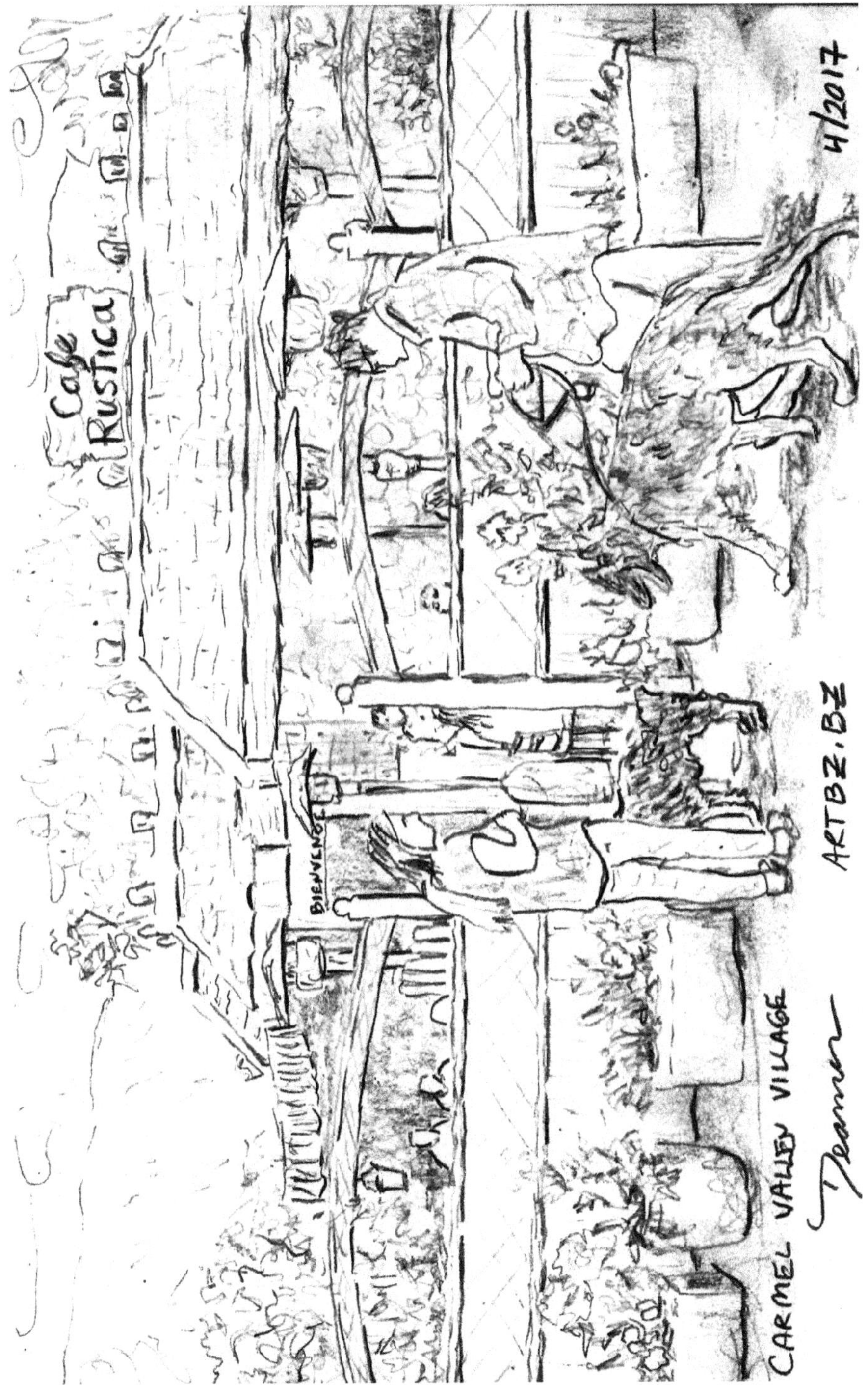
Cafe Rustica
BIENVENUE
CARMEL VALLEY VILLAGE
AKTBZ.BZ
4/2017

86

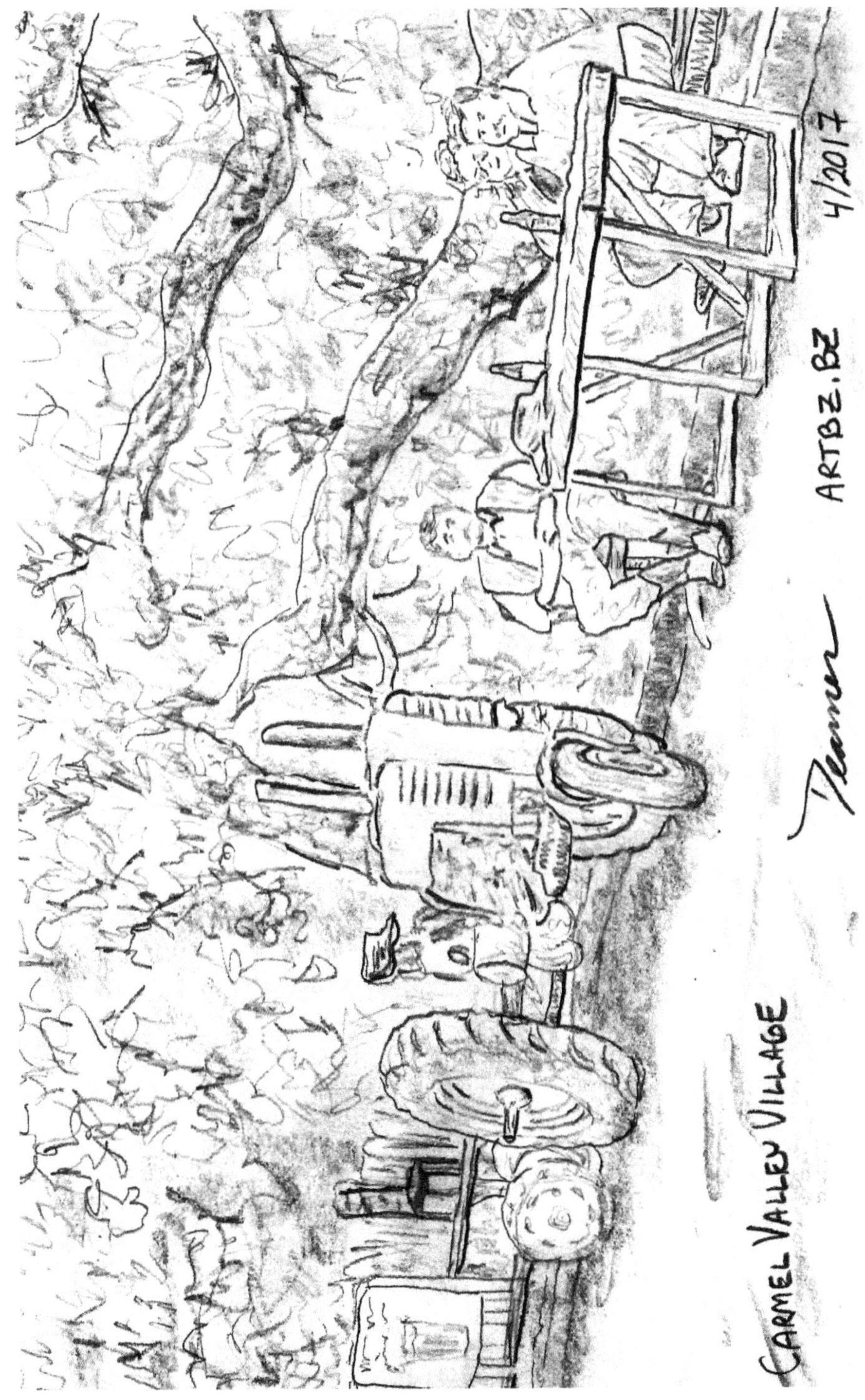
CARMEL VALLEY VILLAGE
ARTBZ.BZ
4/2017

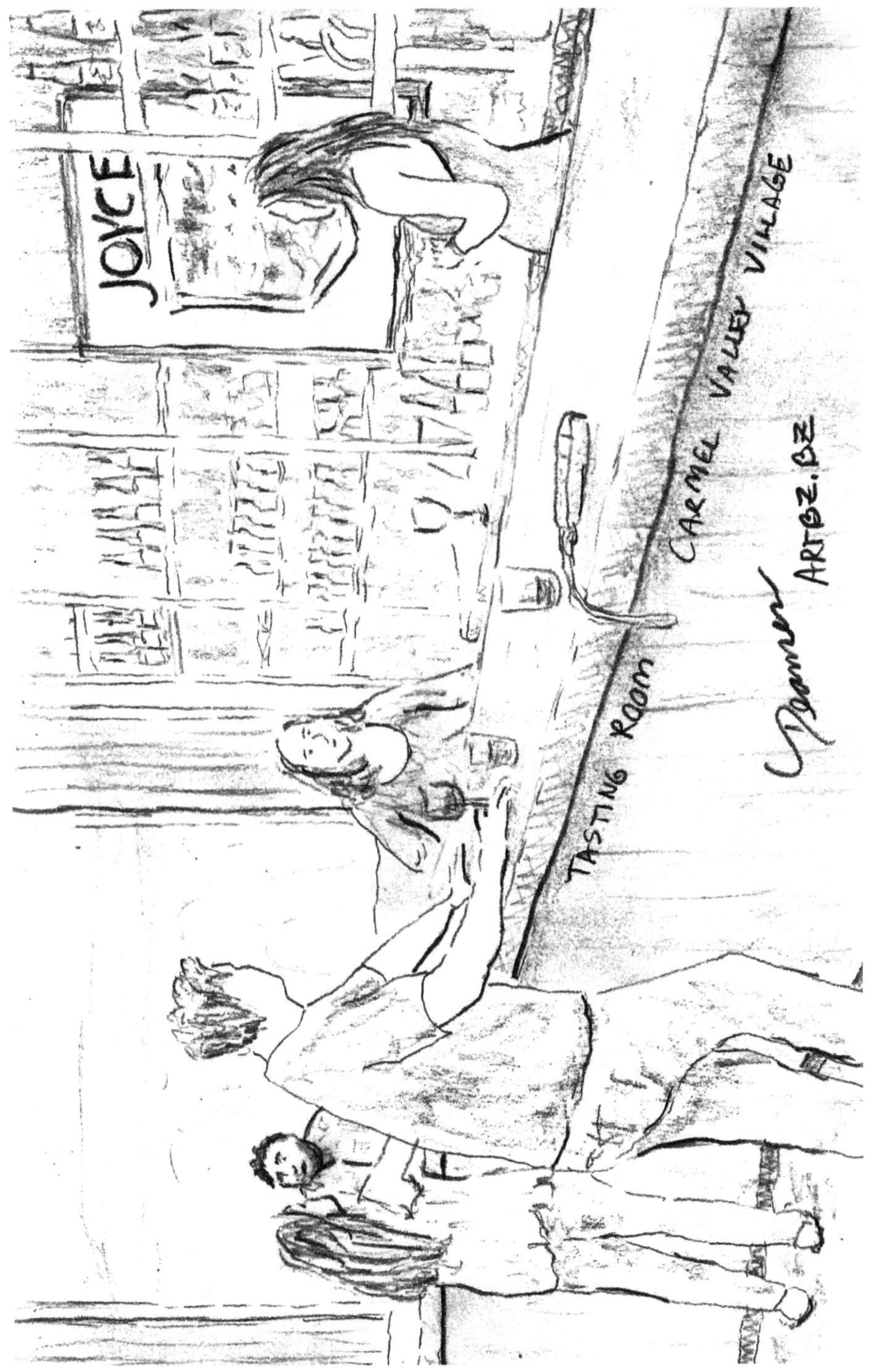

JOYCE
TASTING ROOM
CARMEL VALLEY VILLAGE
ARTG2.0Z

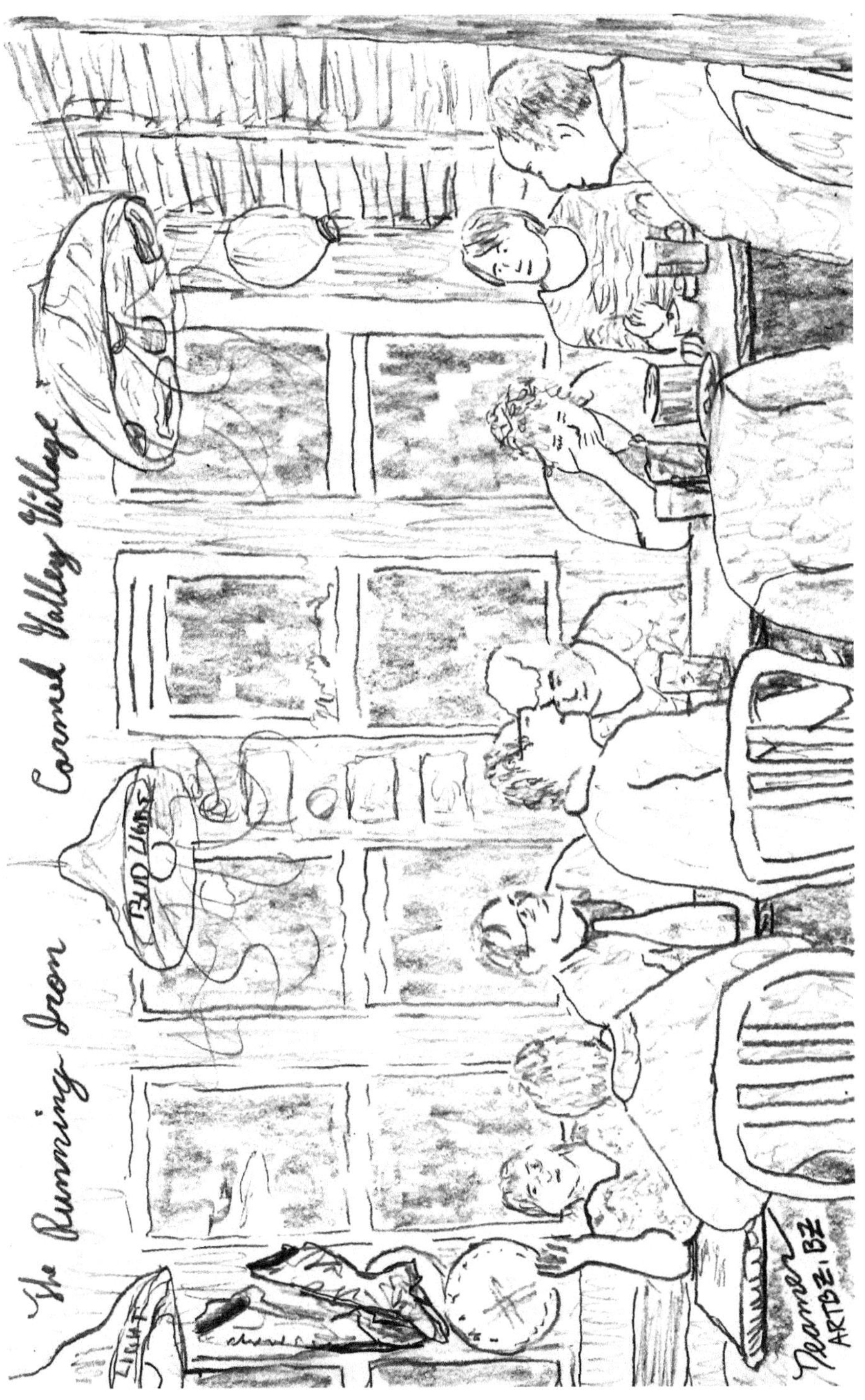
The Running Iron
Carmel Valley Village
BUD LIGHT

92

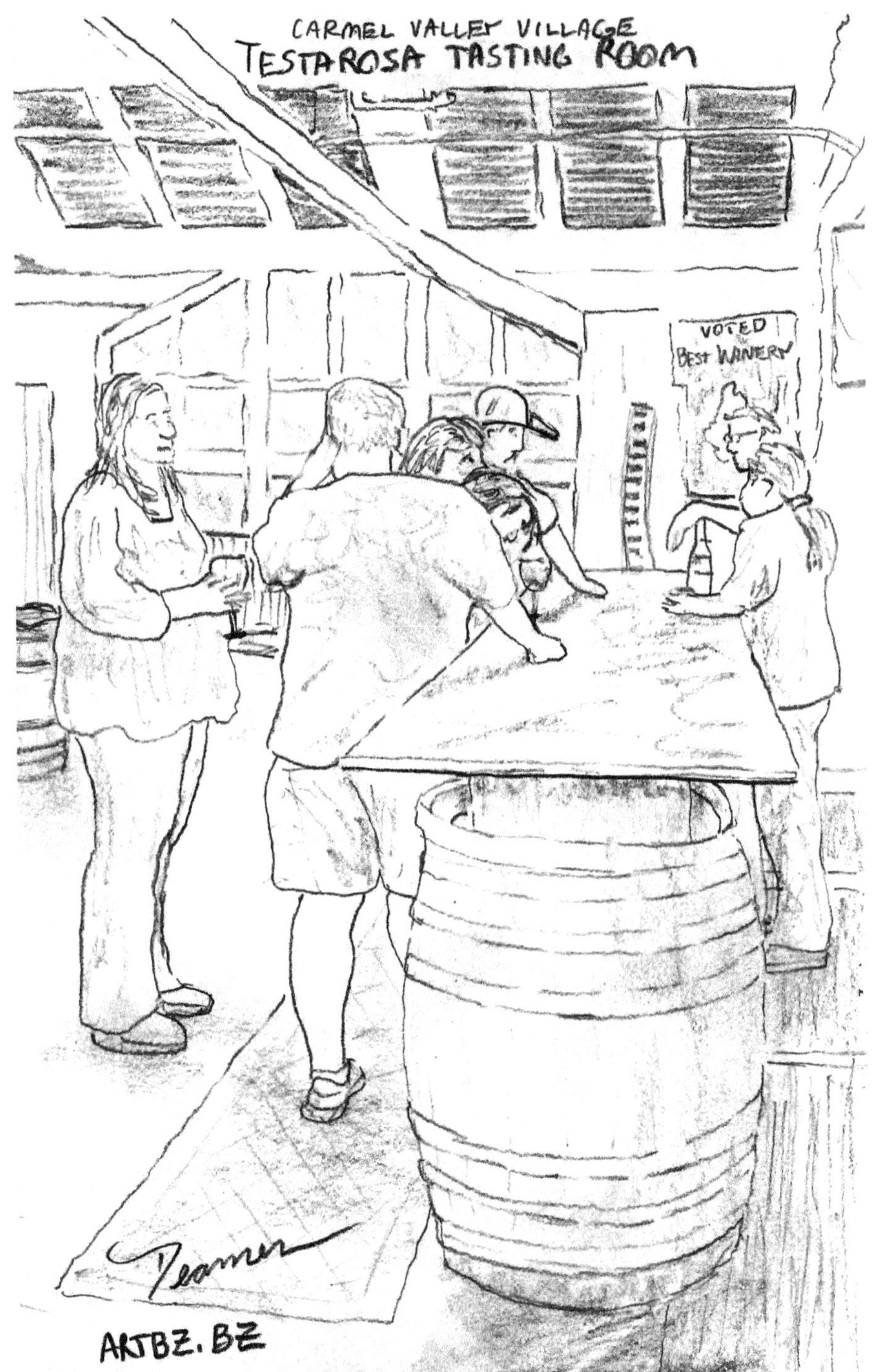
CARMEL VALLEY VILLAGE
TESTAROSA TASTING ROOM
VOTED BEST WINERY
ARTBZ.BZ

DEAMER DUNN

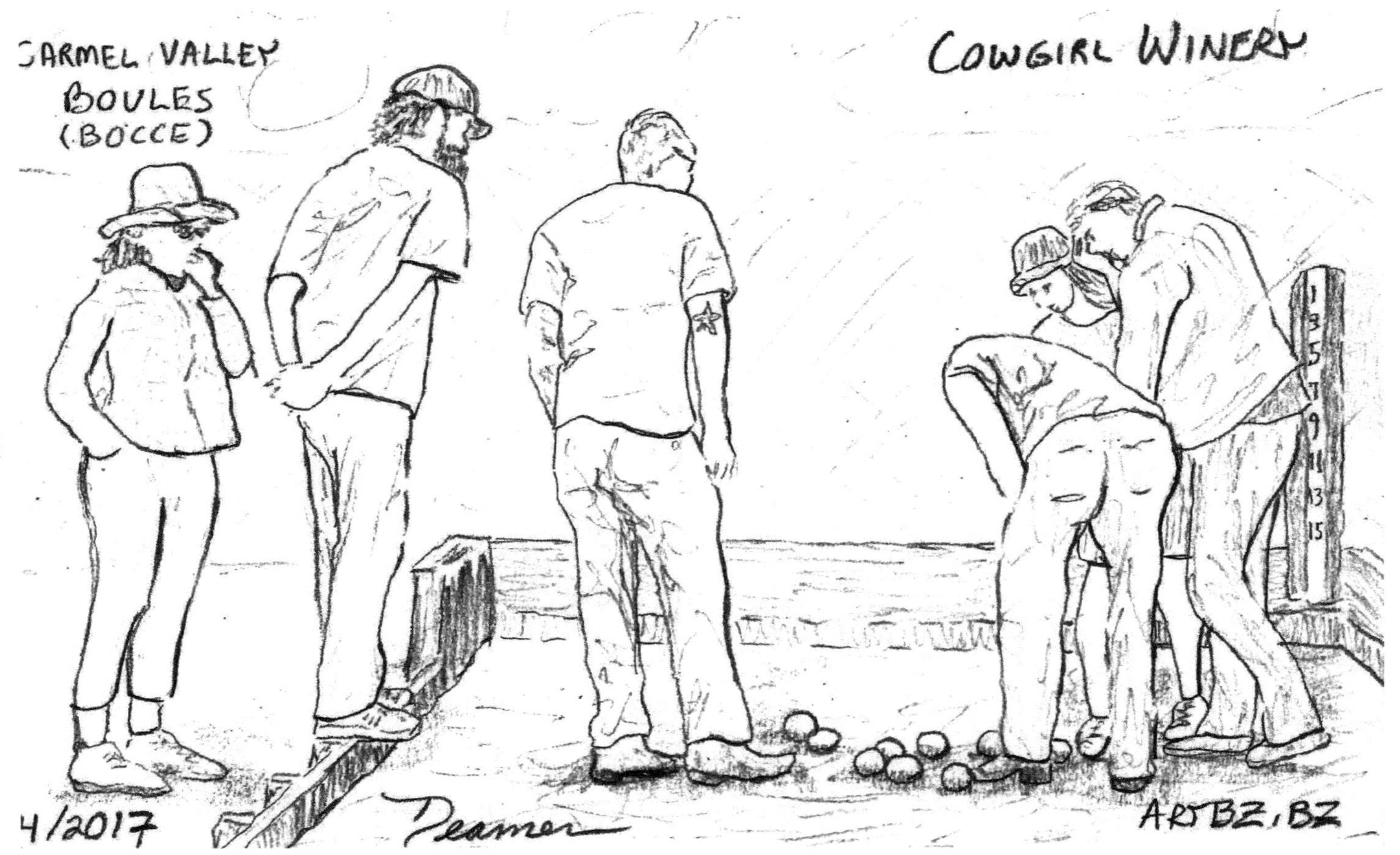
CARMEL VALLEY
BOULES
(BOCCE)
COWGIRL WINERY
4/2017
Pearson
ARTBZ.BZ

96

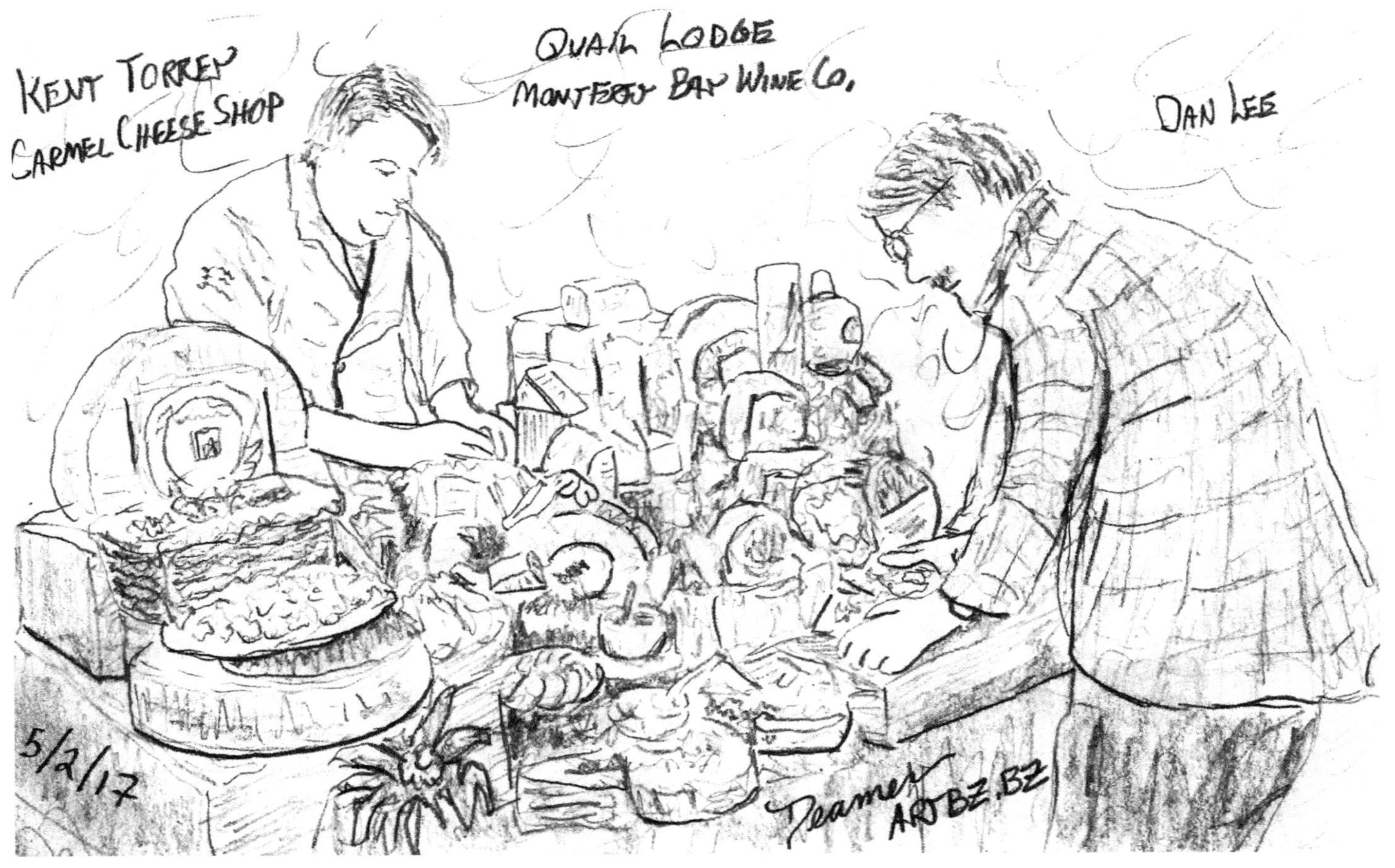
Kent Torrey
Carmel Cheese Shop
Quail Lodge
Monterey Bay Wine Co.
Dan Lee
5/2/17
Deamer ART BZ. BZ

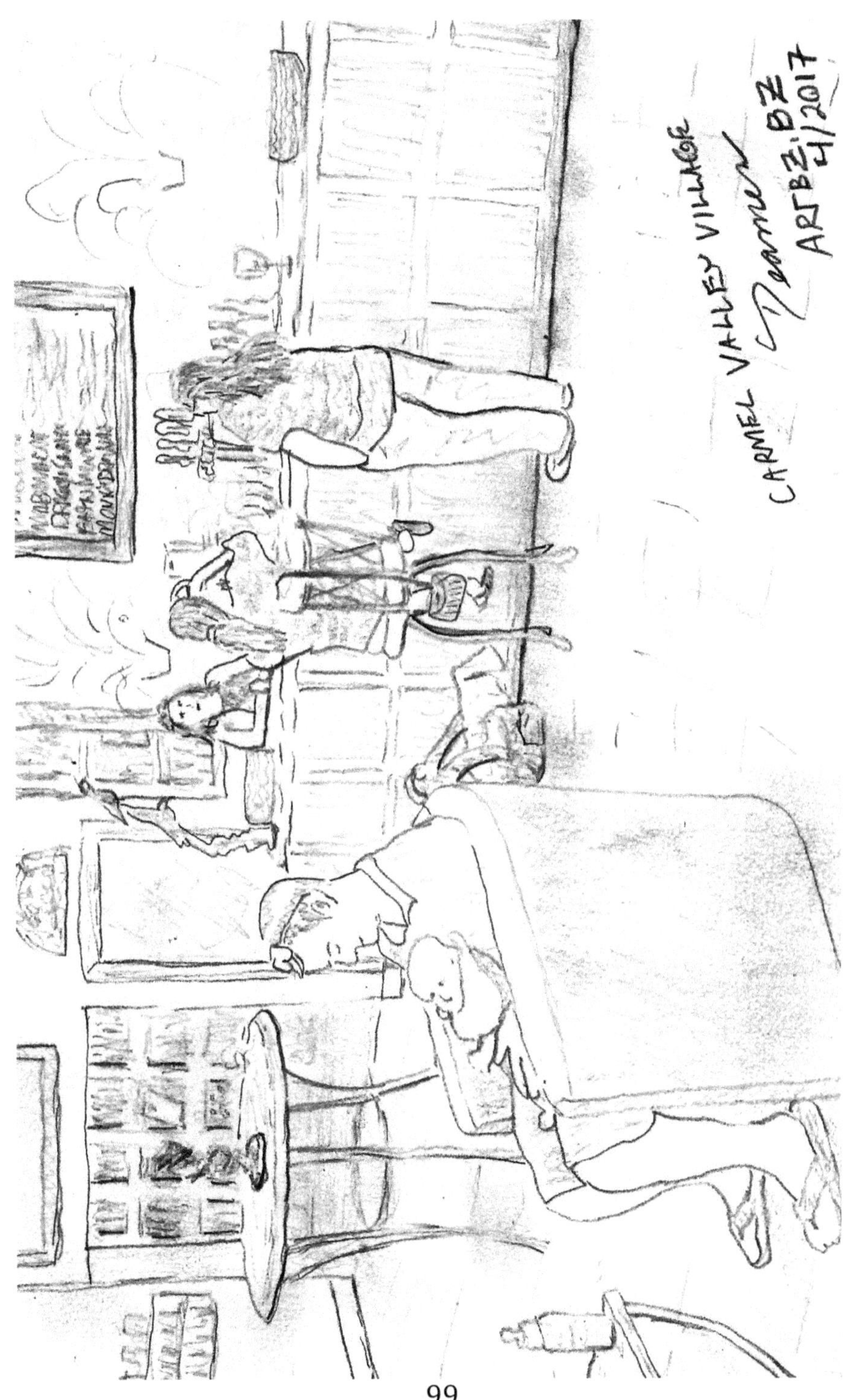
CARMEL VALLEY VILLAGE
Pearmen
APRIL/2017

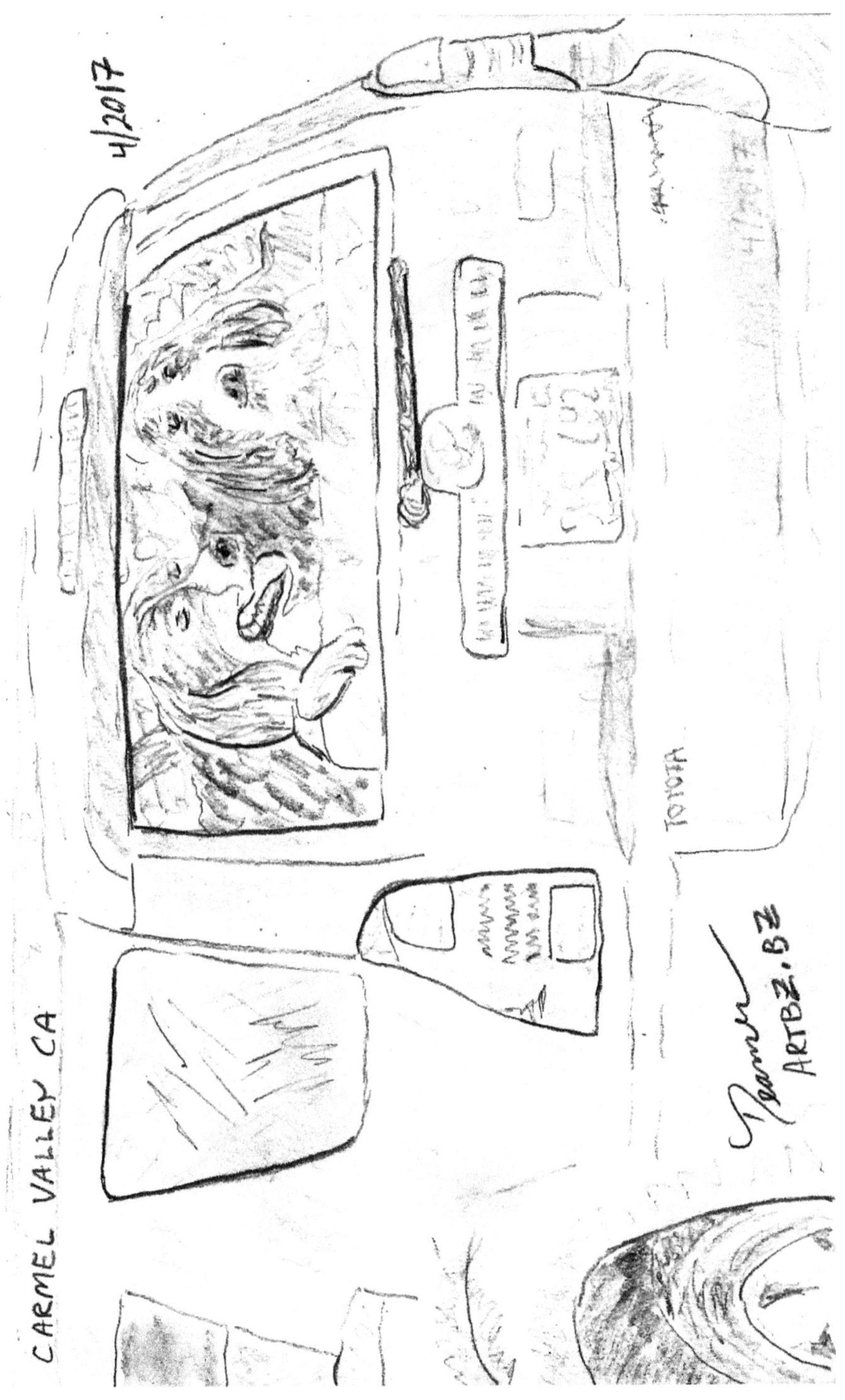
4/2017
CARMEL VALLEY CA
TOYOTA
ARTBZ.BZ

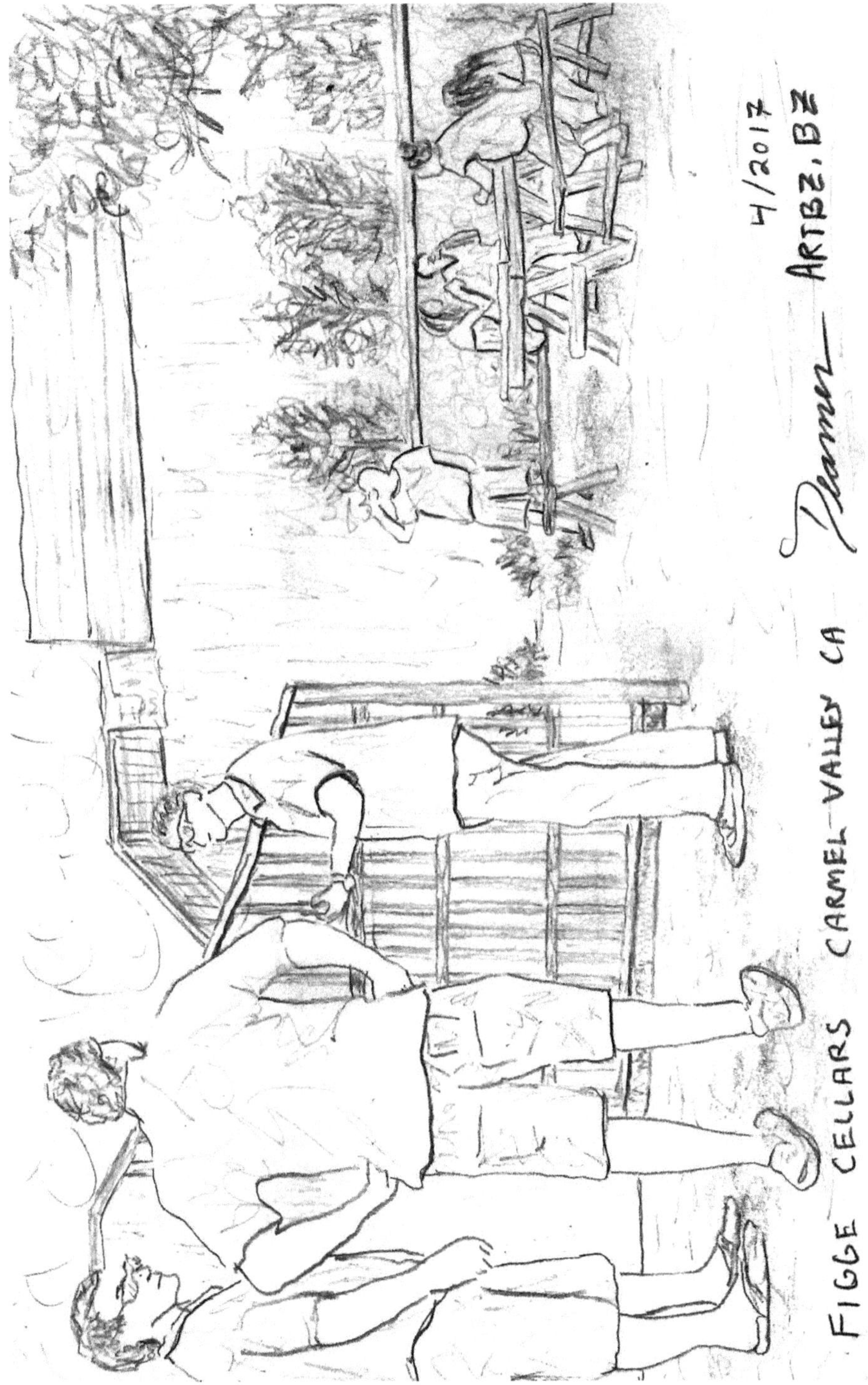
FIGGE CELLARS CARMEL VALLEY CA
4/2017
ARTBZ.BZ

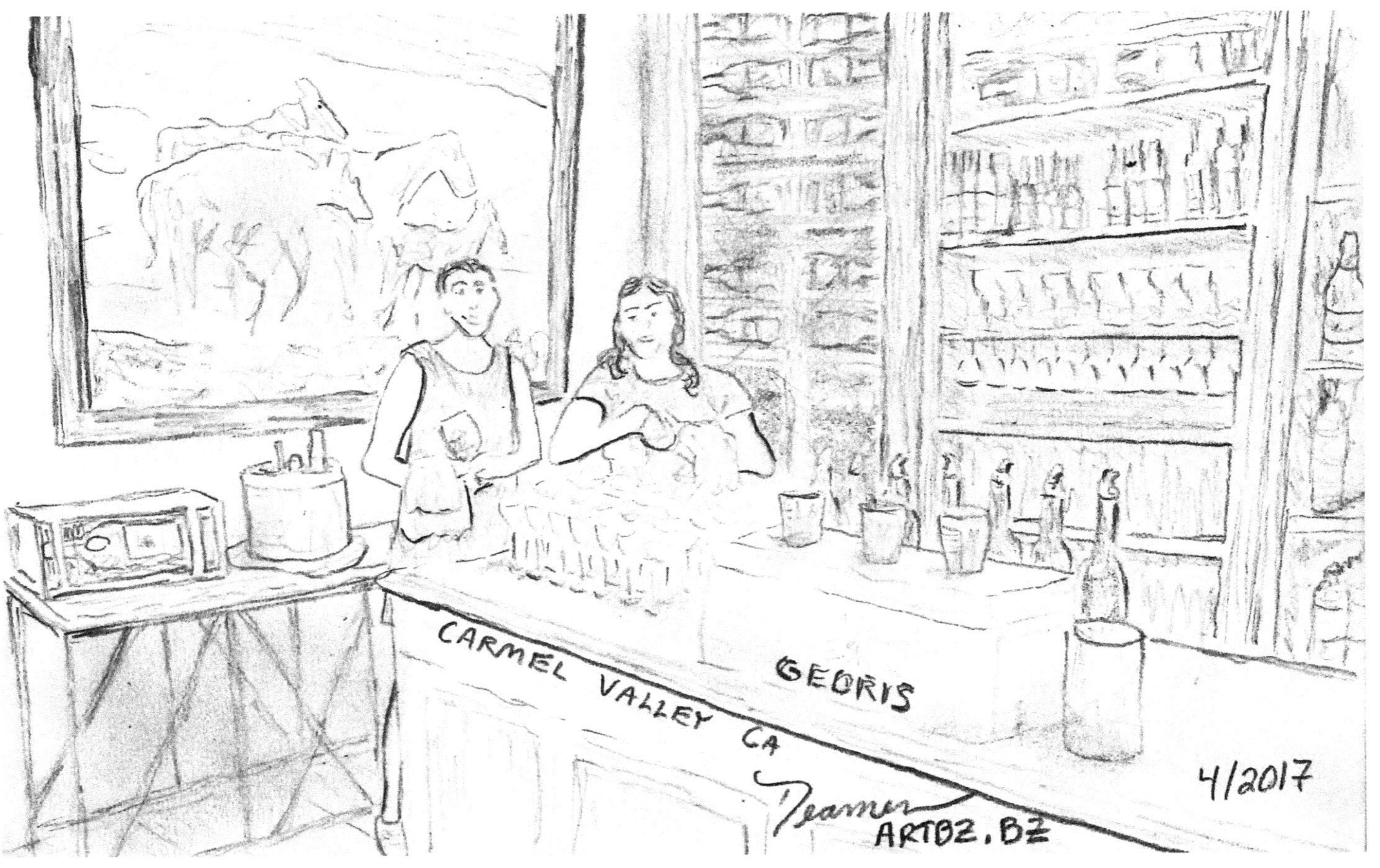
CARMEL VALLEY CA
GEORIS
ART02.BZ
4/2017

106

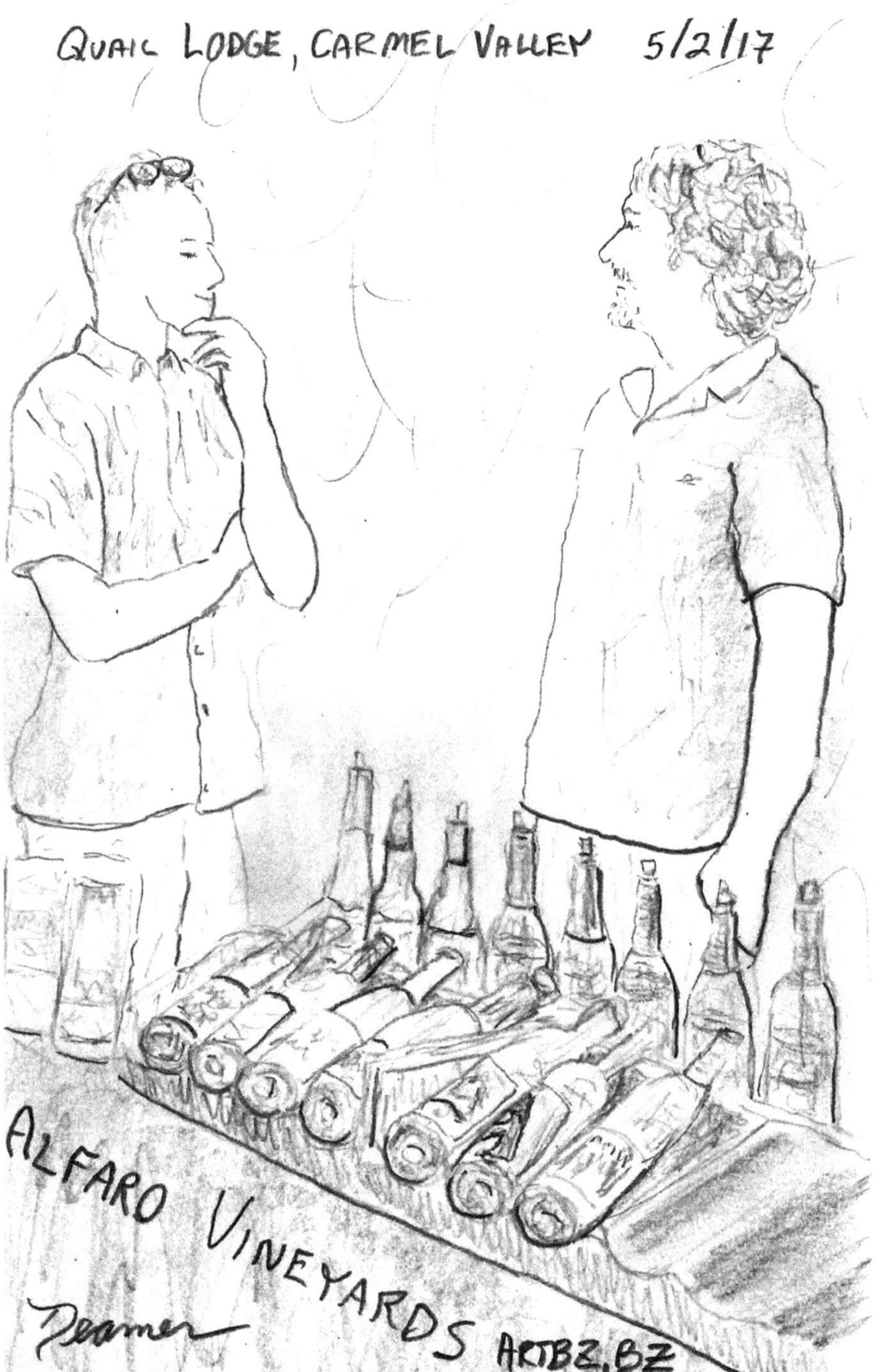
QUAIL LODGE, CARMEL VALLEY 5/2/17
ALFARO VINEYARDS
ARTBZ.BZ

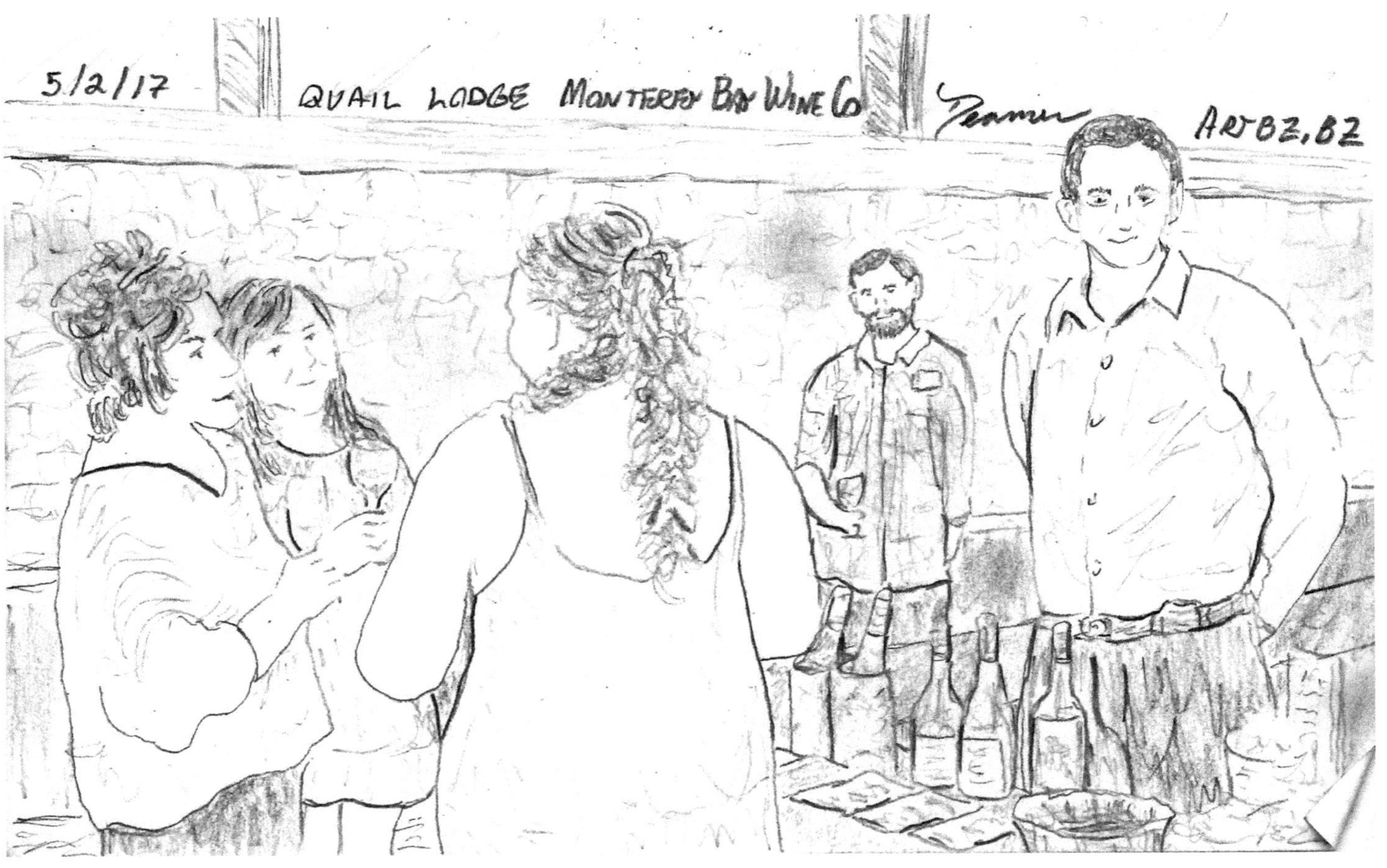
5/2/17   QUAIL LODGE   Monterey Bay Wine Co
Aug 82, 82

110

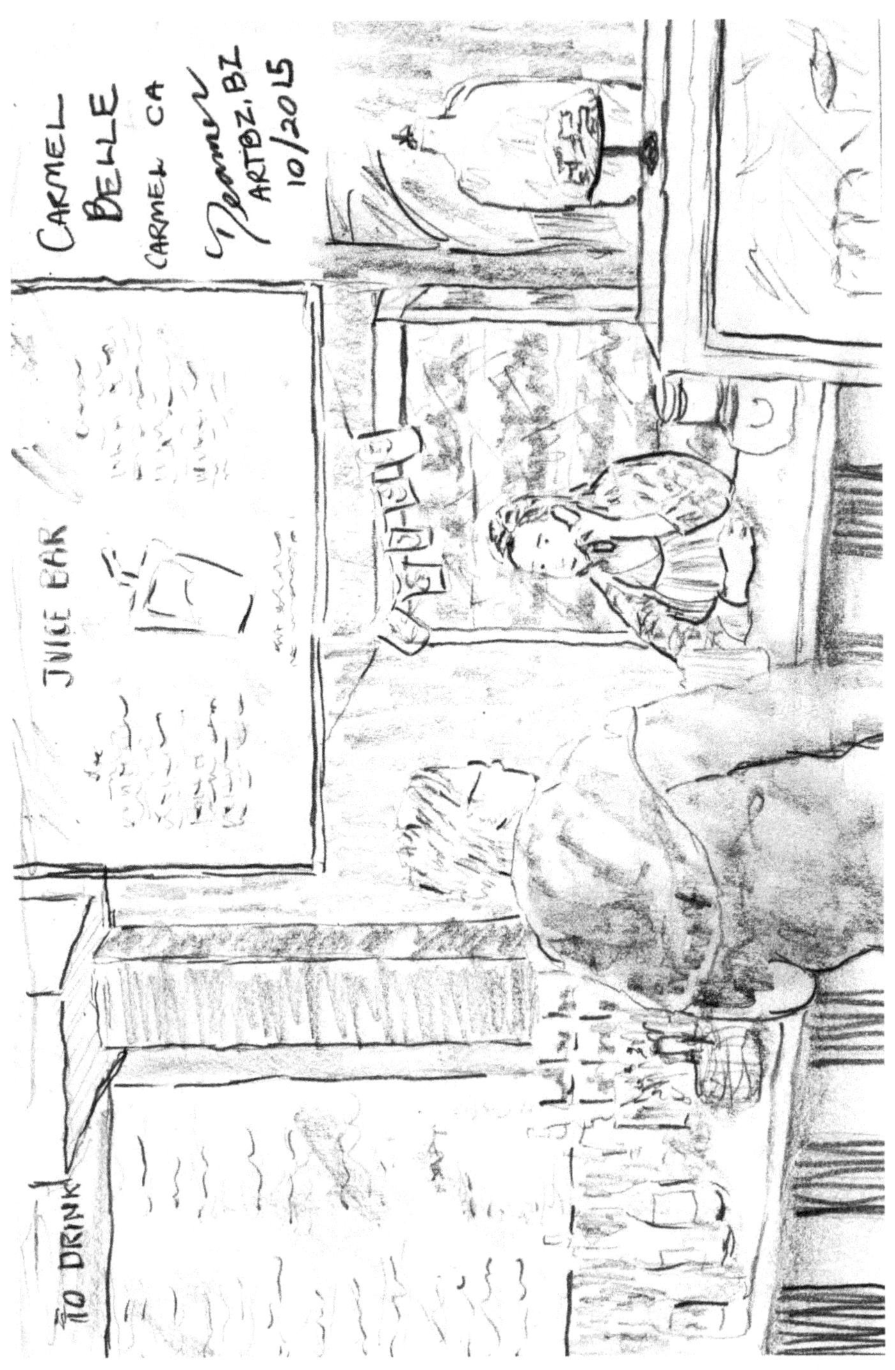
CARMEL
BELLE
CARMEL CA
Yeoman
ARTOZ, BZ
10/20 15
JUICE BAR
TO DRINK

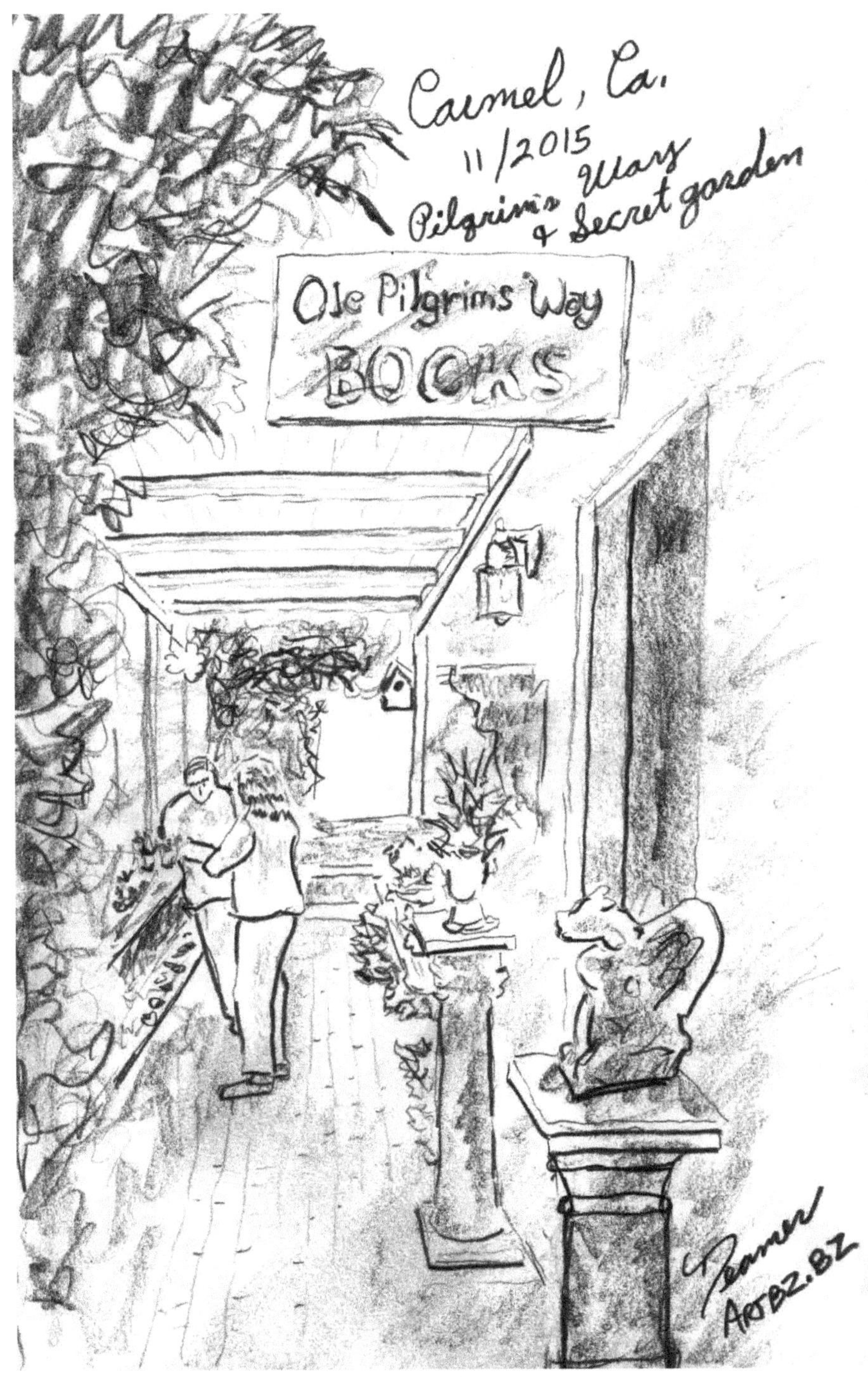
Carmel, Ca.
11/2015
Pilgrims Way
& Secret garden
Ole Pilgrims' Way
BOOKS

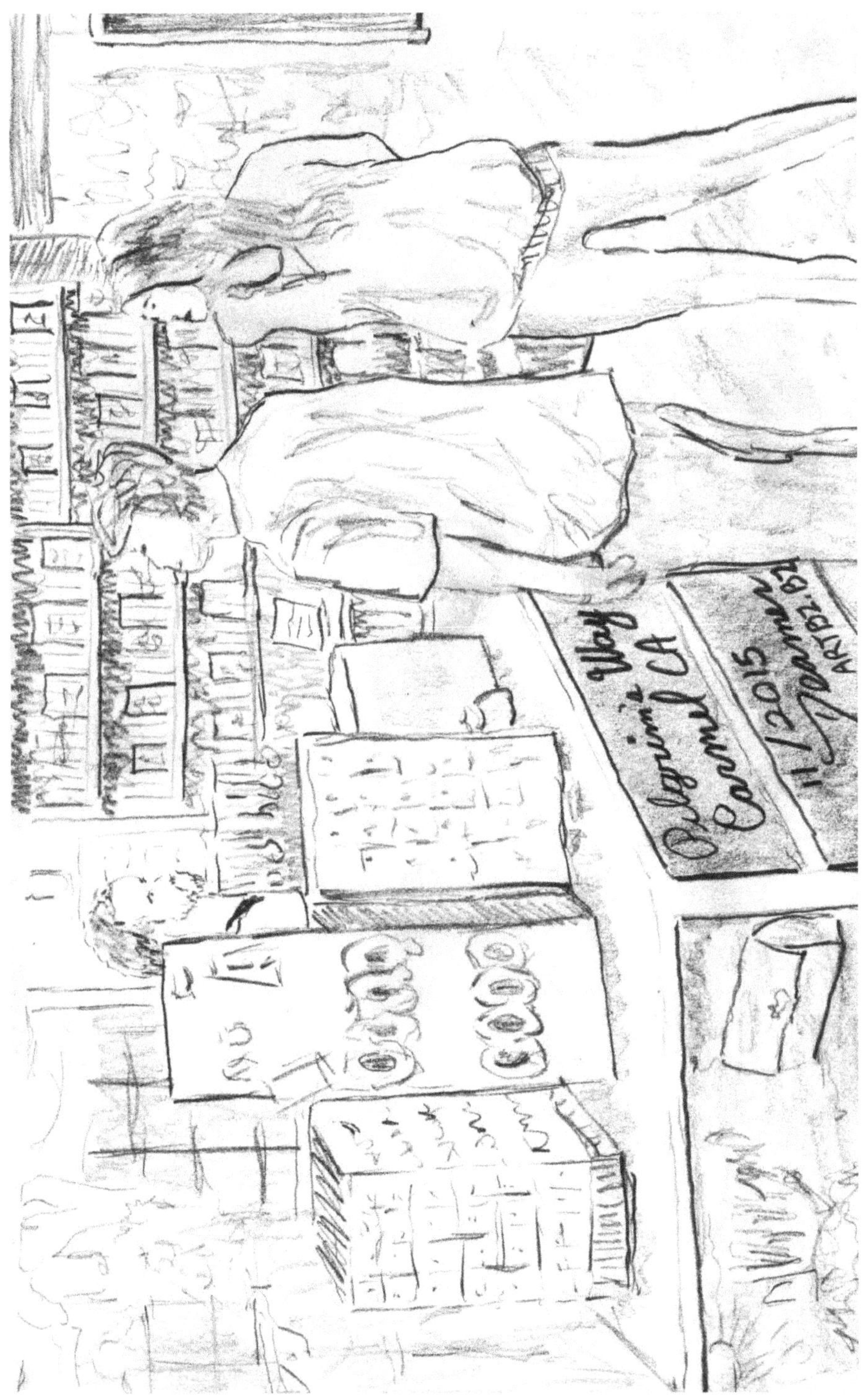

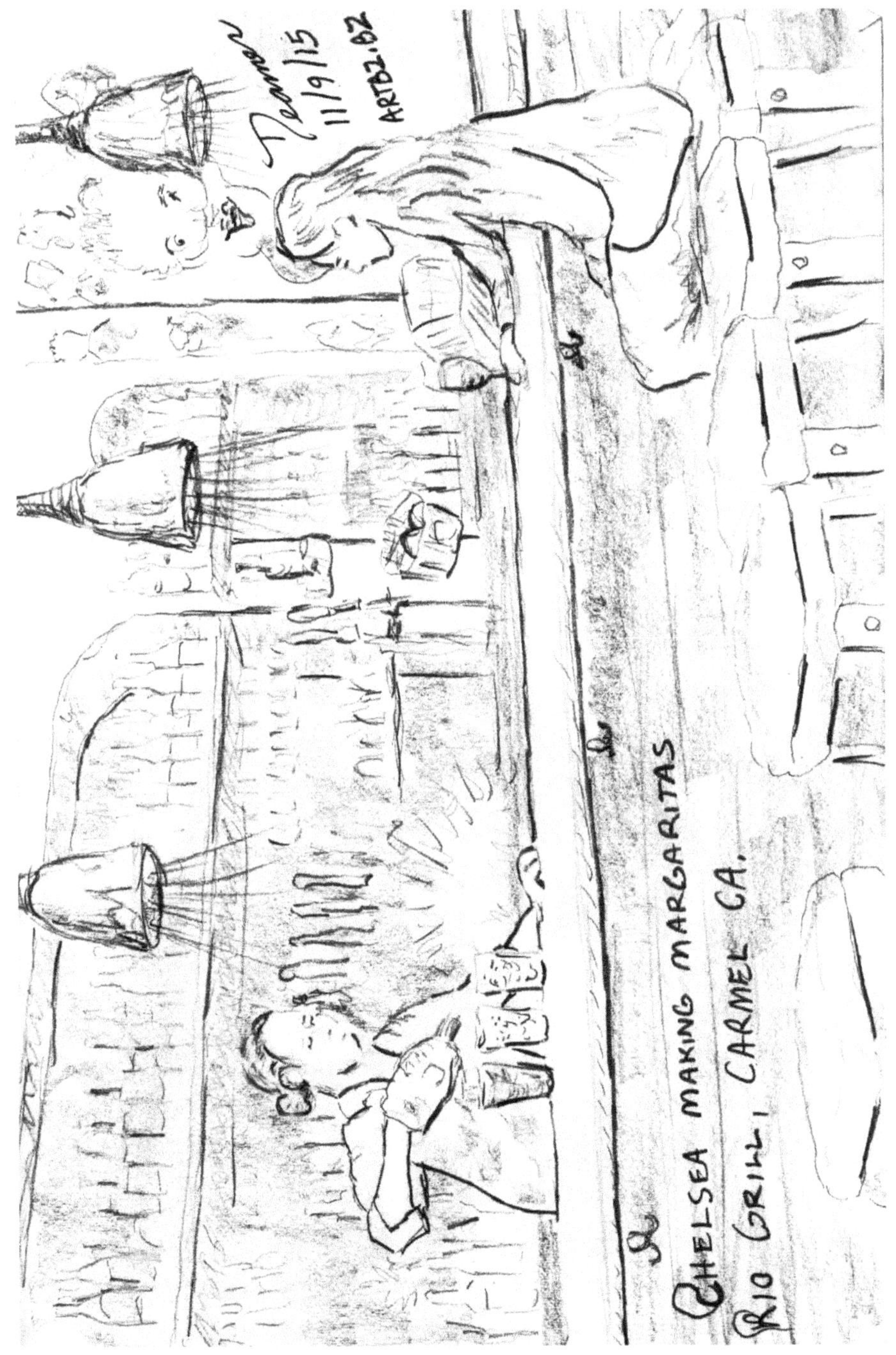
Pearman
11/9/15
ARTB2.62
Chelsea making margaritas
Rio Grill, Carmel CA.

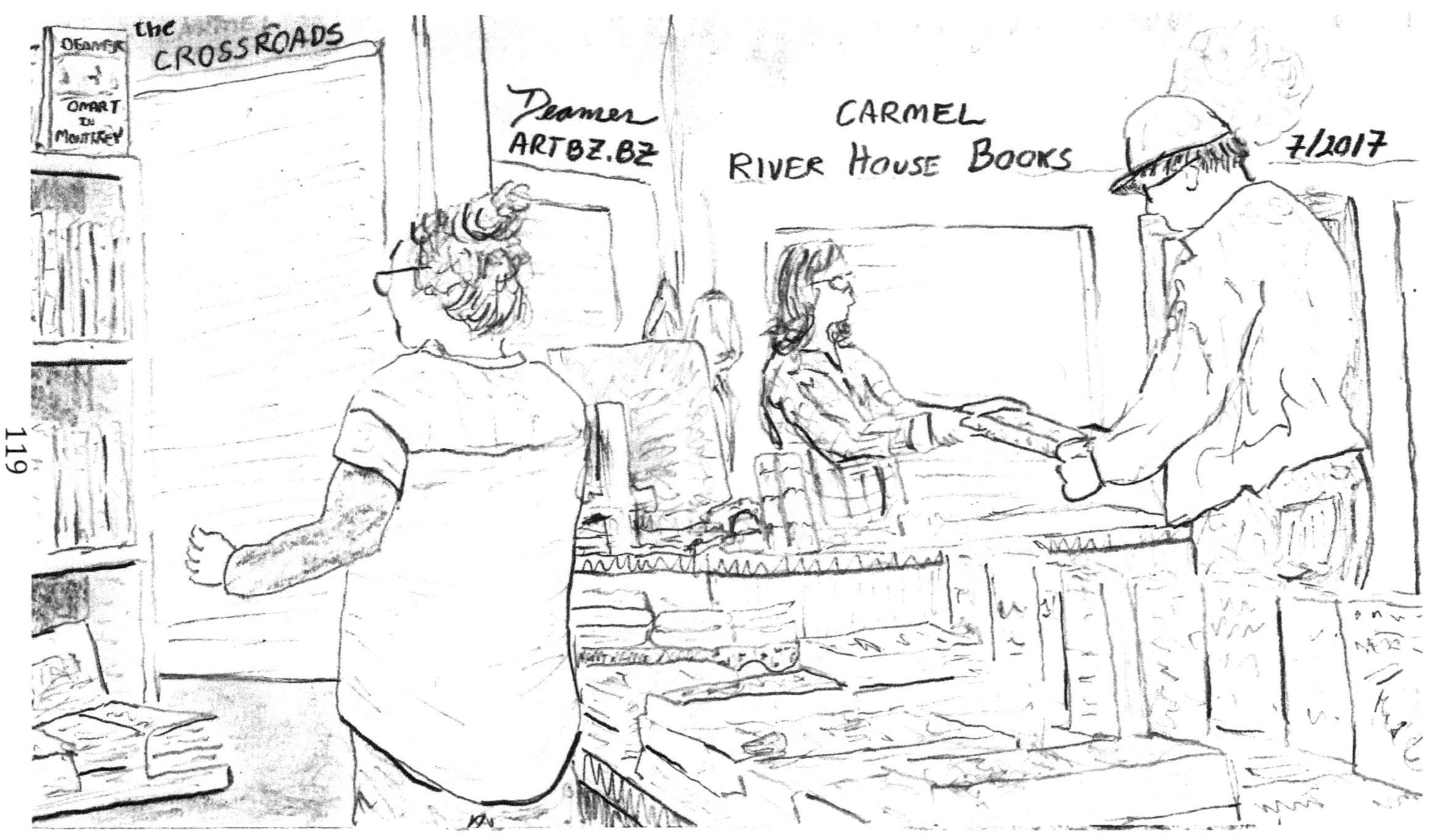

the CROSSROADS
OBANER
OMART TO MONTEREY
Deamer
ARTBZ.BZ
CARMEL
RIVER HOUSE BOOKS
7/2017

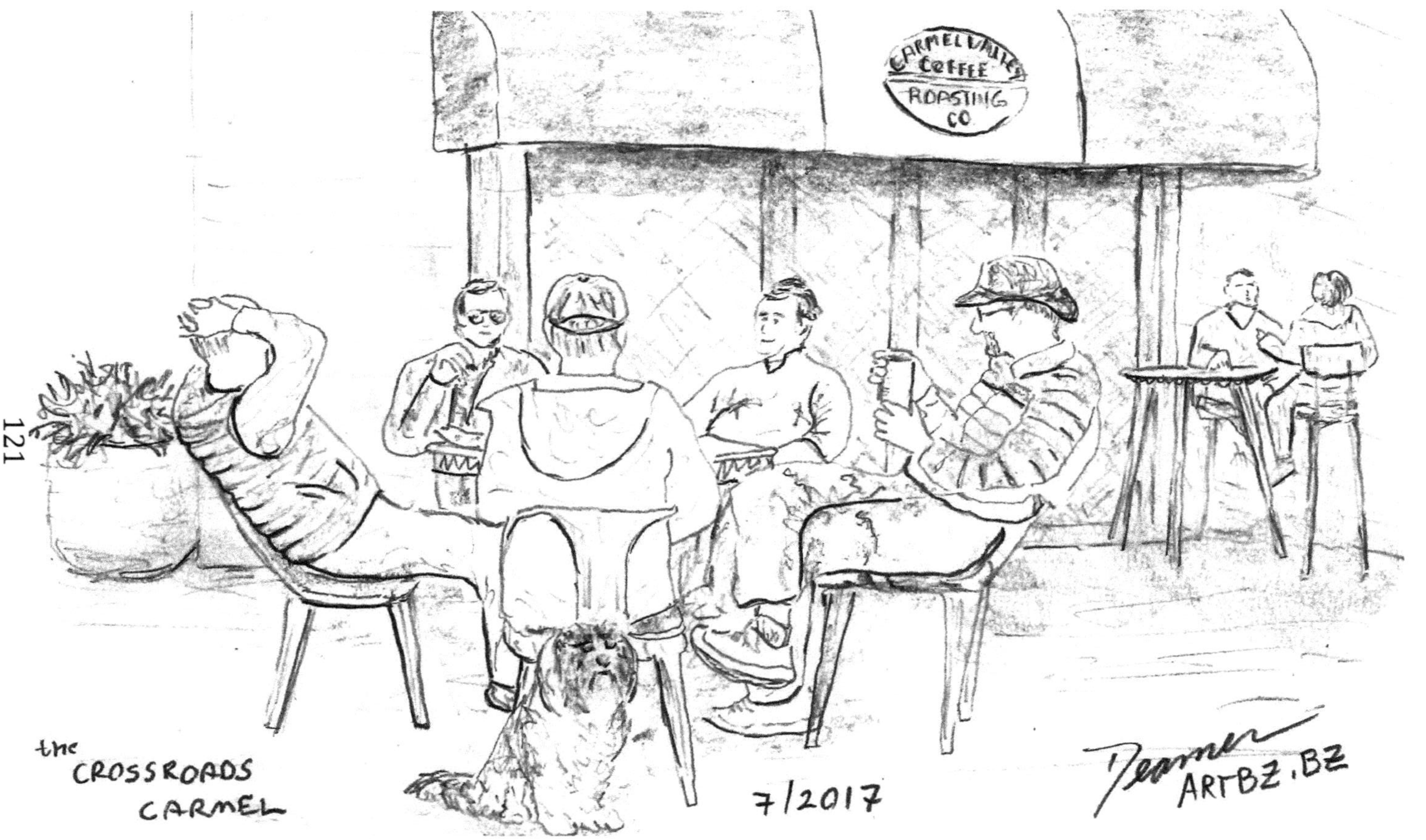
CARMEL VALLEY Coffee ROASTING CO
the CROSSROADS CARMEL
7/2017
ArtBZ.BZ

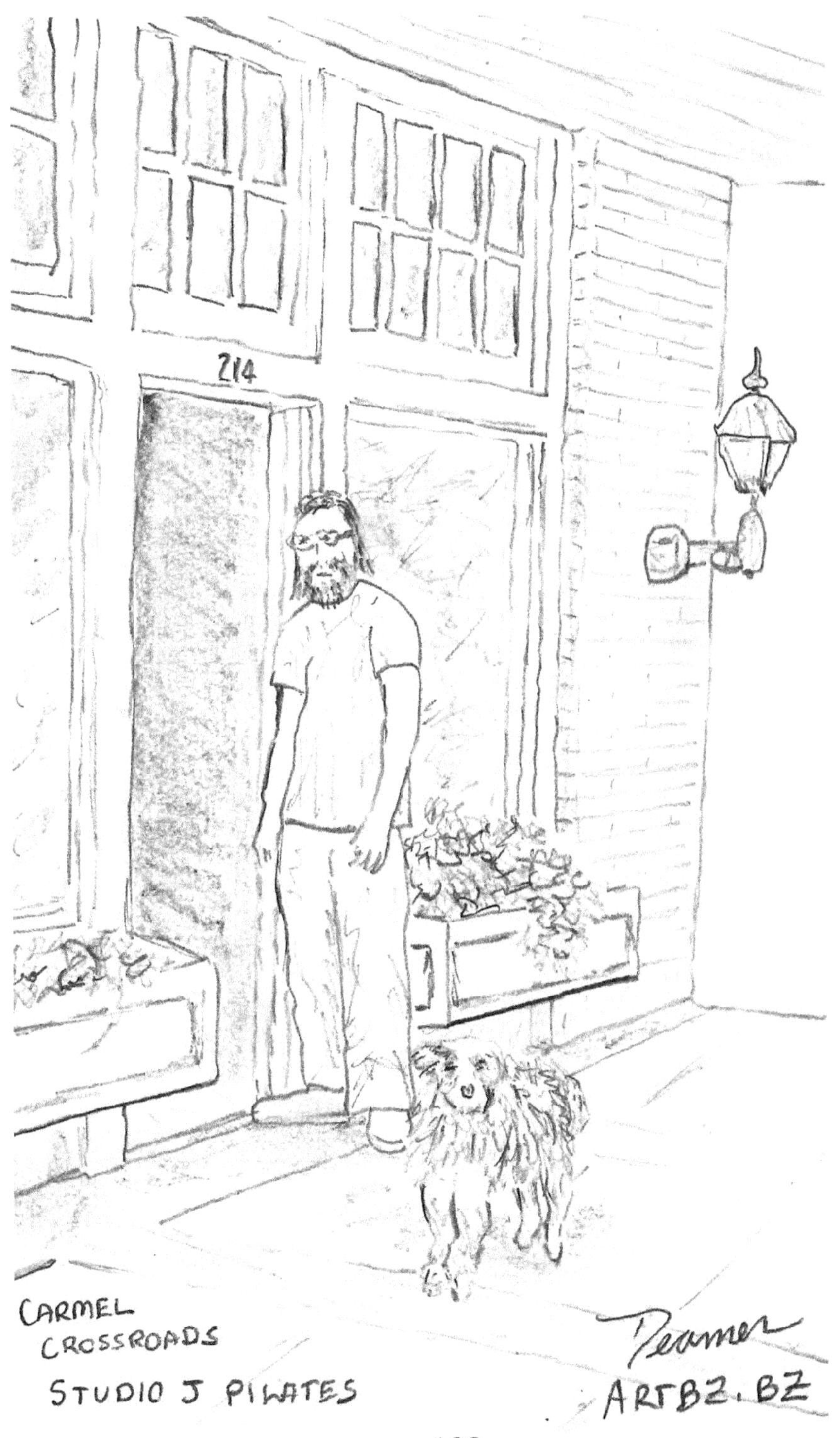
214
CARMEL
CROSSROADS
STUDIO J PILATES
ARTBZ.BZ

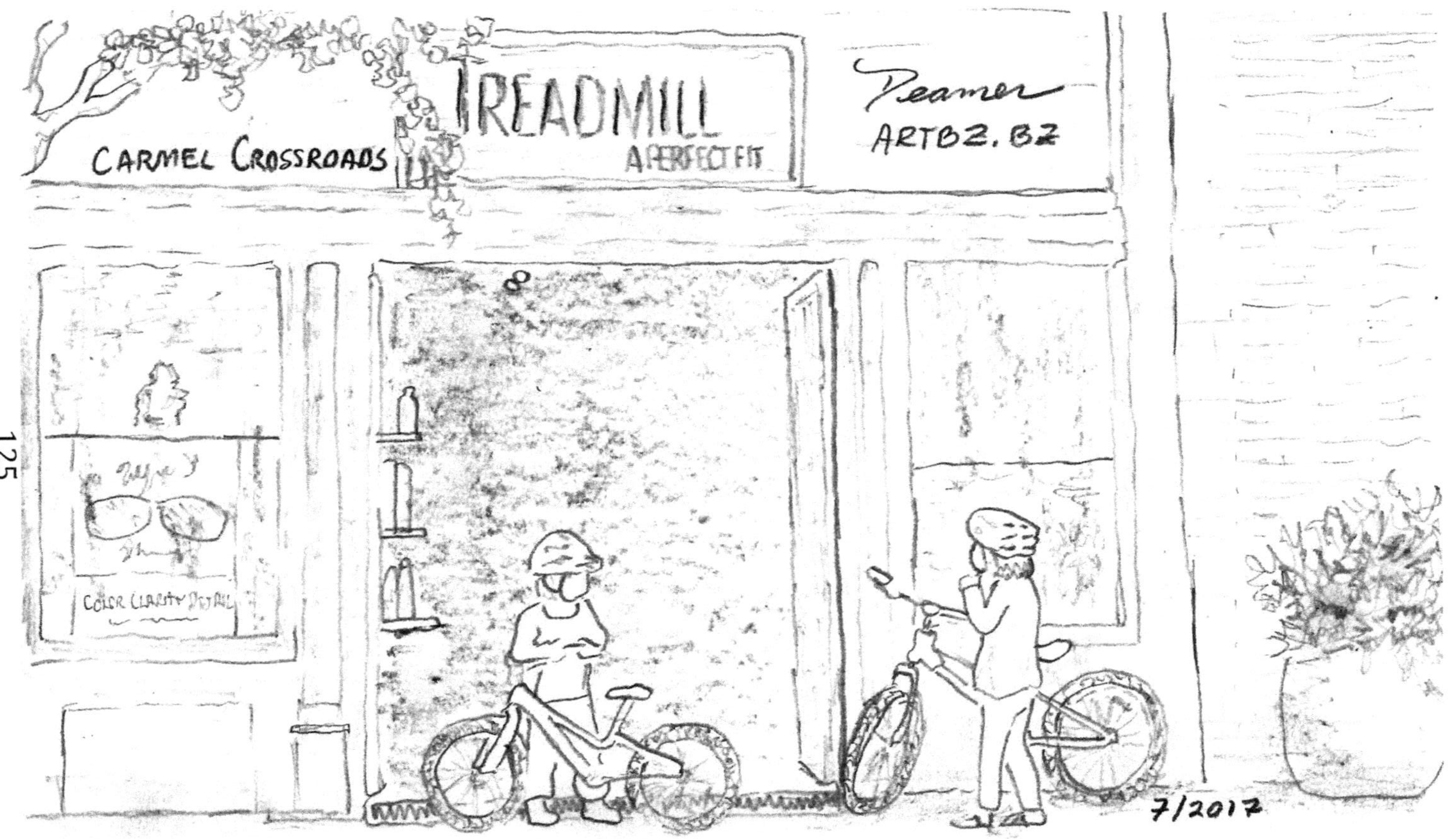
CARMEL CROSSROADS
TREADMILL
A PERFECT FIT
Reamer ARTB2.B2
COLOR CLARITY DETAIL
7/2017

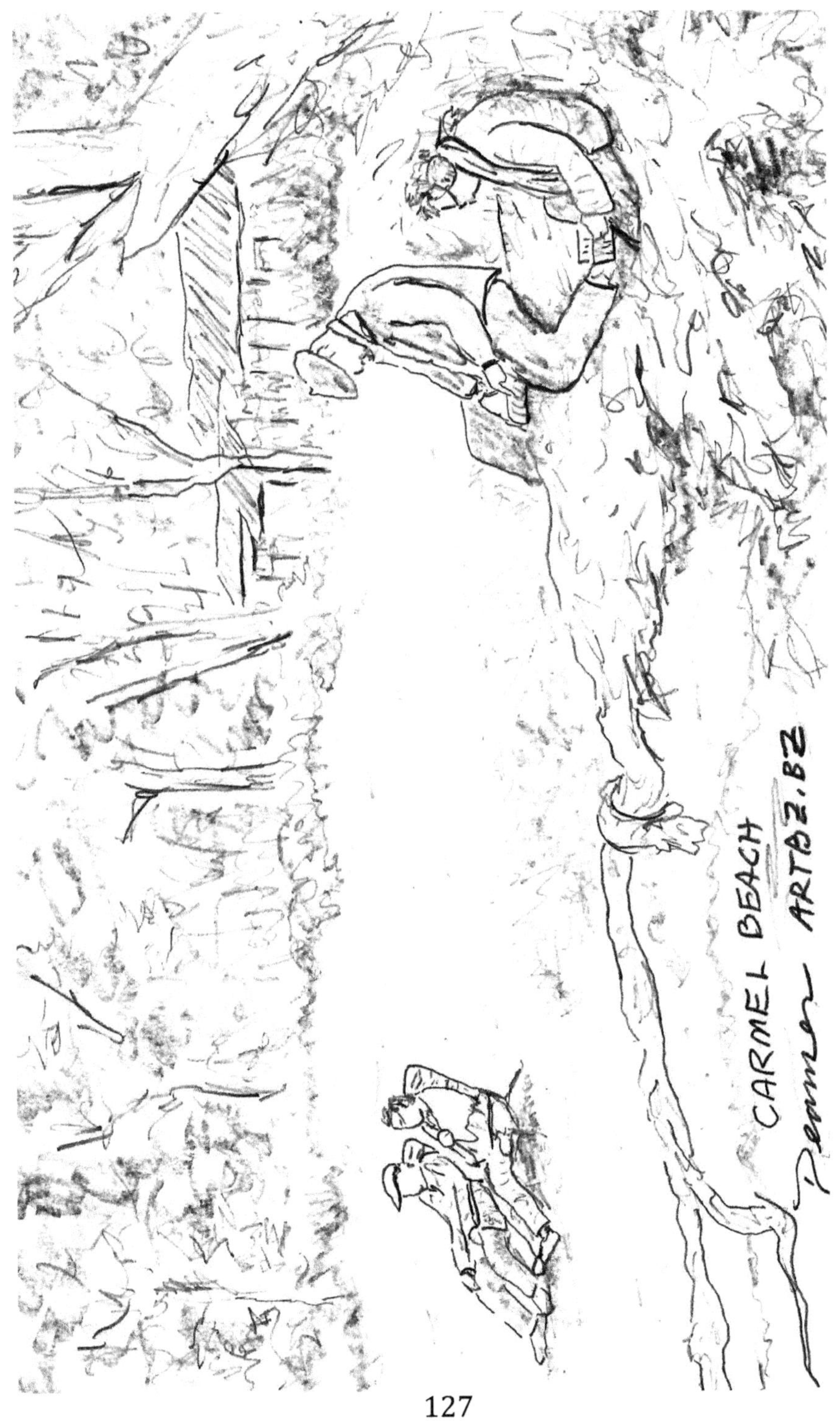
CARMEL BEACH
Penman ART82.B2

128

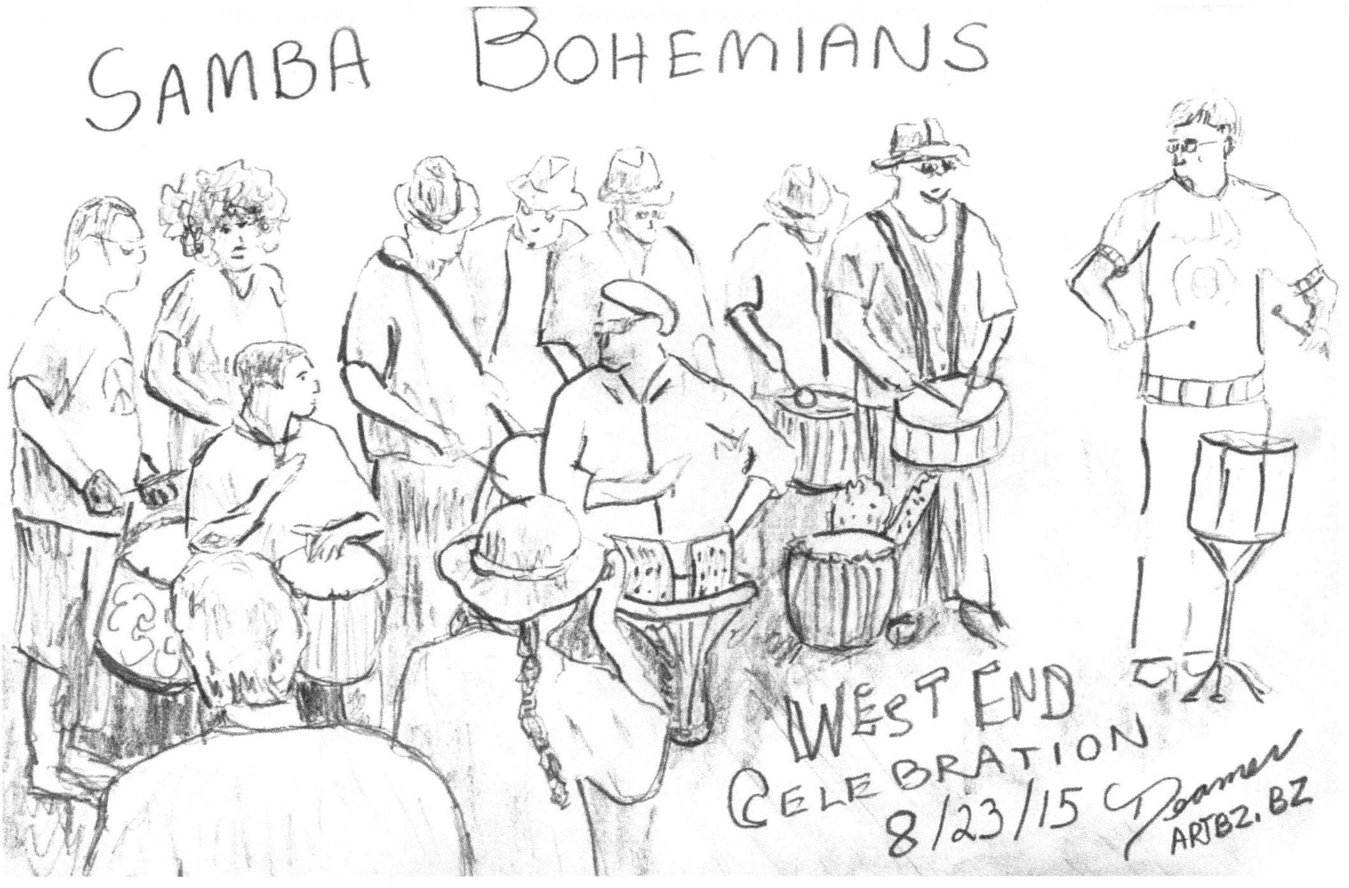
SAMBA BOHEMIANS
WEST END
CELEBRATION
8/23/15
ARTB2.BZ

130

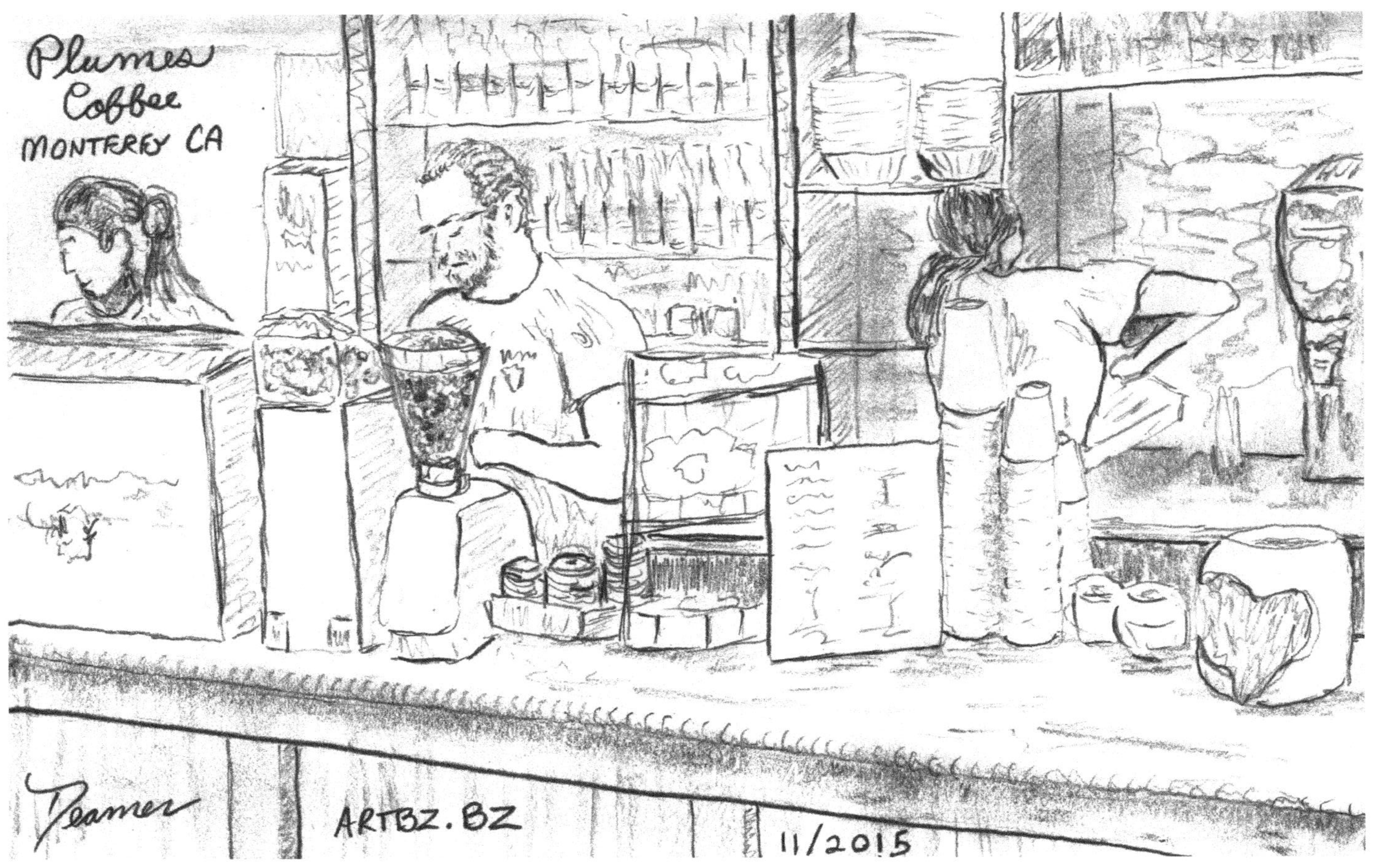

Plumes
Coffee
MONTEREY CA
ARTBZ.BZ
11/2015

DEAMER DUNN

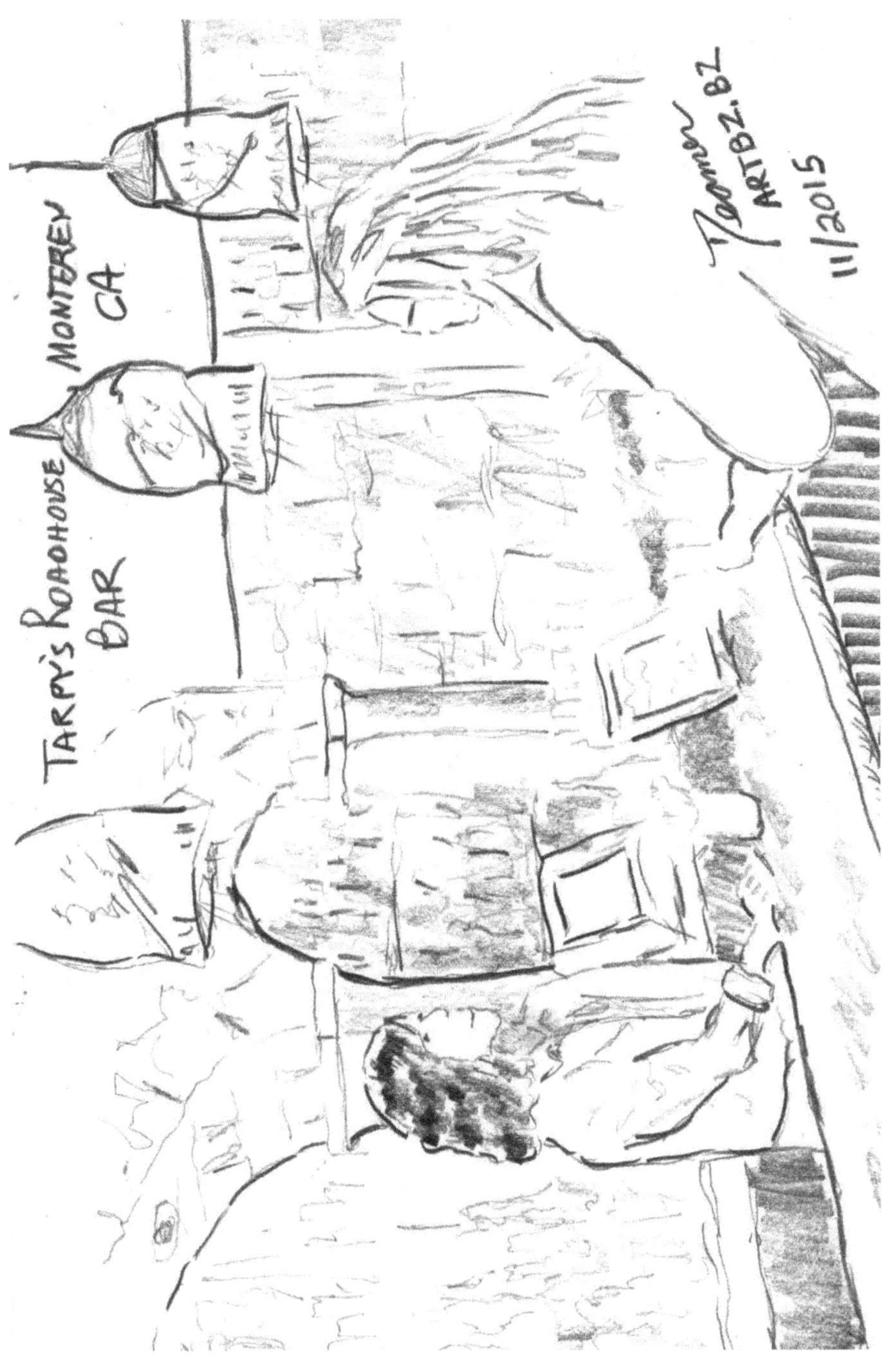
TARPY'S ROADHOUSE
BAR
MONTEREY
CA
Toomer
ART B2.B2
11/2015

134

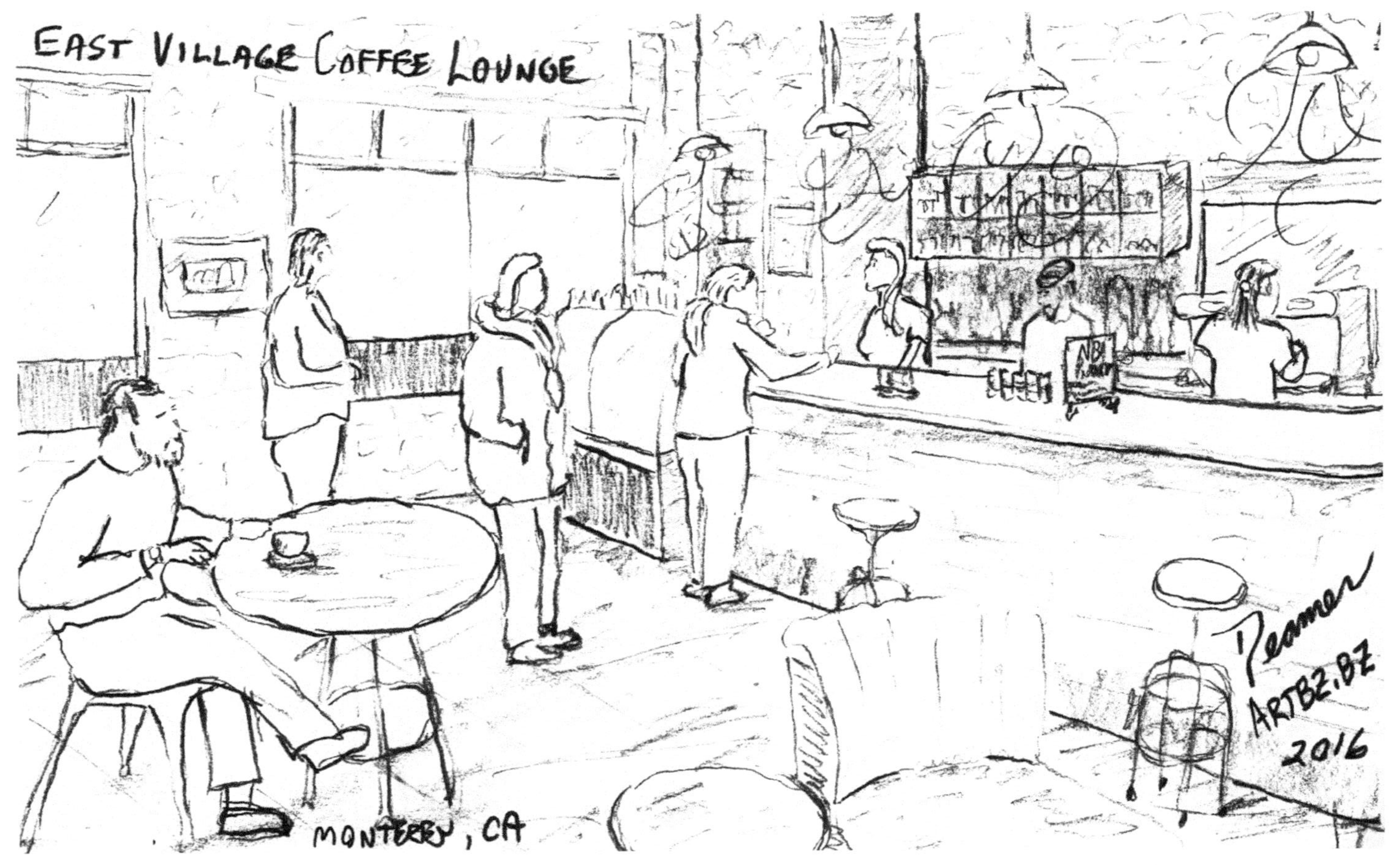
EAST VILLAGE COFFEE LOUNGE
MONTERRY, CA
Reamer
ARTB2.BZ
2016

136

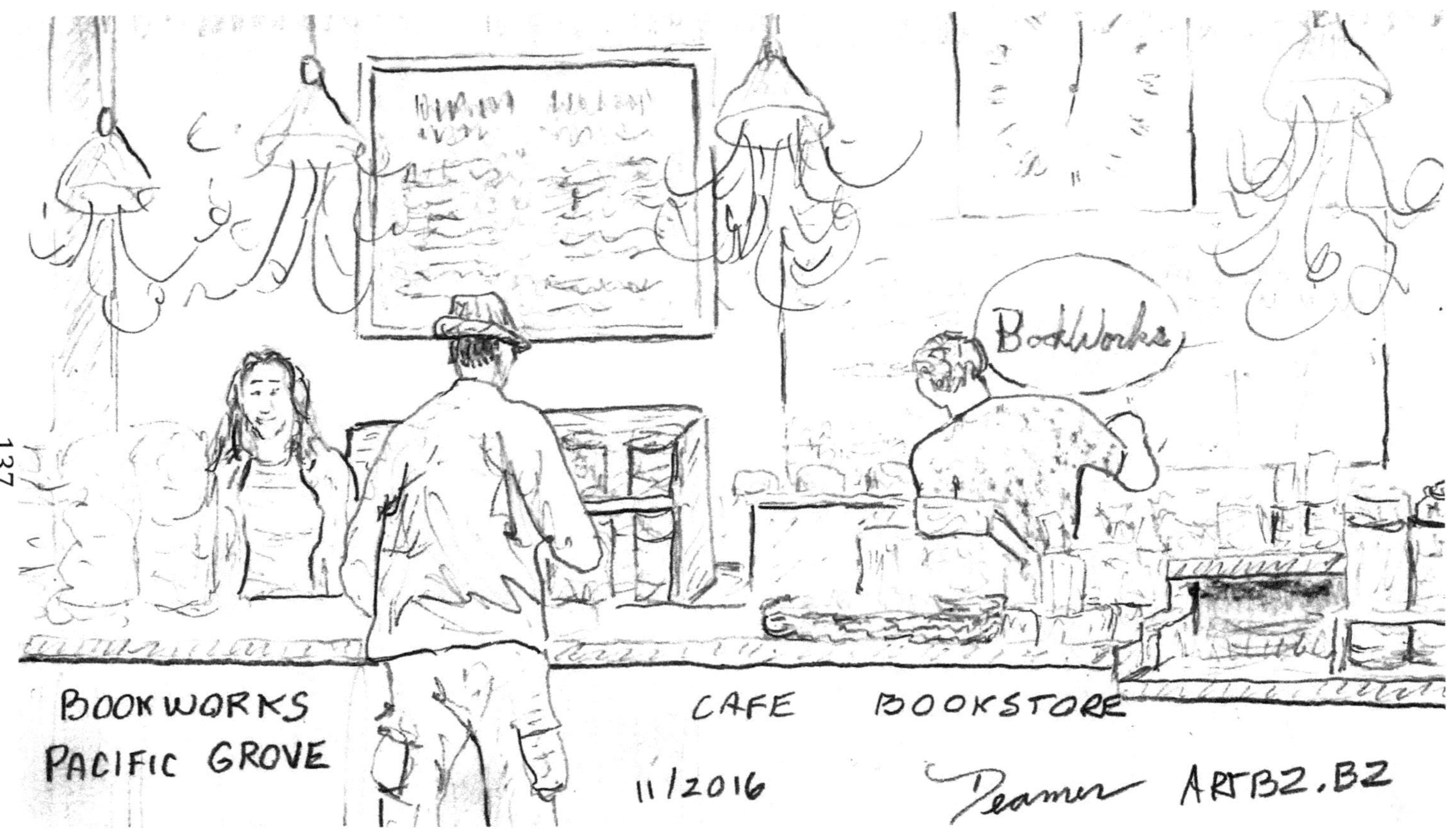
BookWorks
BOOKWORKS
PACIFIC GROVE
CAFE   BOOKSTORE
11/2016
Deamer   ARTB2.BZ

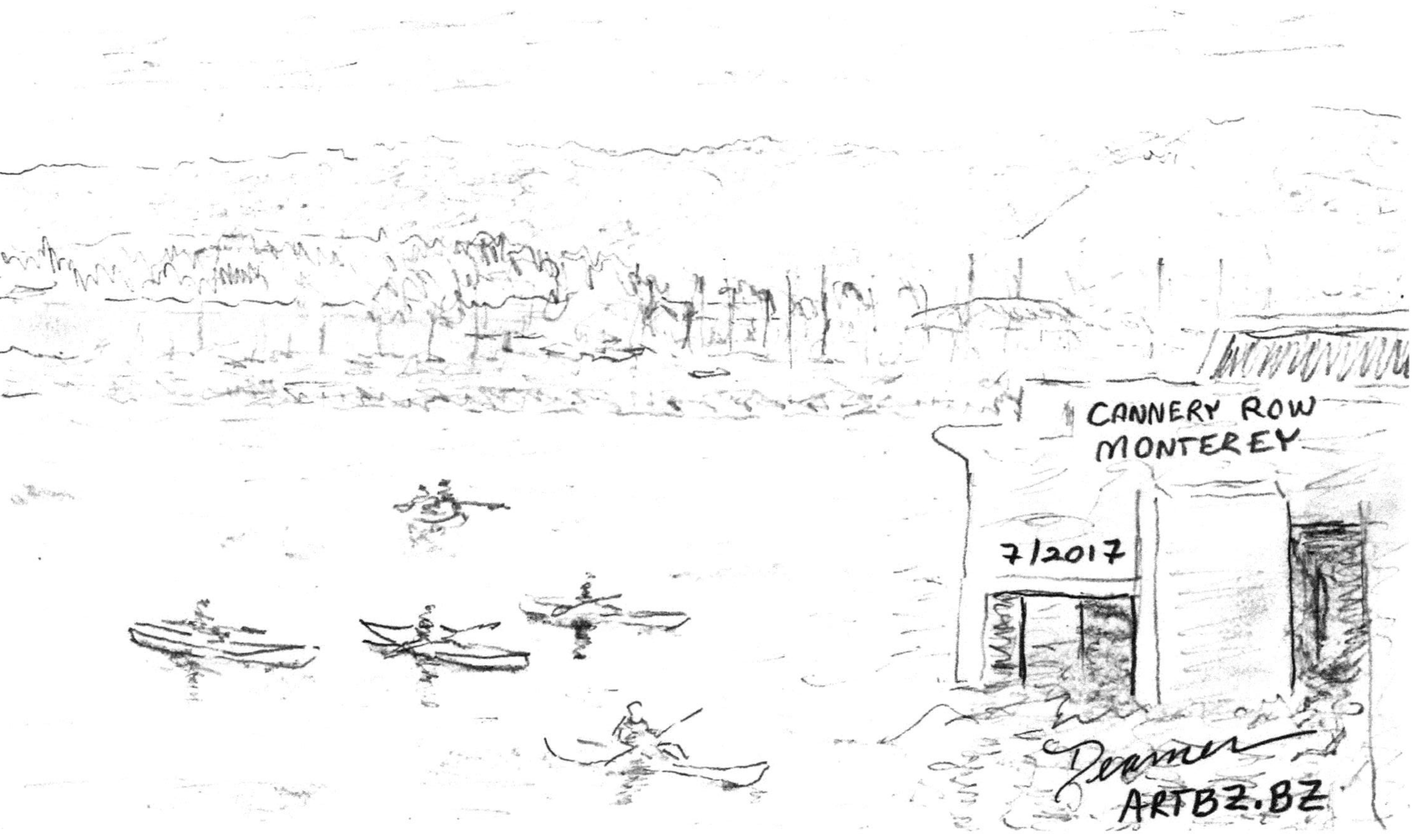

CANNERY ROW
MONTEREY
7/2017
ARTBZ.BZ

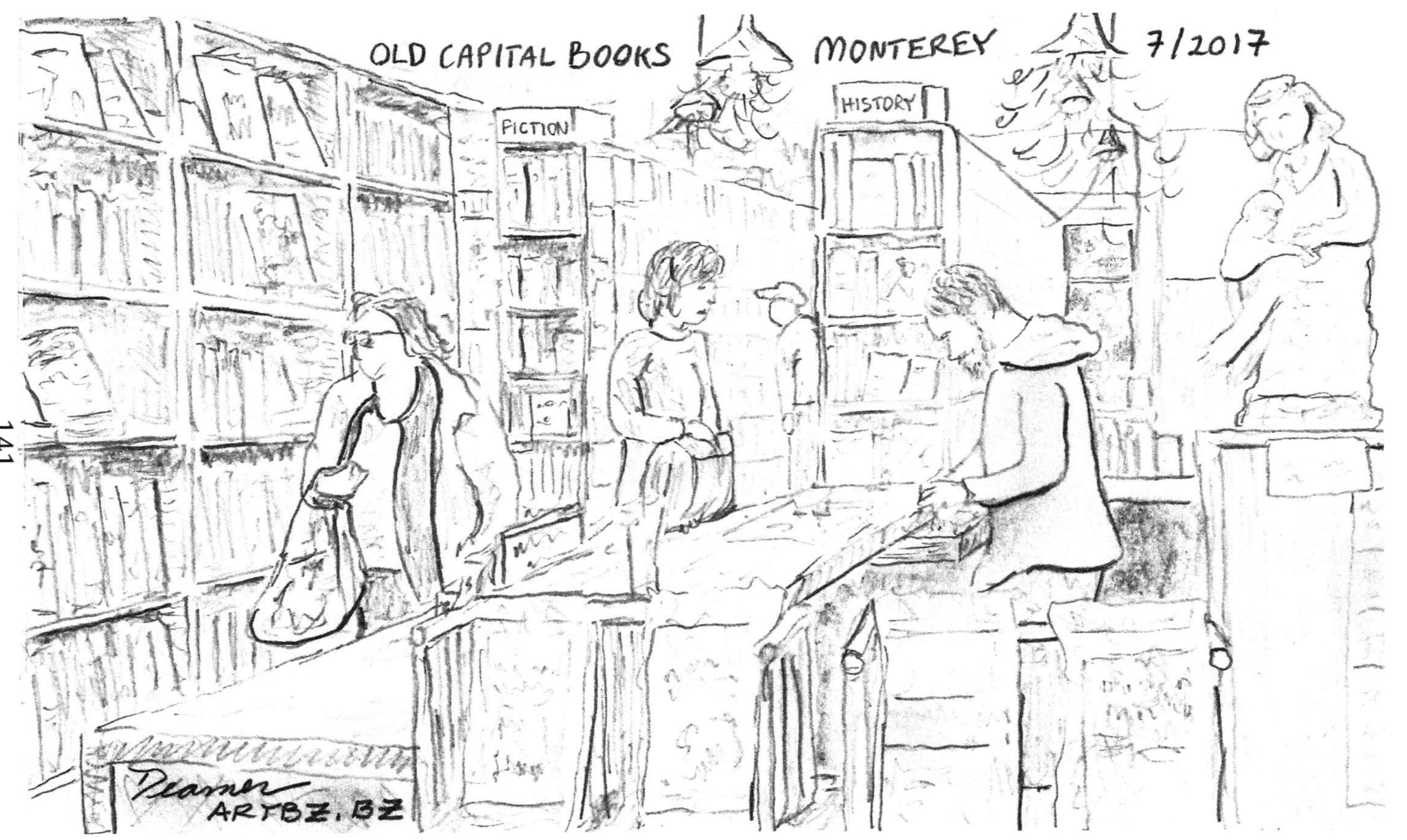

OLD CAPITAL BOOKS
MONTEREY
7/2017
FICTION
HISTORY

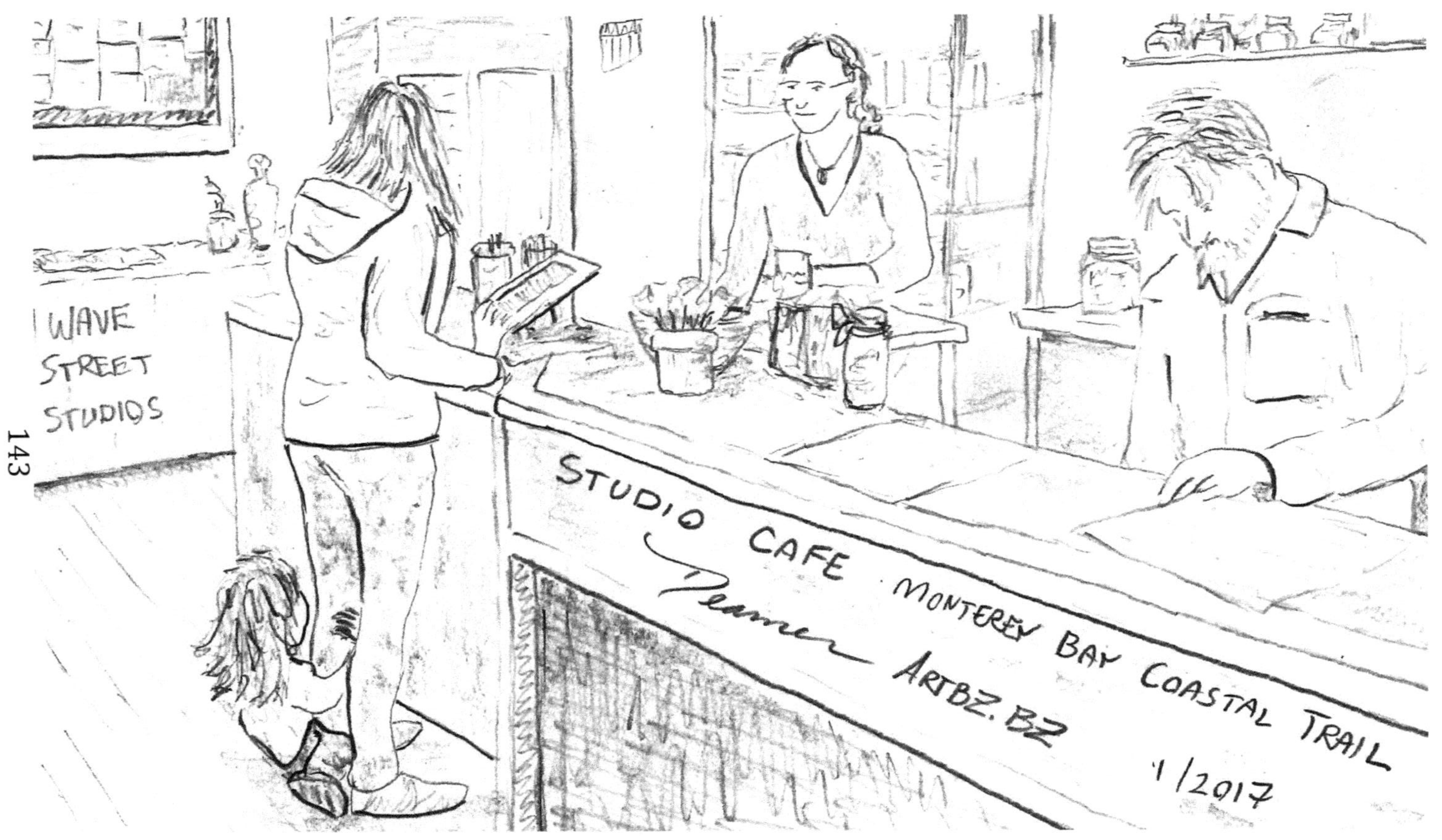
WAVE STREET STUDIOS
STUDIO CAFE · MONTEREY BAY COASTAL TRAIL
Penner ArtBz.BZ
1/2017

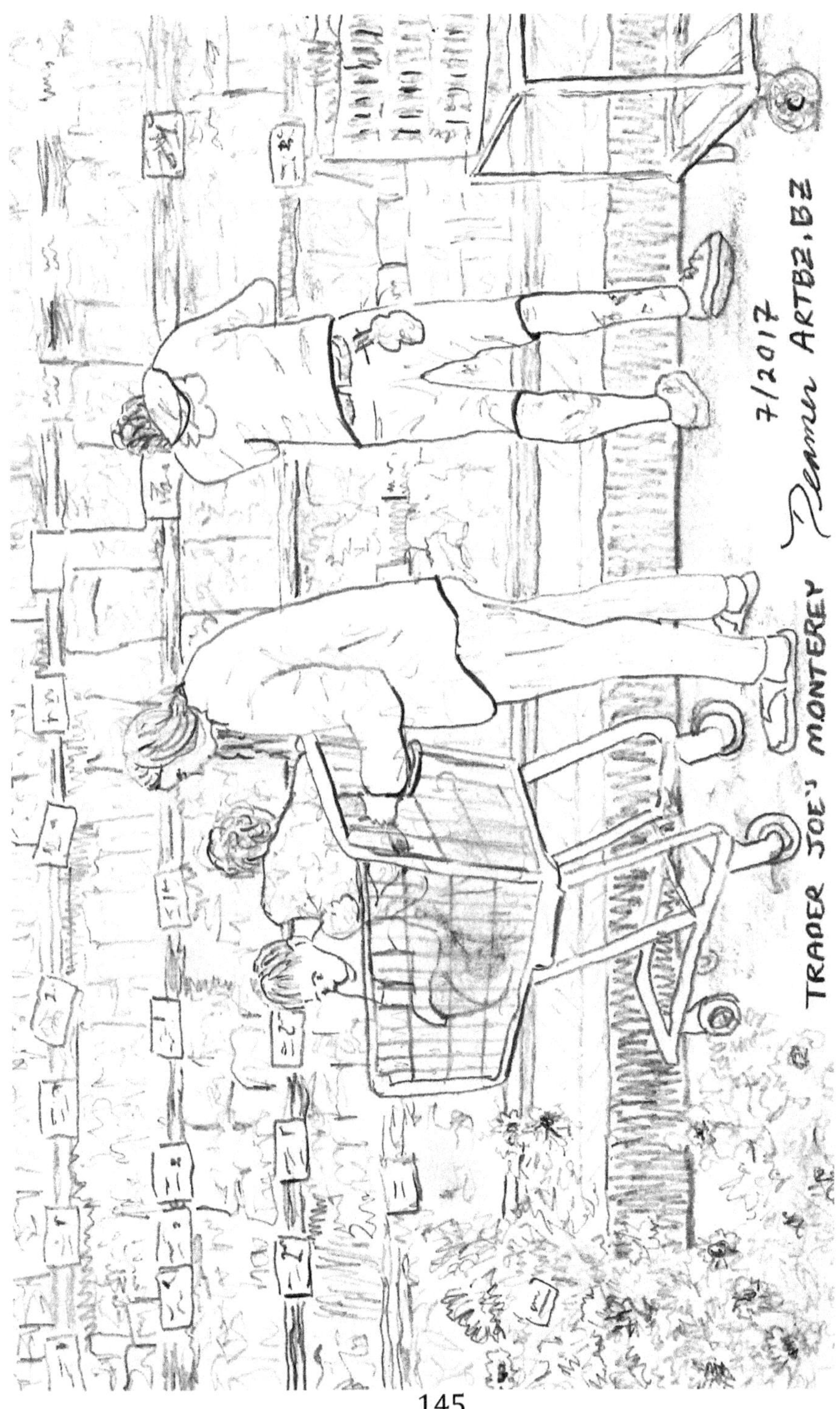
7/2017
TRADER JOE'S MONTEREY

146

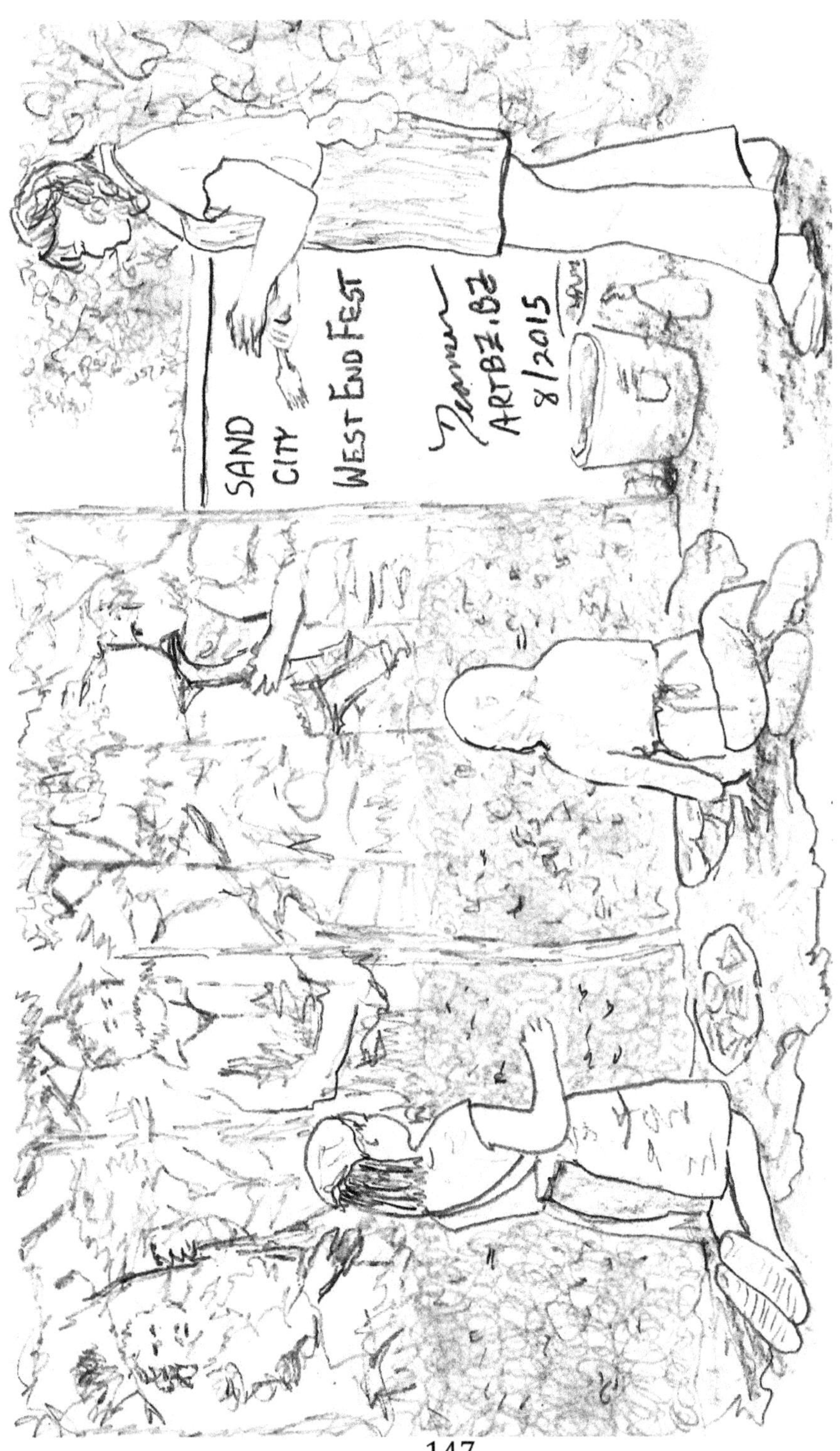
SAND CITY
West End Fest
ARTBZ.BZ
8/2015

148

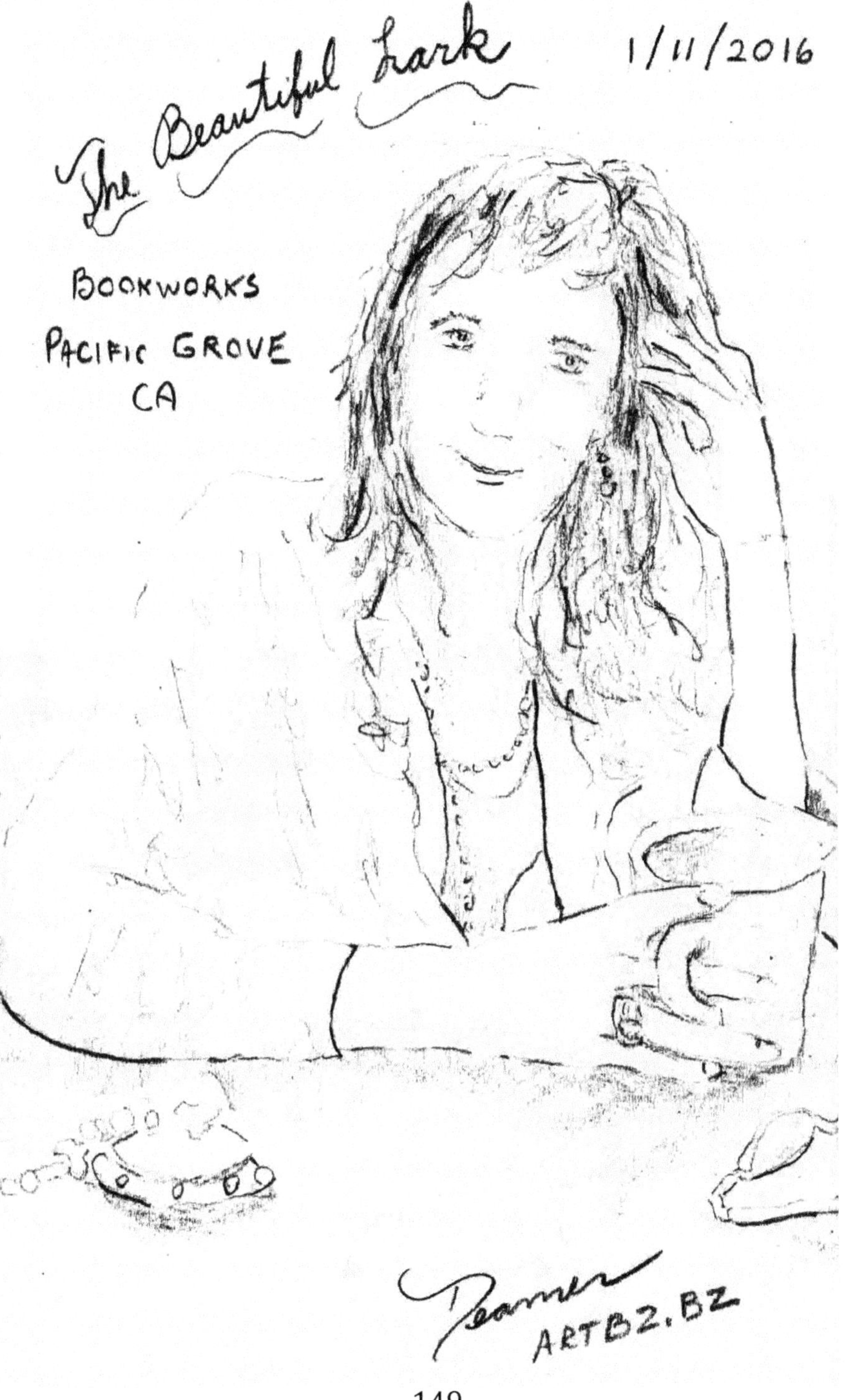
The Beautiful Lark
1/11/2016
BOOKWORKS
PACIFIC GROVE
CA
ARTB2.BZ

150

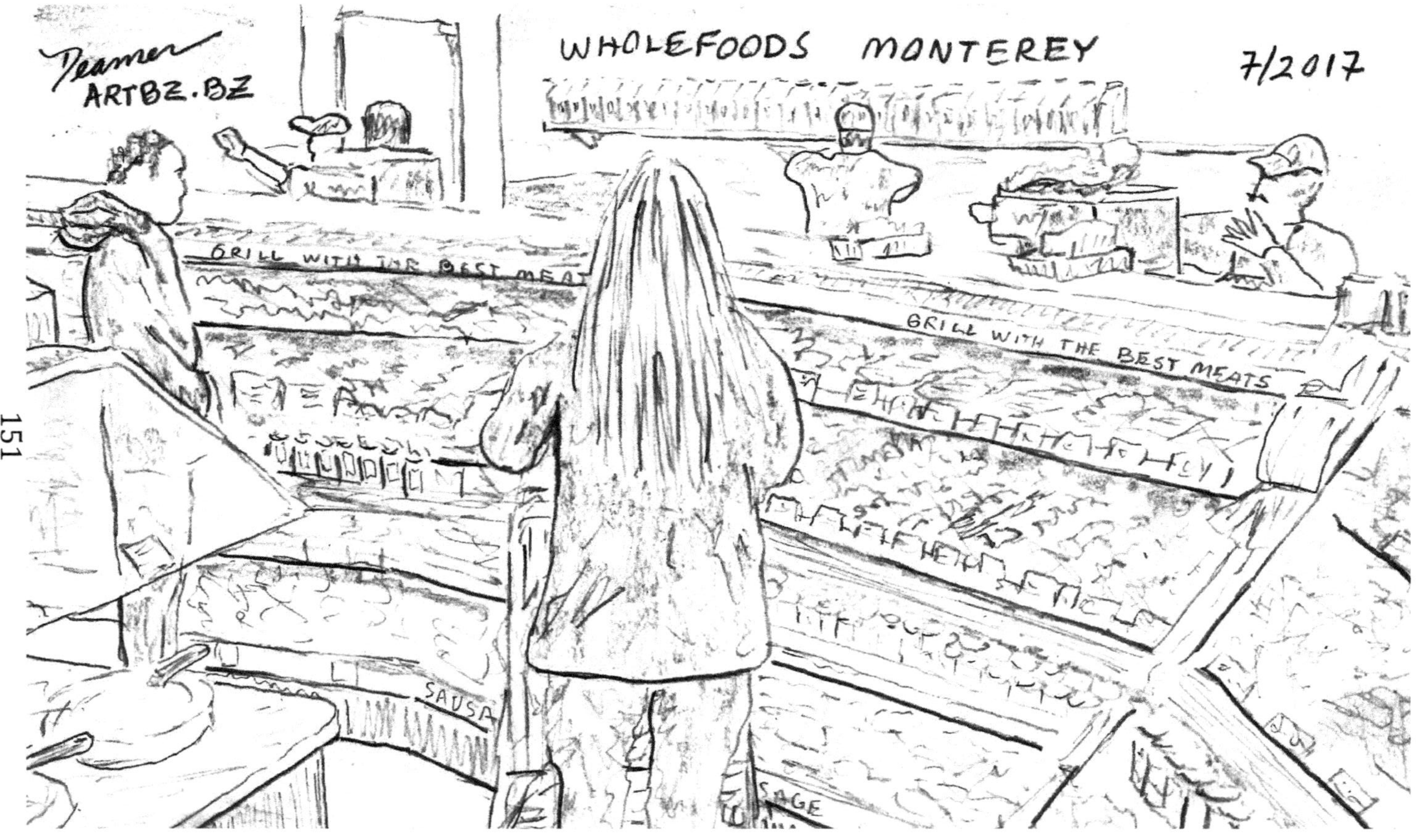

Dreamer
ARTB2.BZ
WHOLEFOODS MONTEREY
7/2017
GRILL WITH THE BEST MEATS
GRILL WITH THE BEST MEATS
SAUSA
SAGE

152

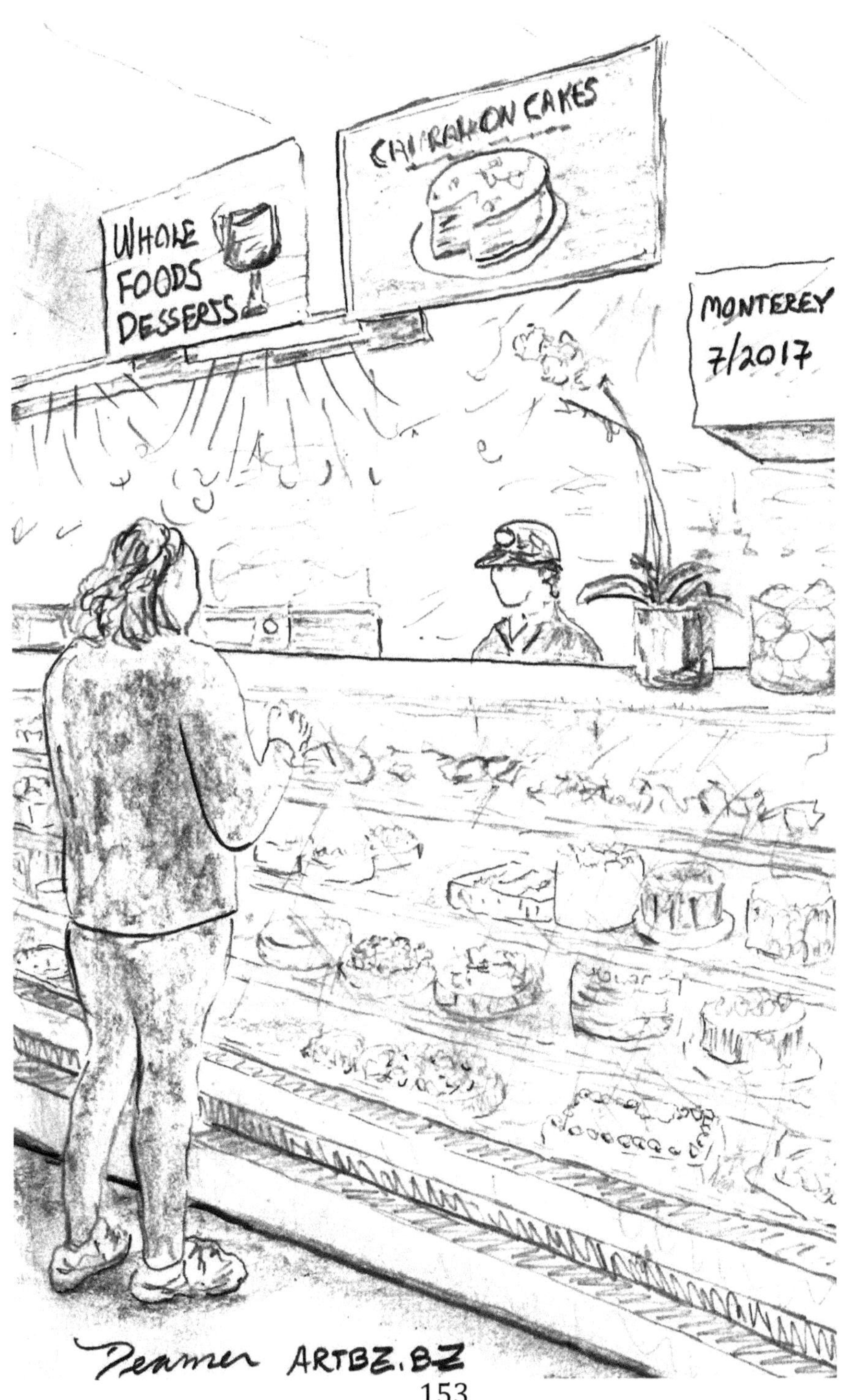
WHOLE FOODS DESSERTS
CHIFFON CAKES
MONTEREY
7/2017
Deamer ARTBZ.BZ

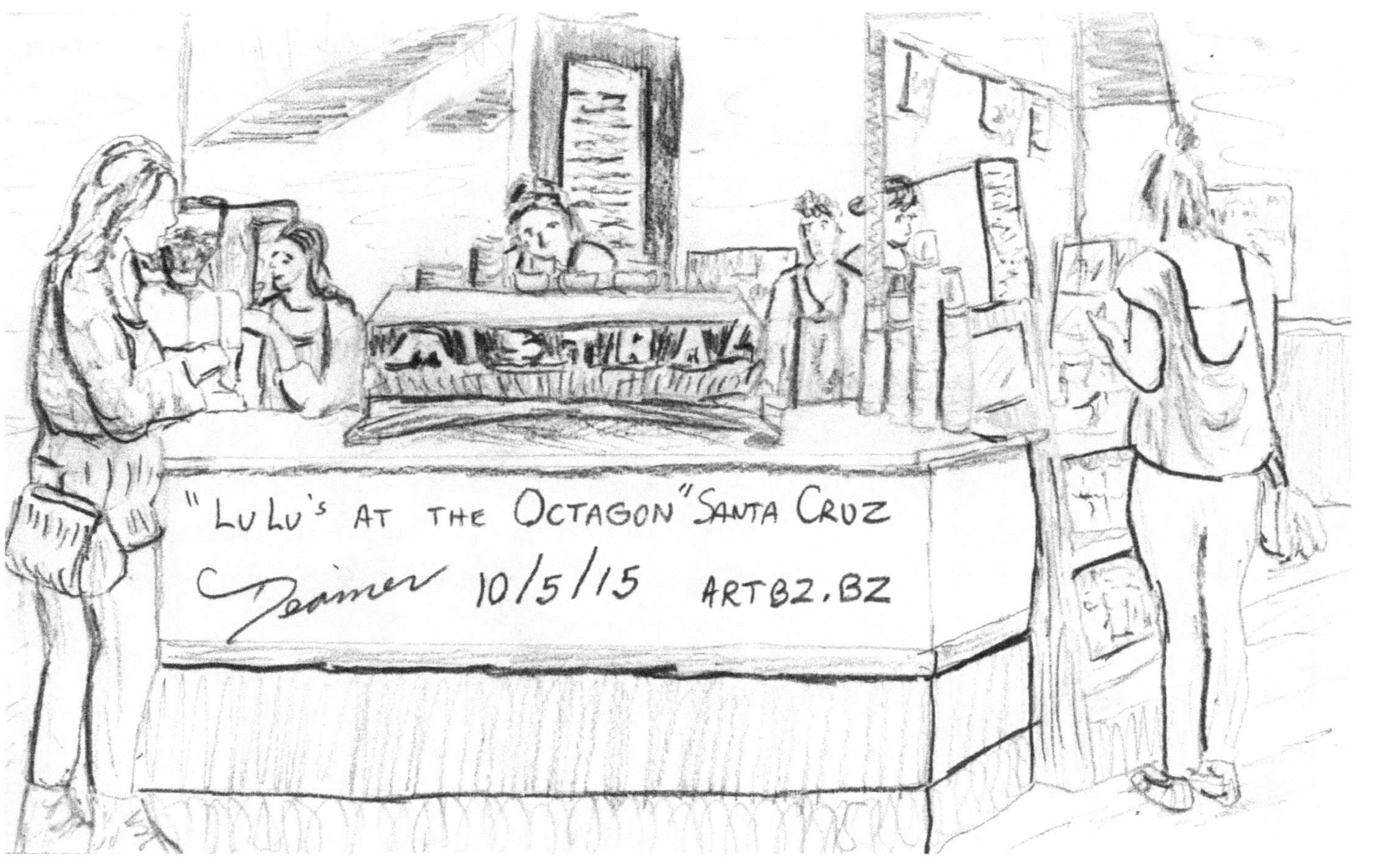

"Lu Lu's at the Octagon" Santa Cruz
Reimer 10/5/15   ARTBZ.BZ

156

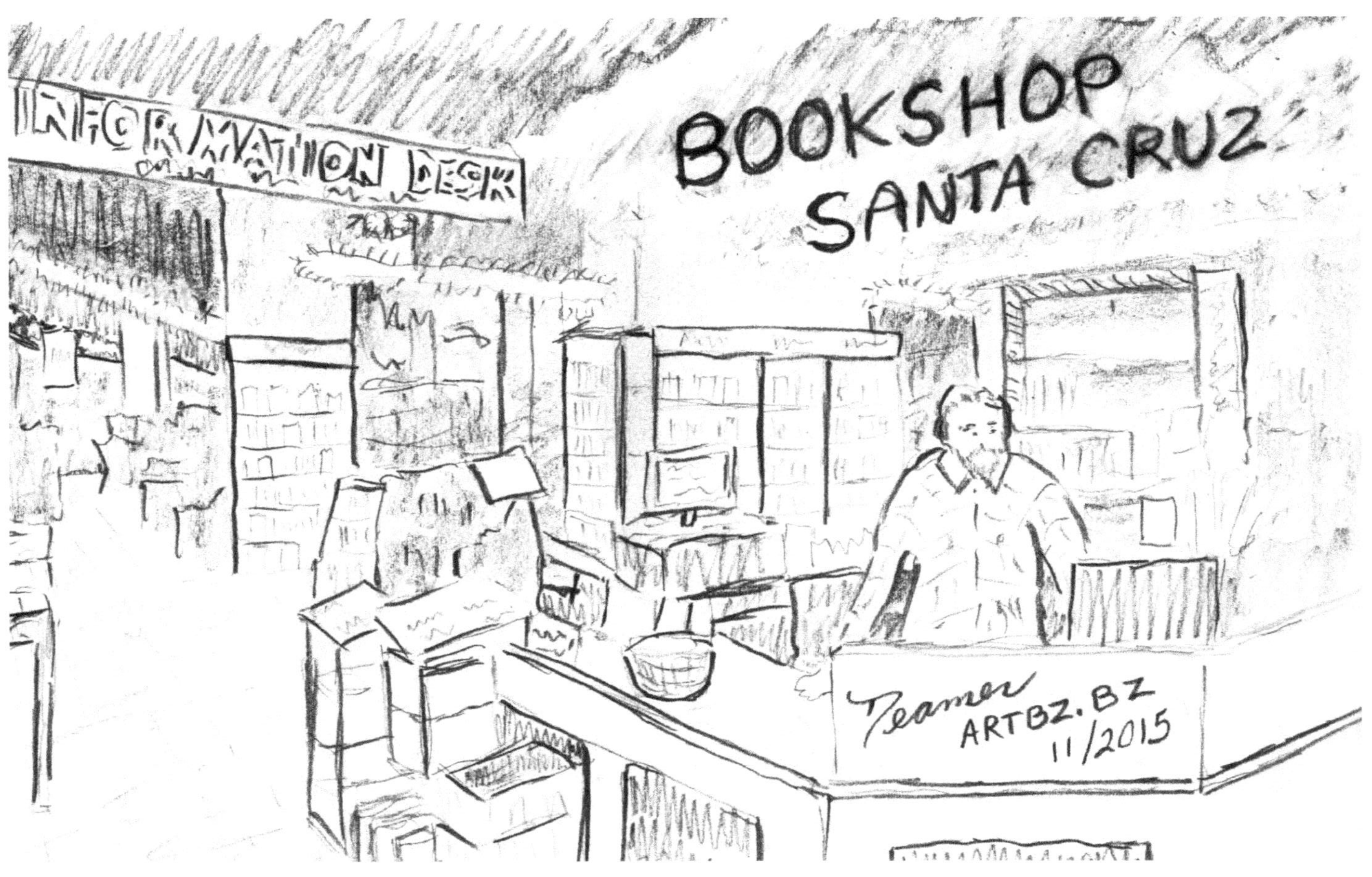
INFORMATION DESK
BOOKSHOP
SANTA CRUZ
Teamer
ARTBZ.BZ
11/2015

Bookshop
SantaCruz
11/2015
Reamer
ArtB2.B2

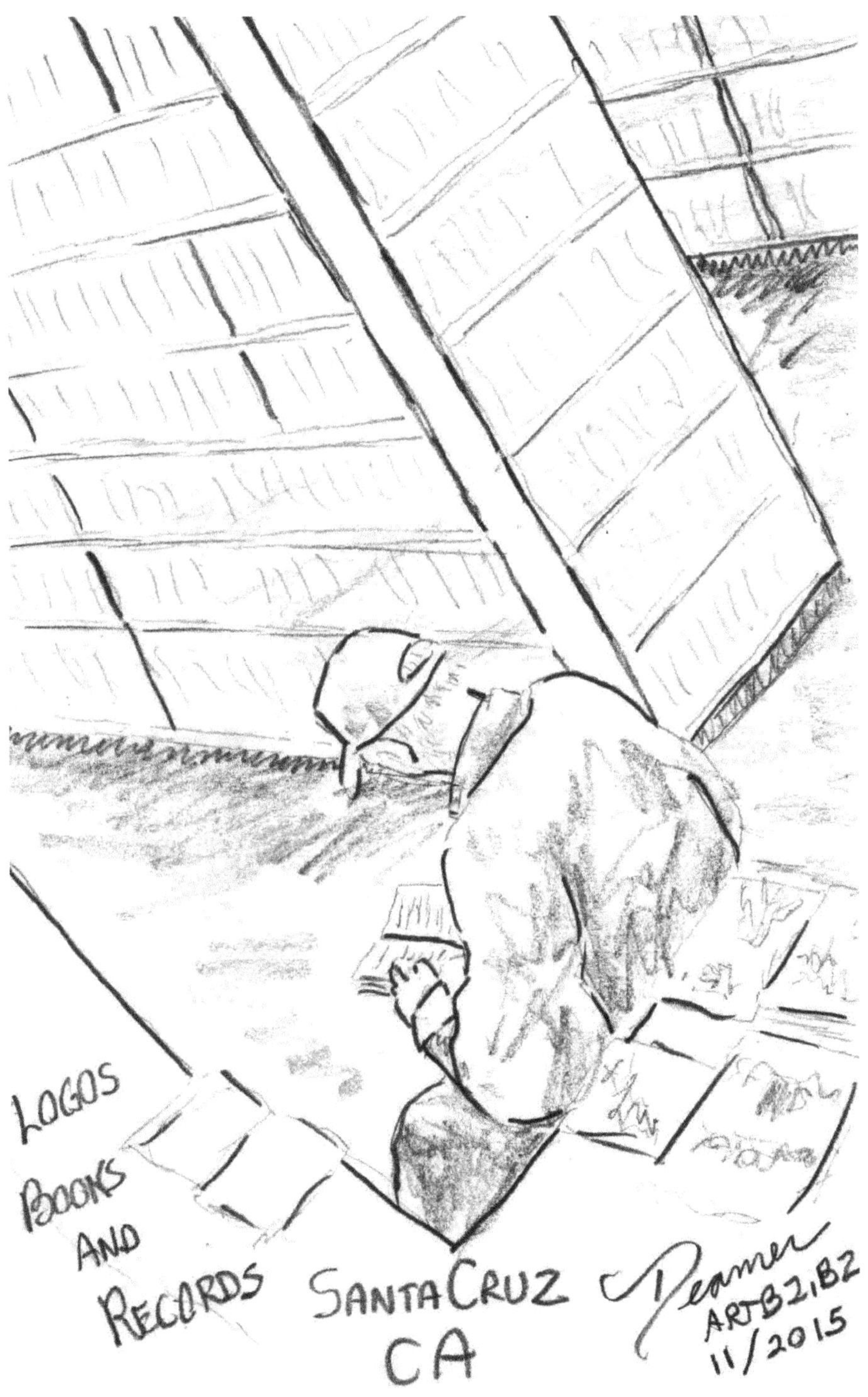

LOGOS
BOOKS
AND
RECORDS SANTA CRUZ
CA

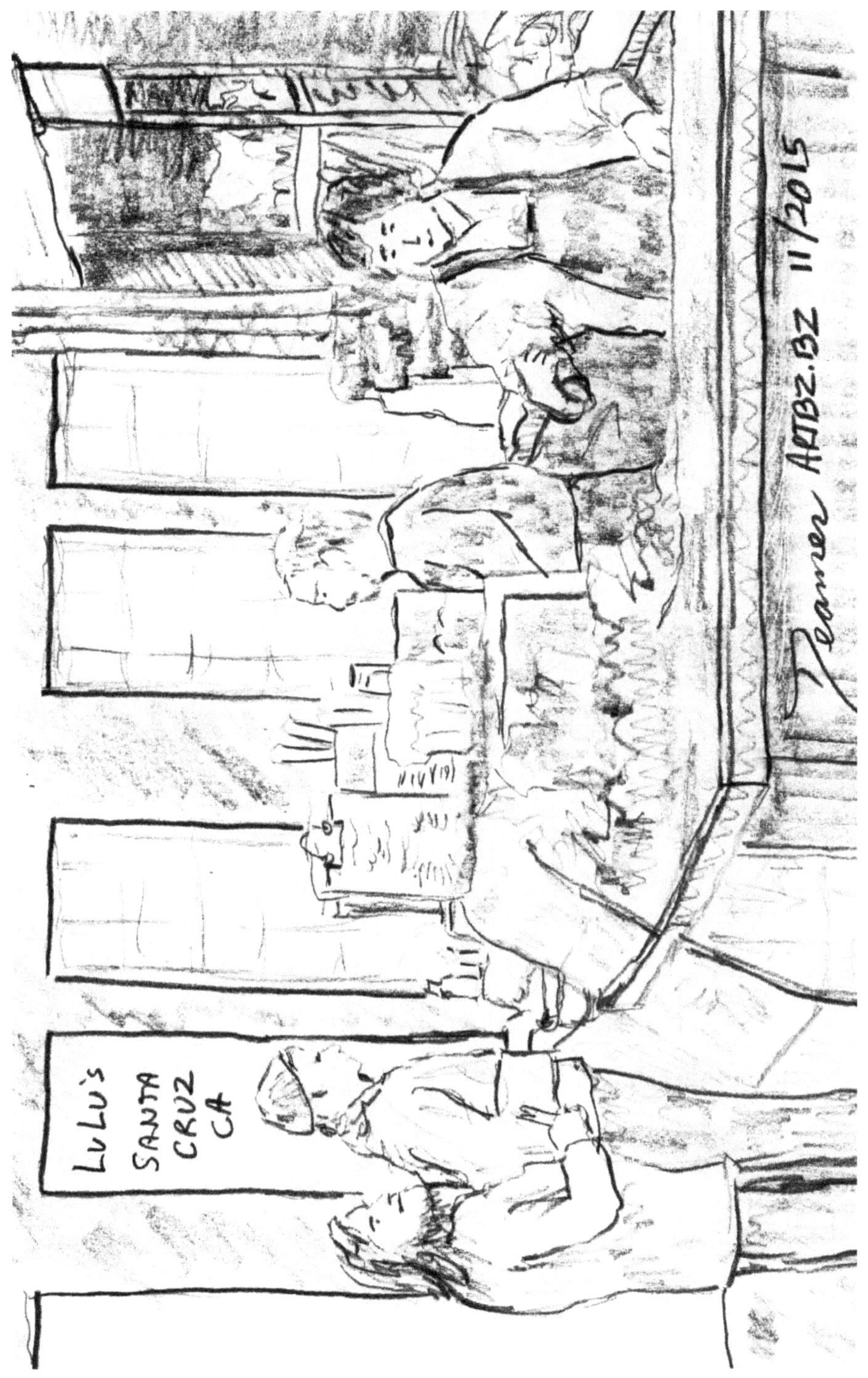
LuLu's
SANTA
CRUZ
CA

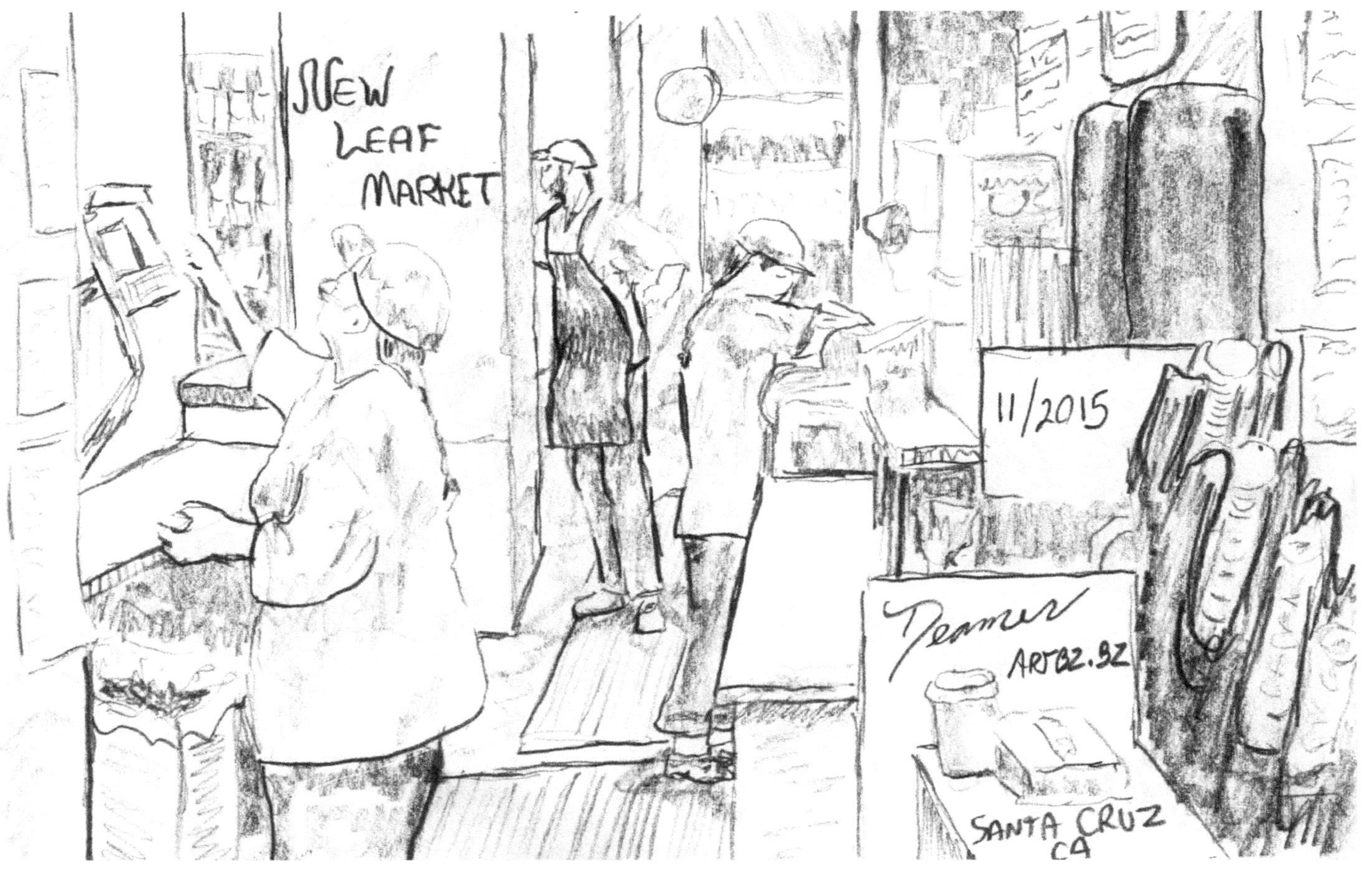
NEW
LEAF
MARKET
11/2015
Deamer
ART32.92
SANTA CRUZ
CA

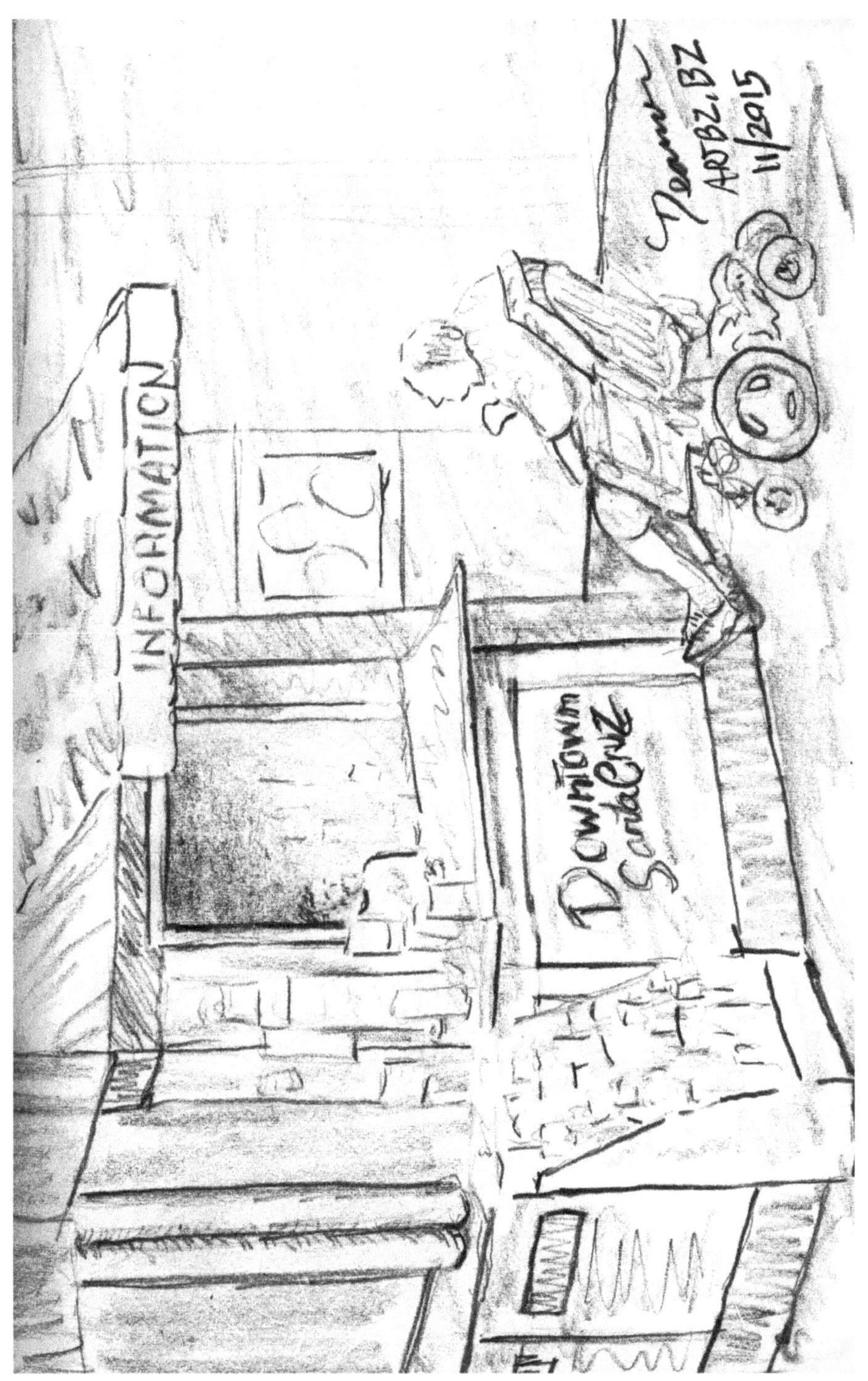

INFORMATION
Downtown Santa Cruz
ARTBZ.BZ
11/2015

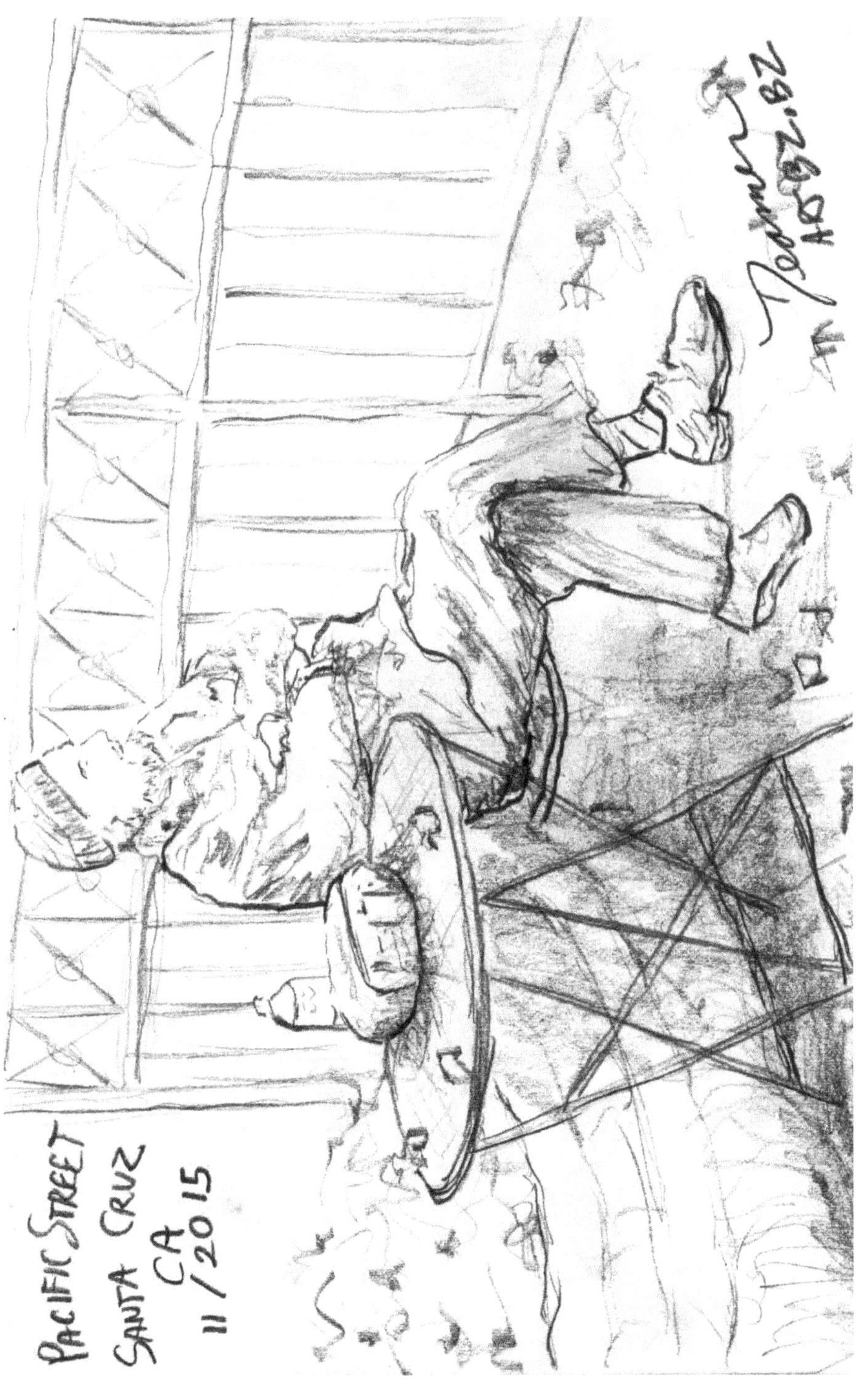
PACIFIC STREET
SANTA CRUZ
CA
11 / 20 15

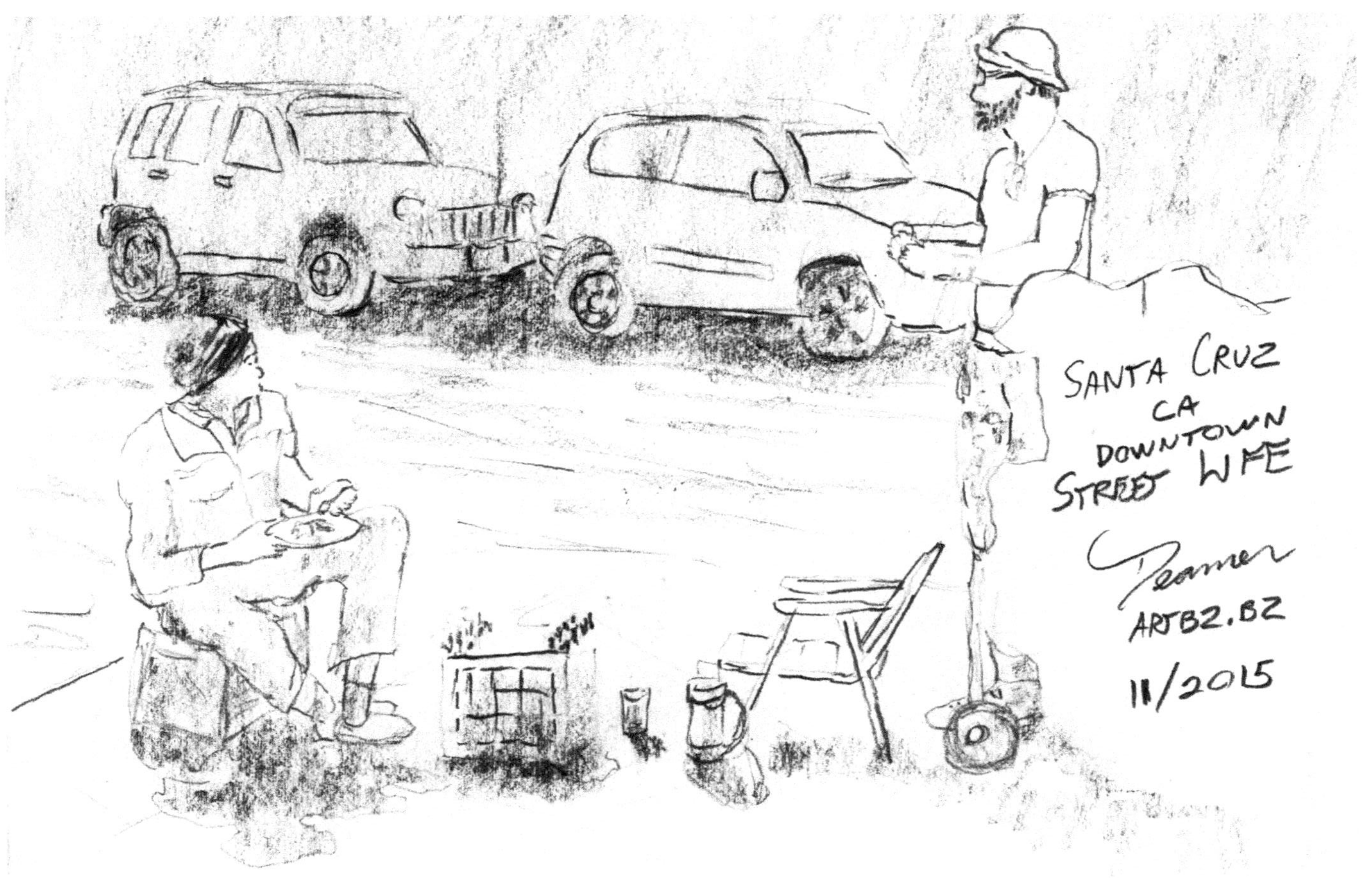
SANTA CRUZ
CA
DOWNTOWN
STREET LIFE
Tanner
ARTB2.B2
11/2015

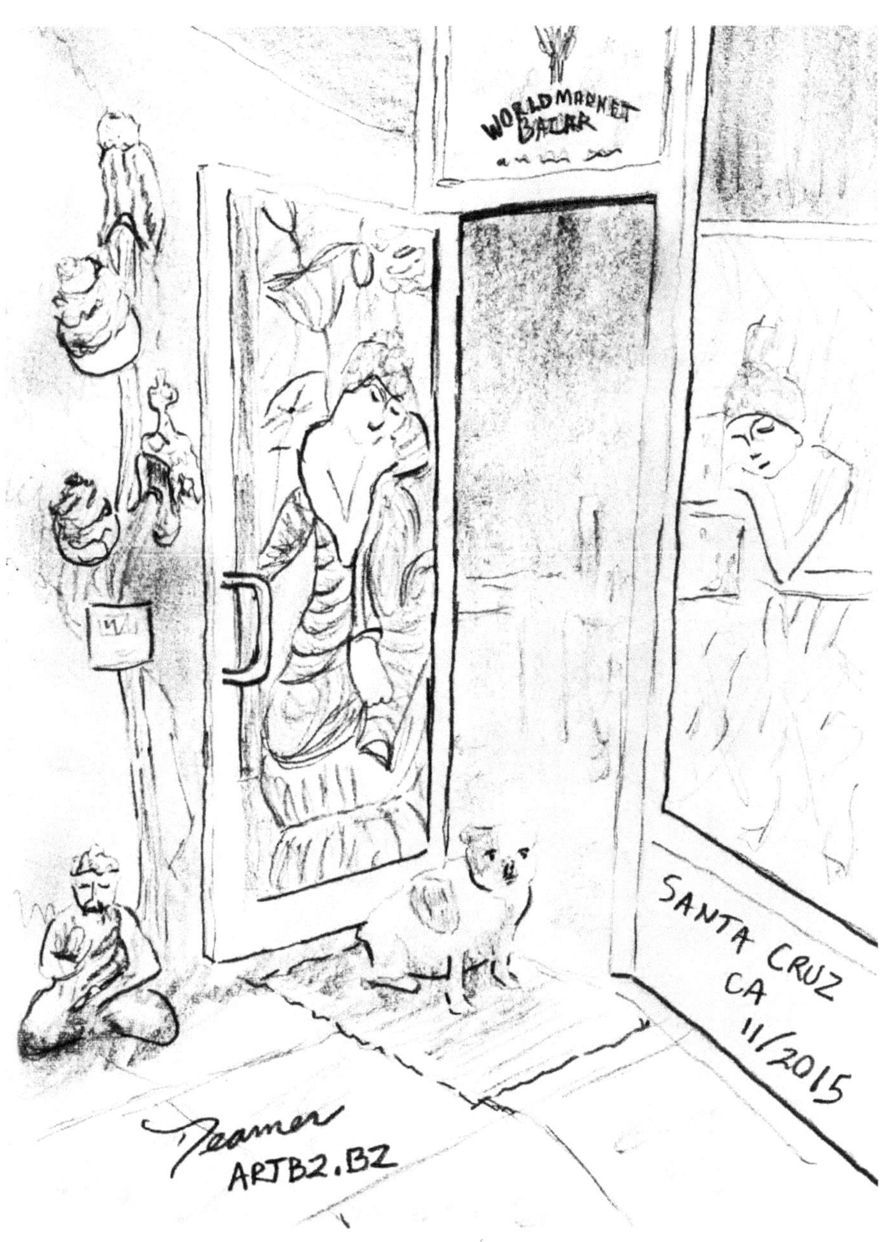
WORLD MARKET
BAZAR
SANTA CRUZ
CA
11/2015
ARTB2.BZ

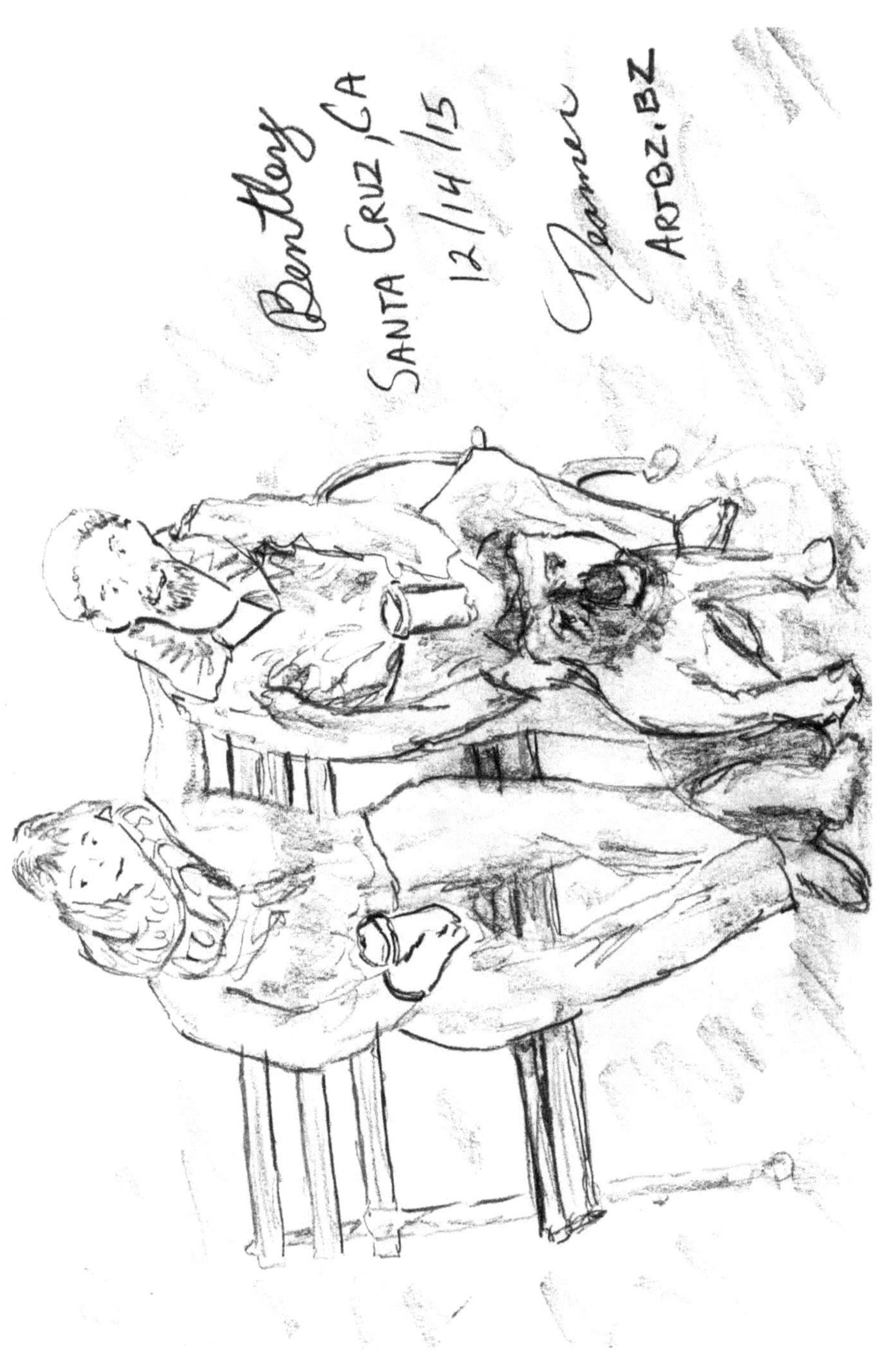

Bentley
Santa Cruz, CA
12/14/15
Arroz.BZ

176

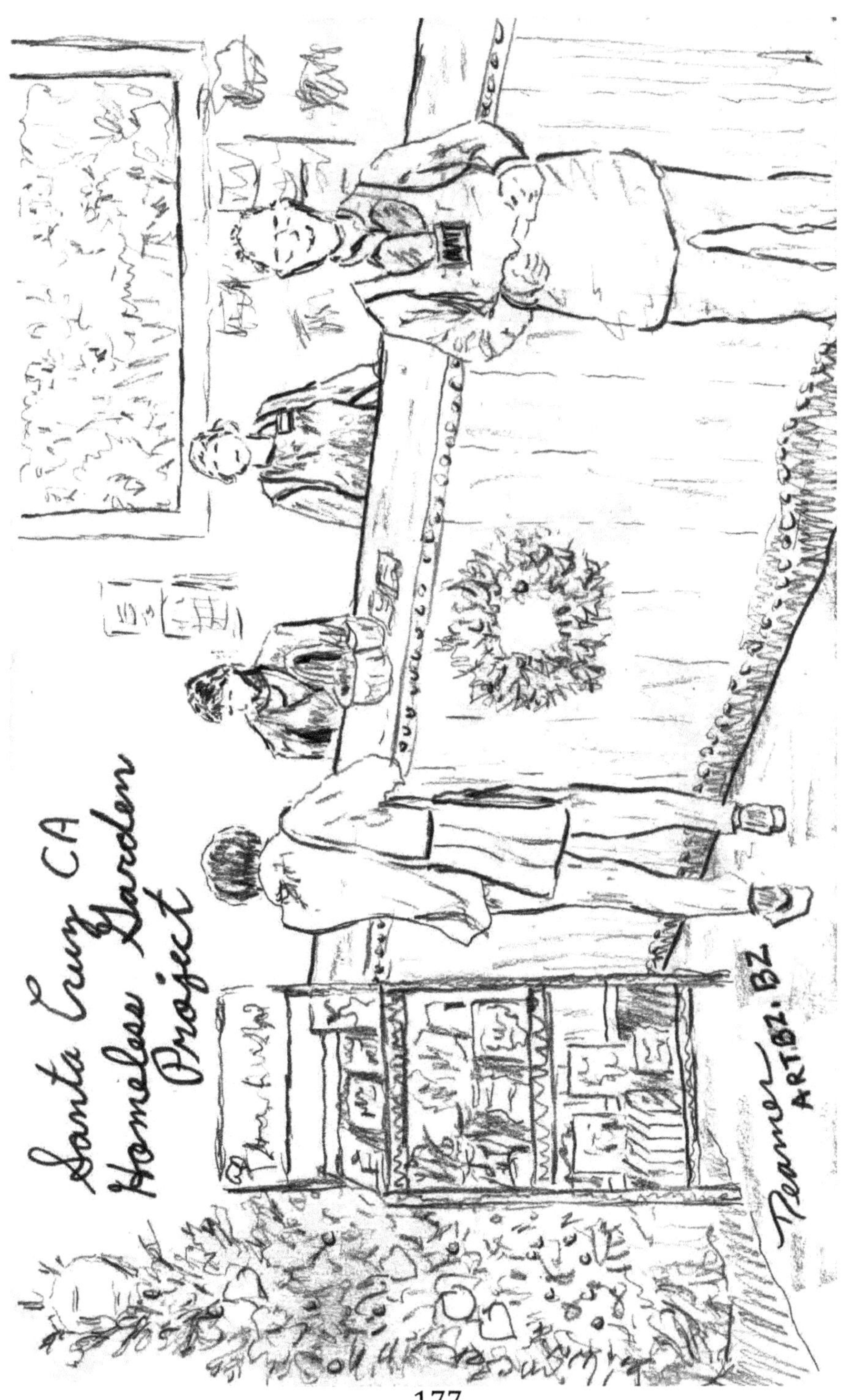

Santa Cruz CA
Homeless Garden
Project
Renner
ART.62. B2

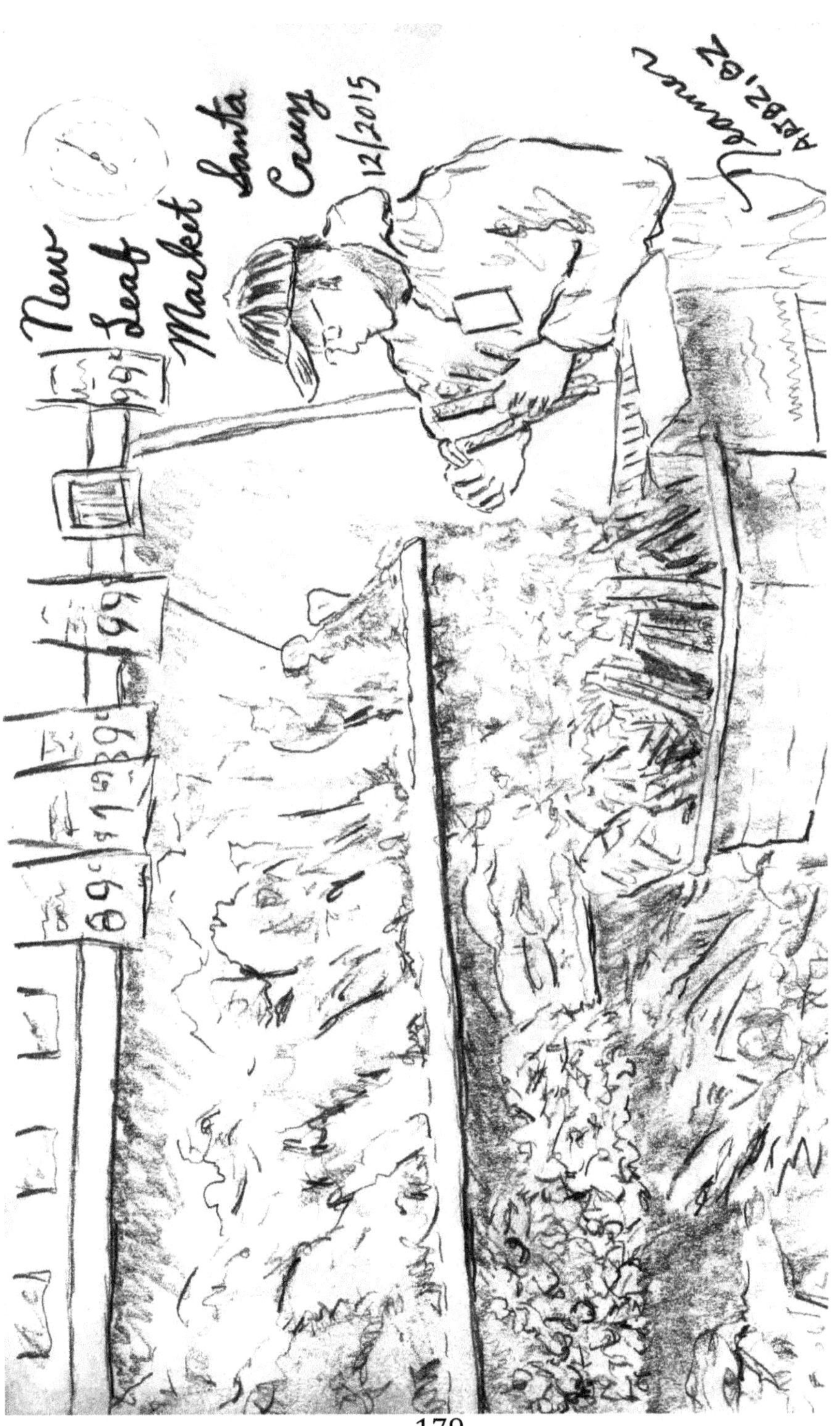
New
Leaf
Market
Santa
Cruz
12/2015

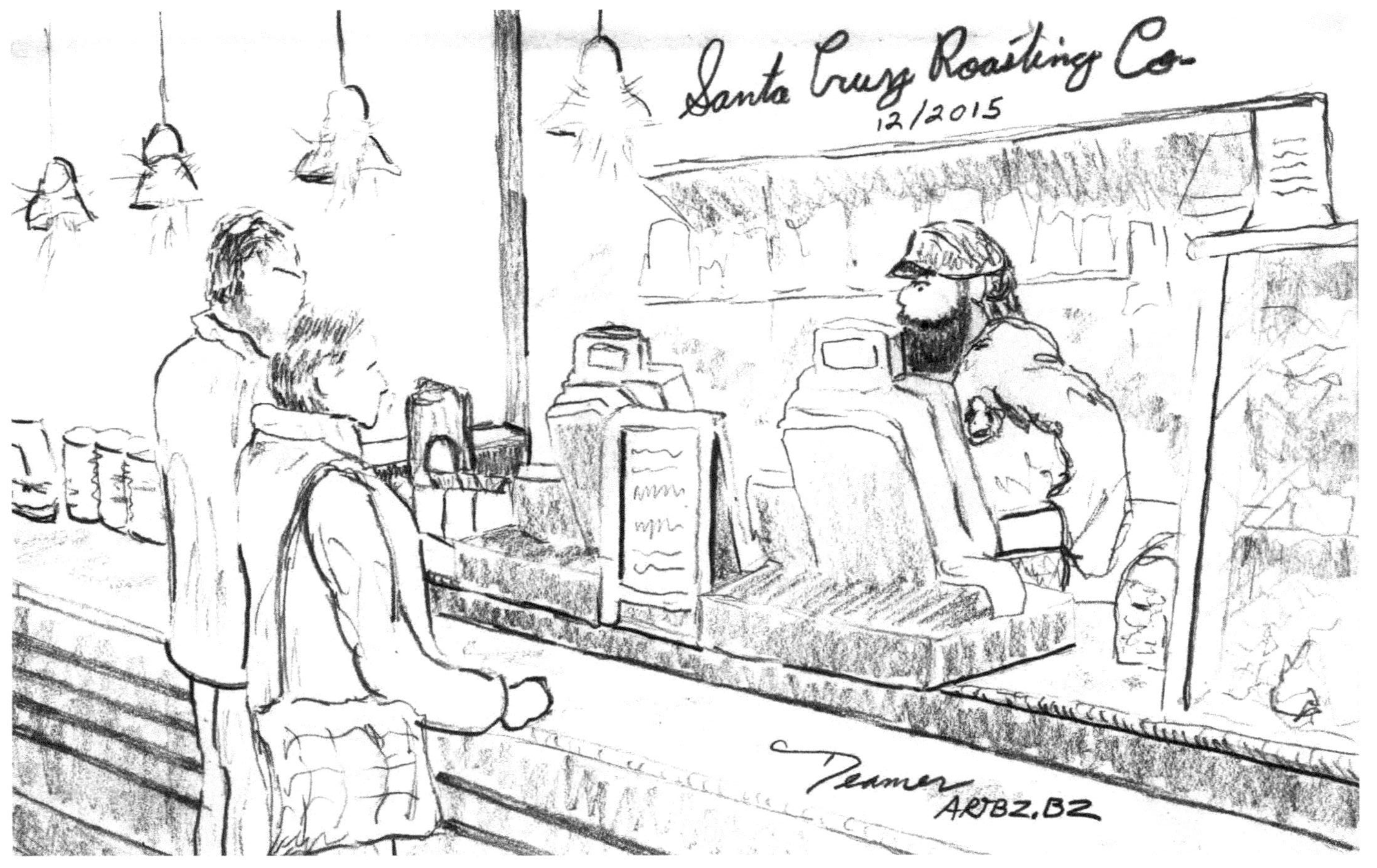
Santa Cruz Roasting Co
12/2015

DEAMER DUNN

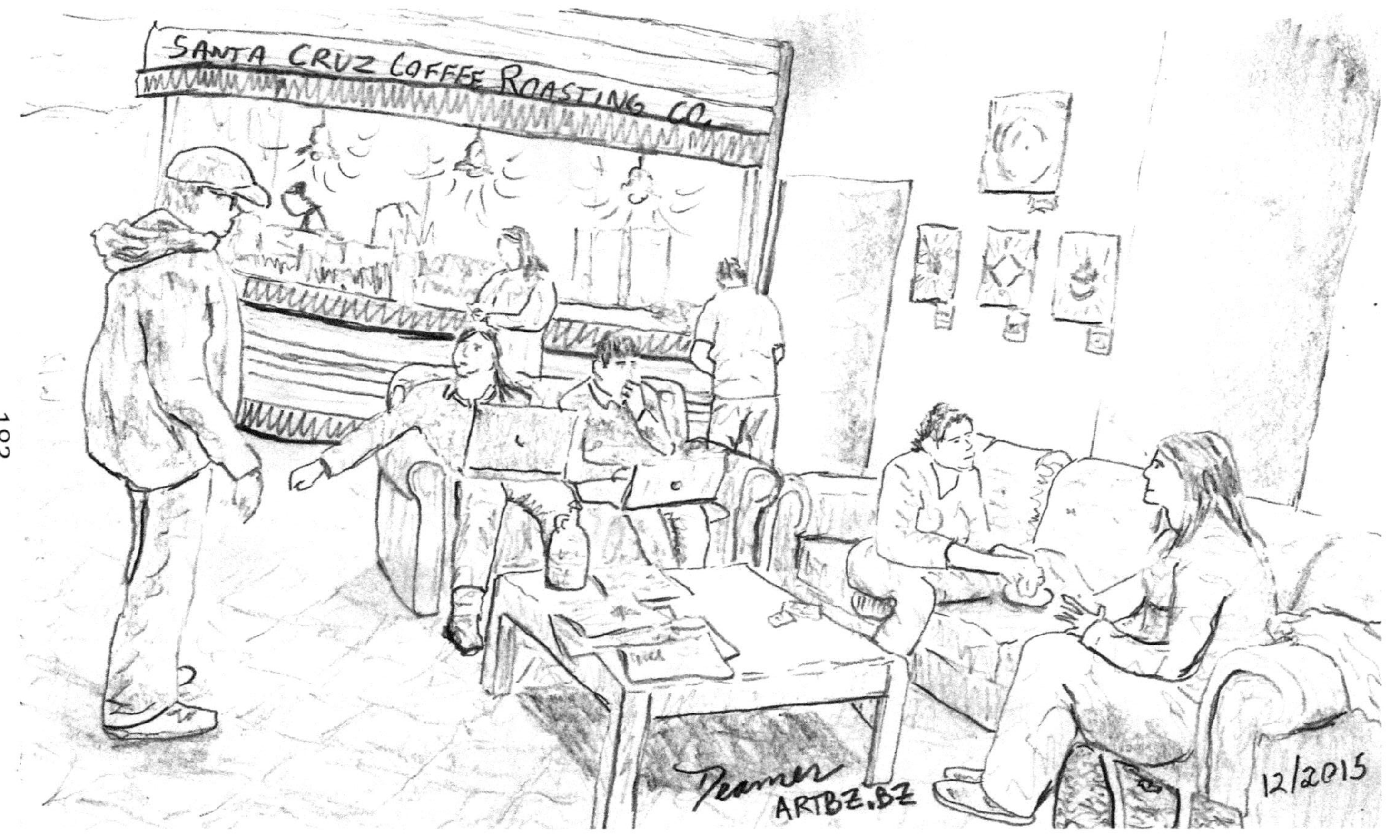

SANTA CRUZ COFFEE ROASTING Co.
ARTBZ.BZ
12/2015

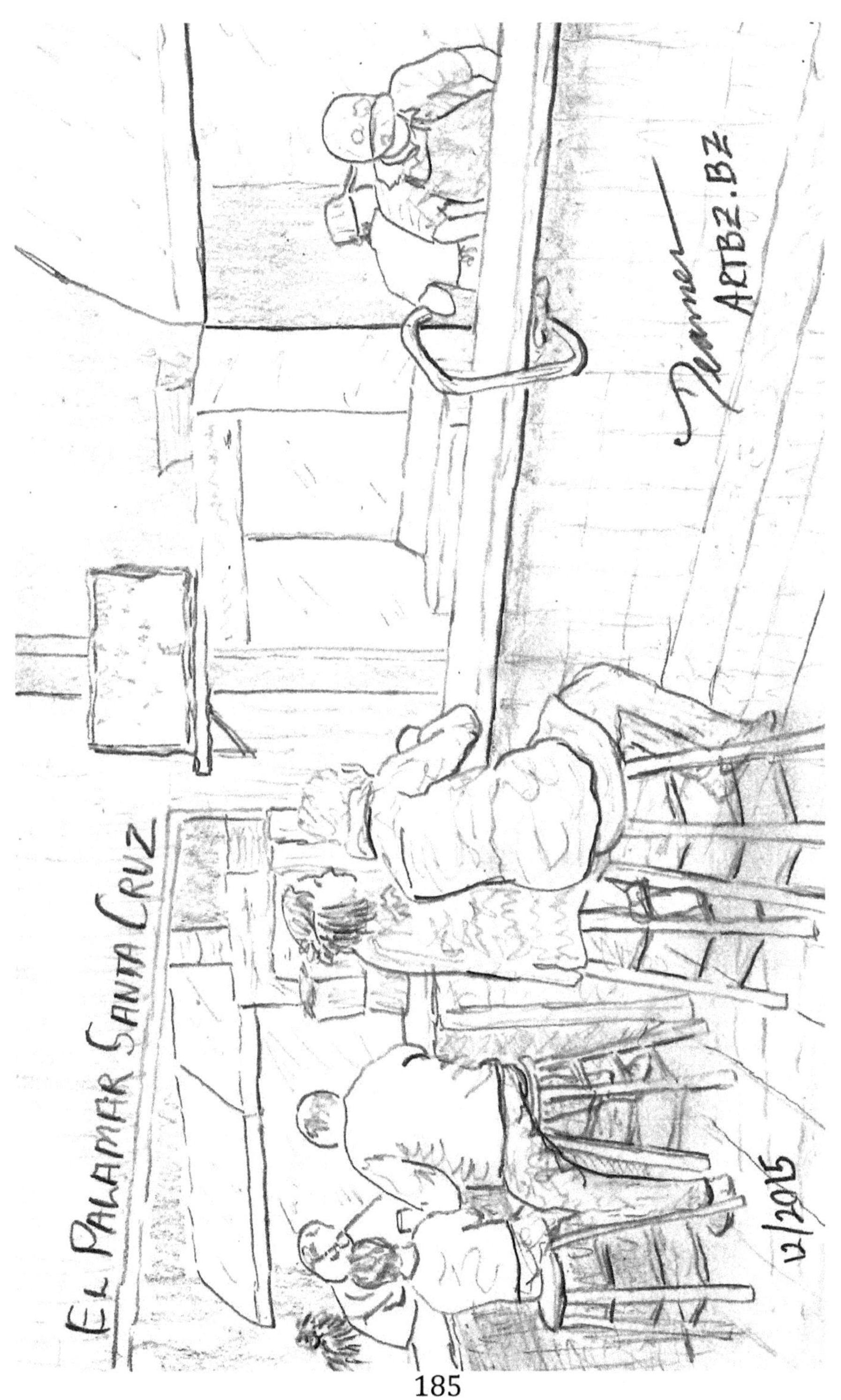

EL PALAMAR SANTA CRUZ
ARTB2.BZ
12/2015

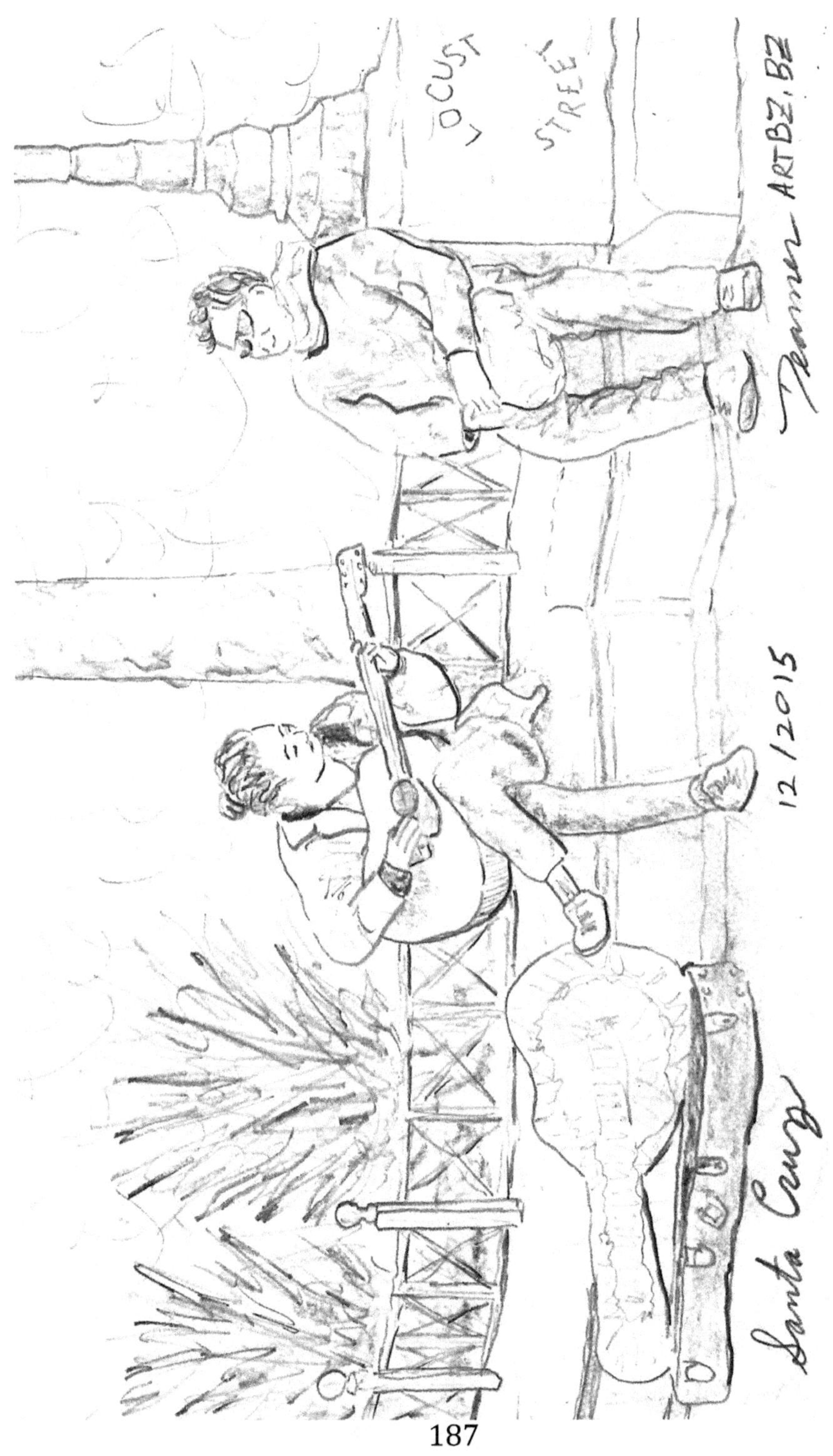
LOCUST STREET
ART BZ, BZ
12/2015
Santa Cruz

188

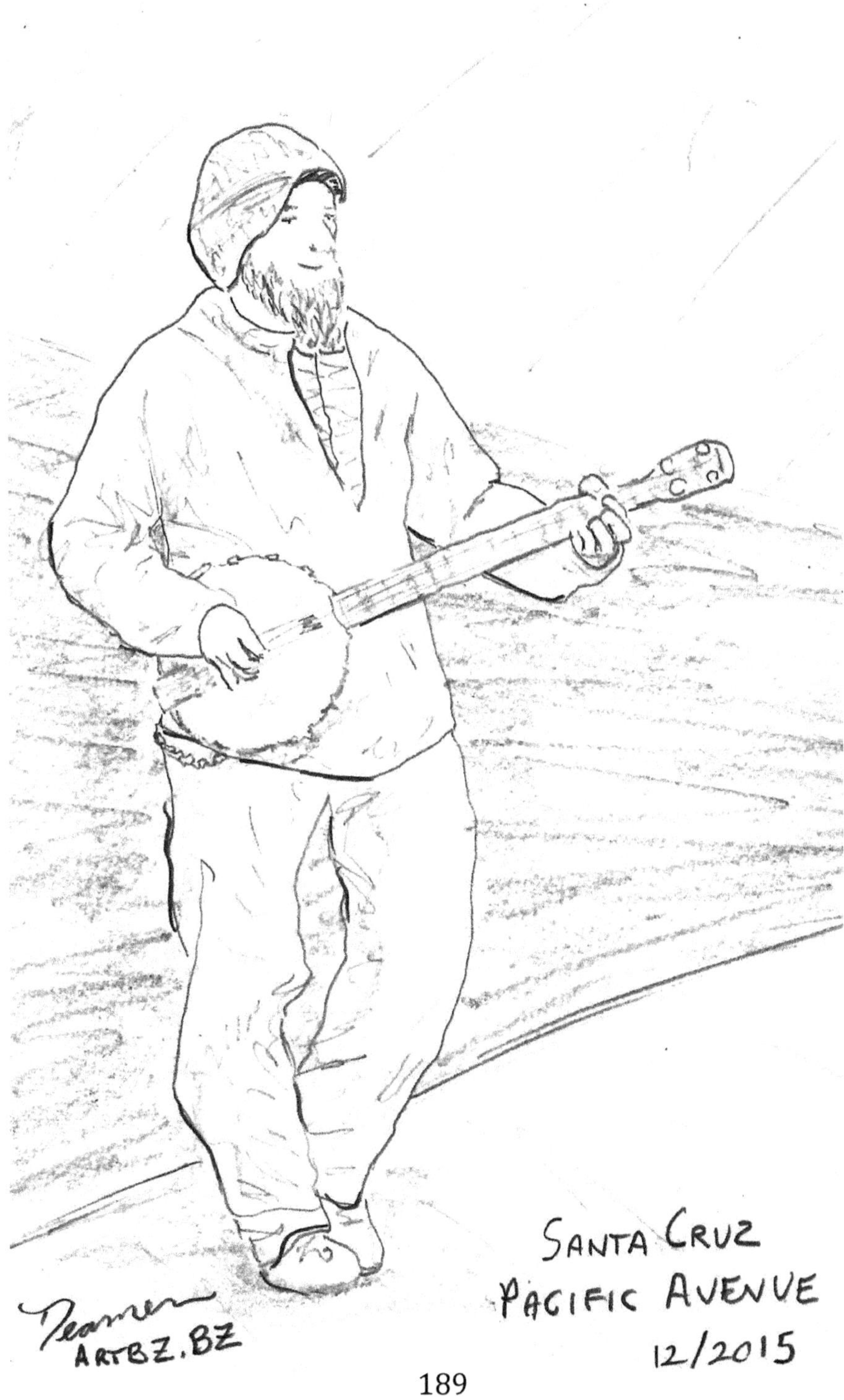

Pearson
ARTBZ.BZ
SANTA CRUZ
PACIFIC AVENUE
12/2015

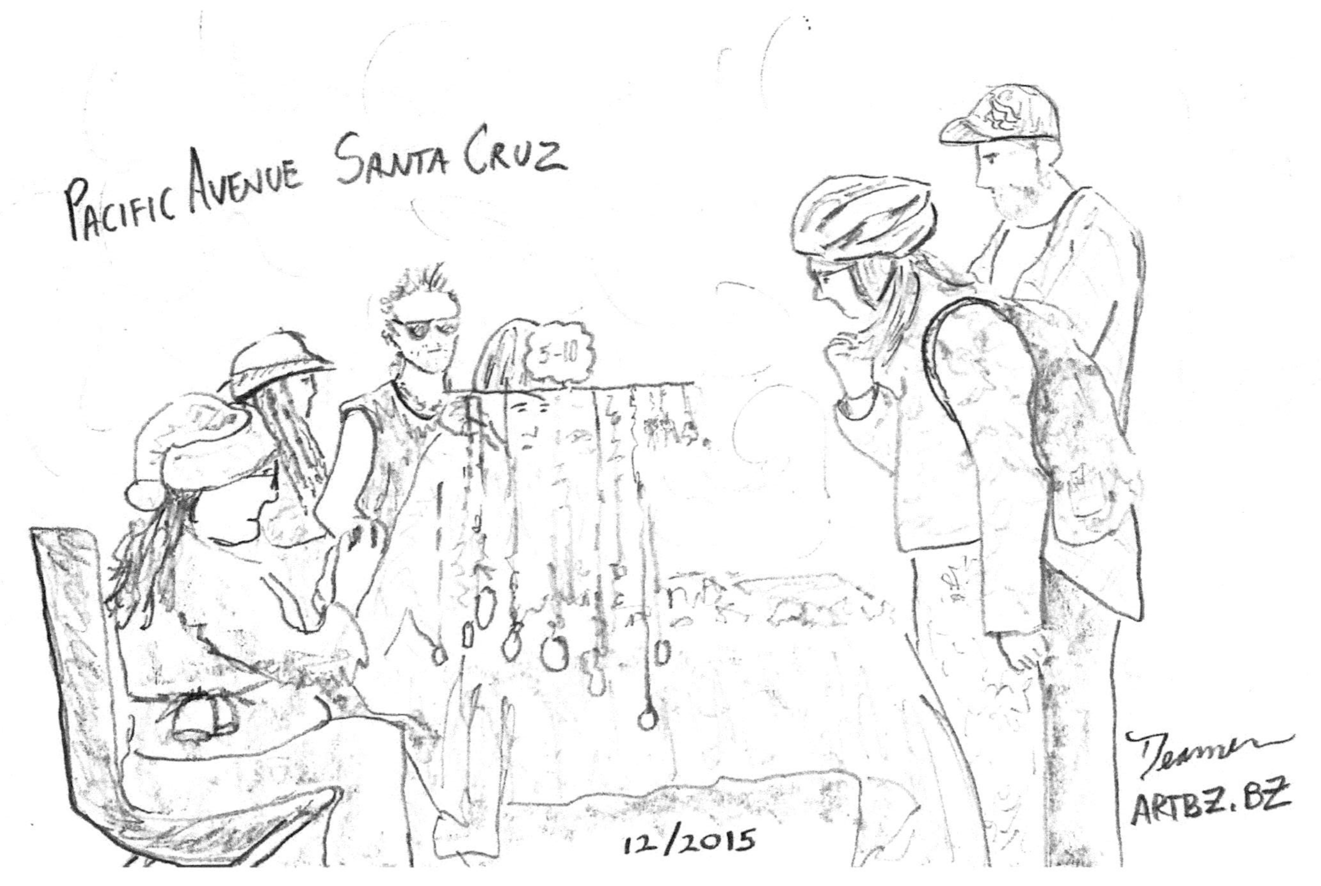
PACIFIC AVENUE SANTA CRUZ
5-10
12/2015
ARTBZ.BZ

192

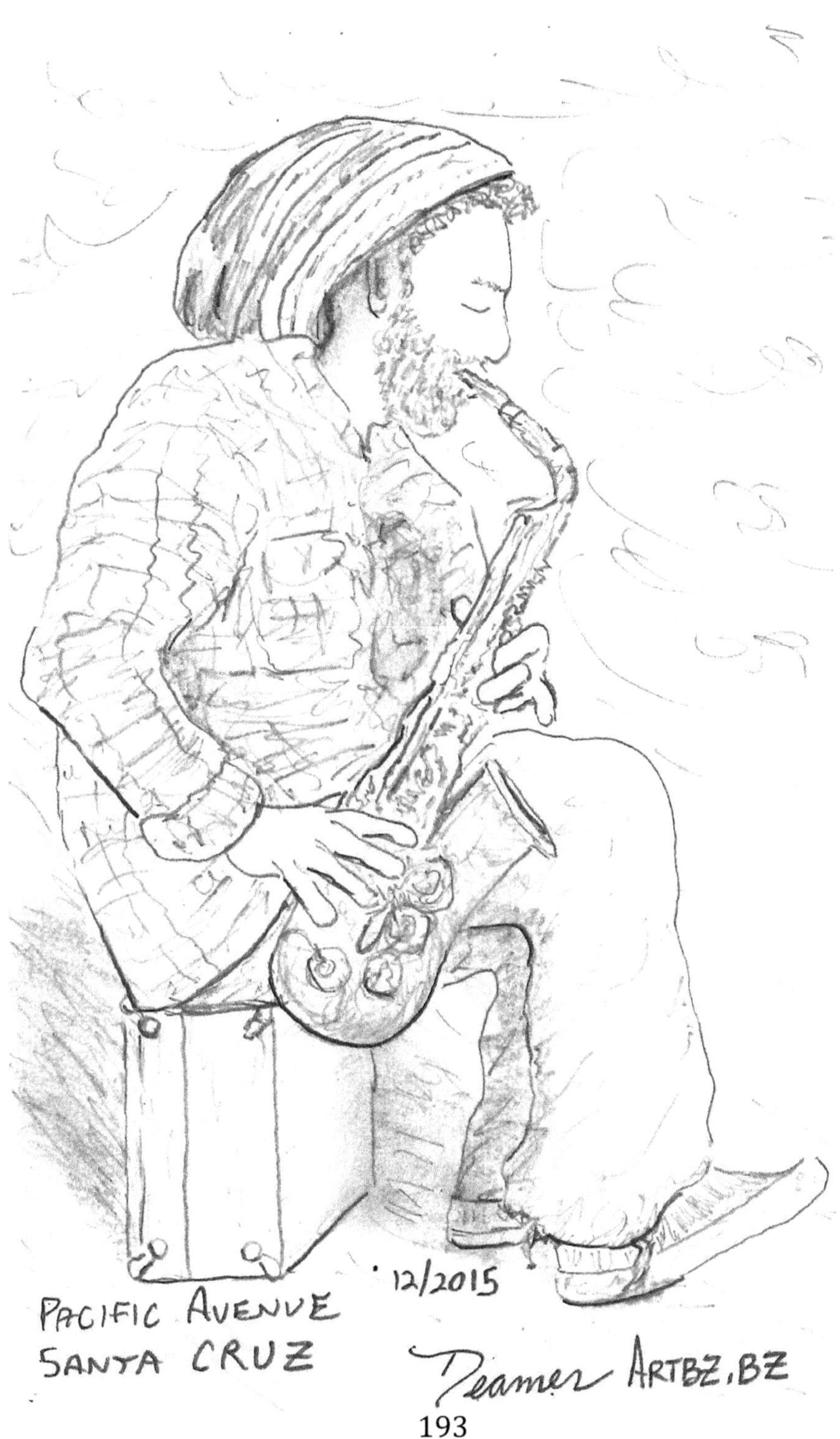

PACIFIC AVENUE
SANTA CRUZ

· 12/2015

Deamer ARTBZ.BZ

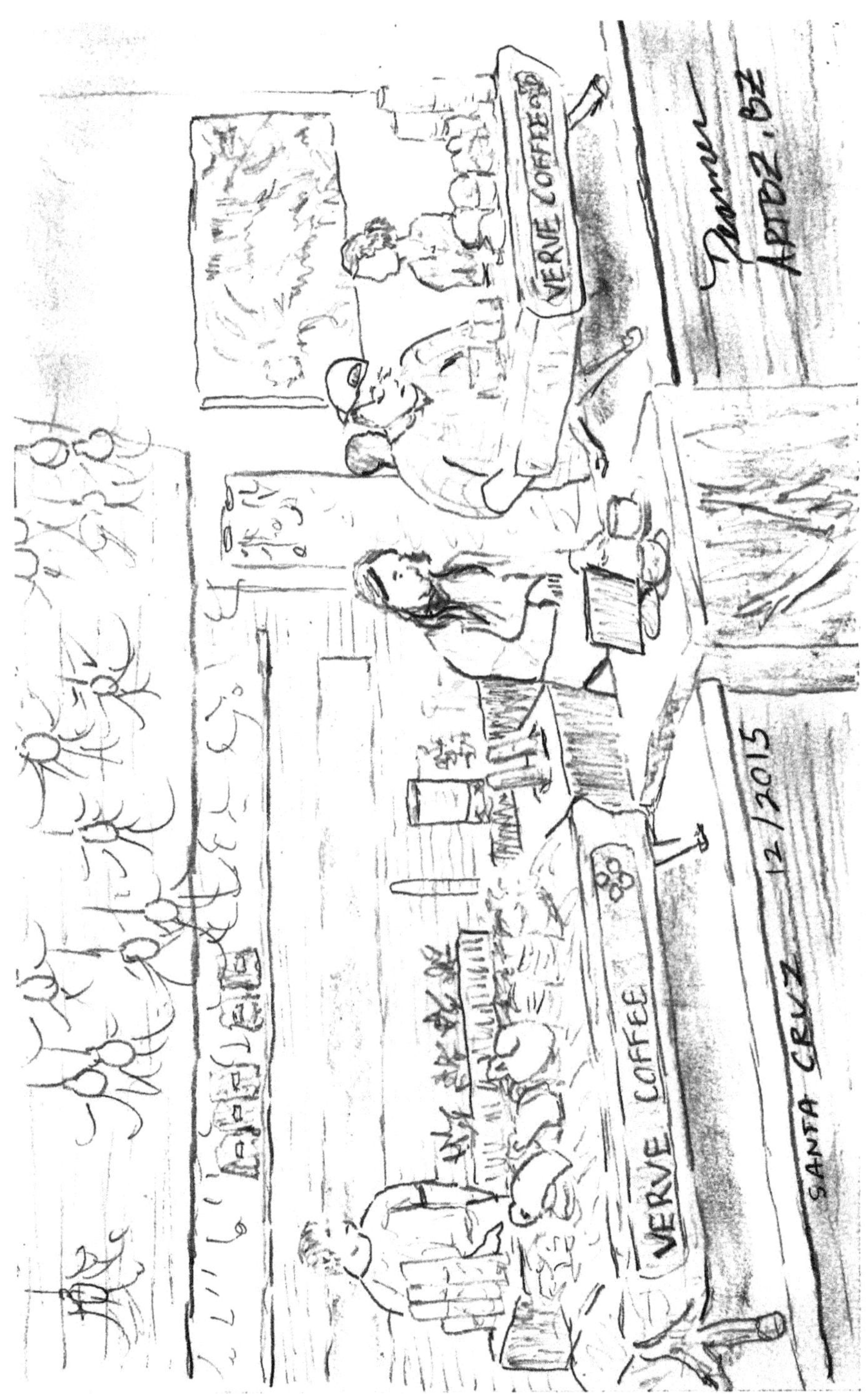
VERVE COFFEE
VERVE COFFEE
SANTA CRUZ
12/2015

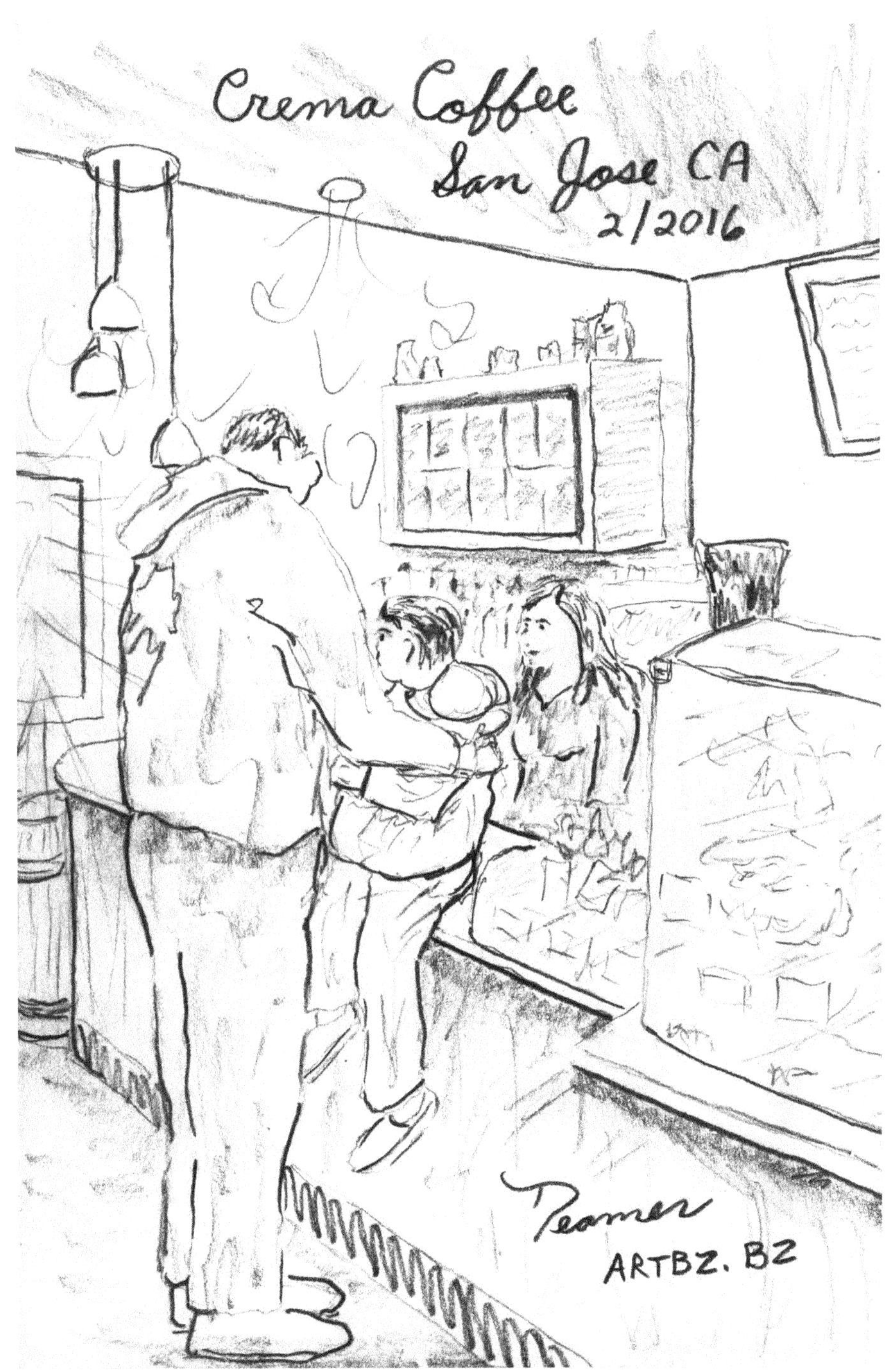
Crema Coffee
San Jose CA
2/2016
ARTBZ. BZ

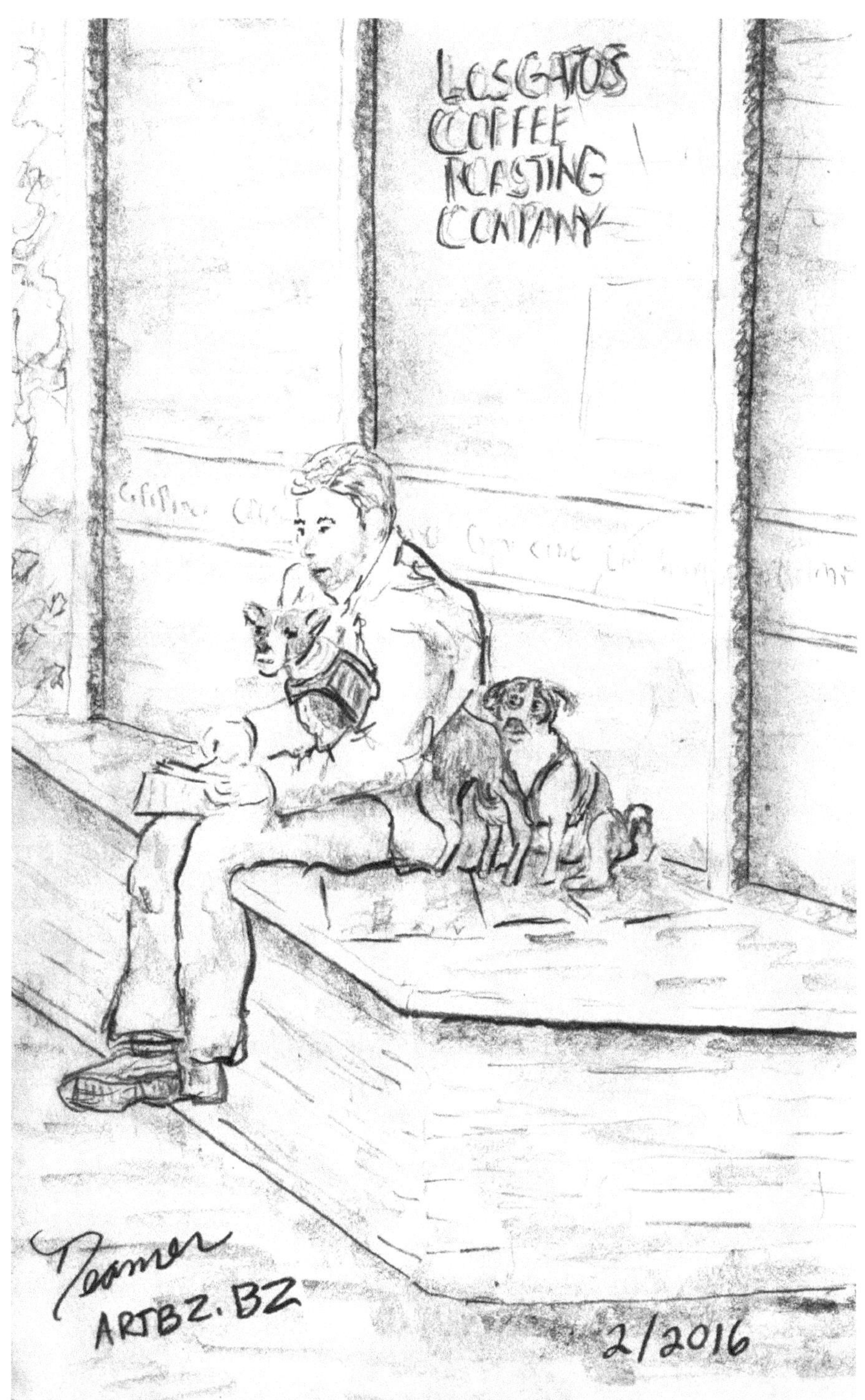
LOS GATOS
COFFEE
ROASTING
COMPANY
ARTBZ.BZ
2/2016

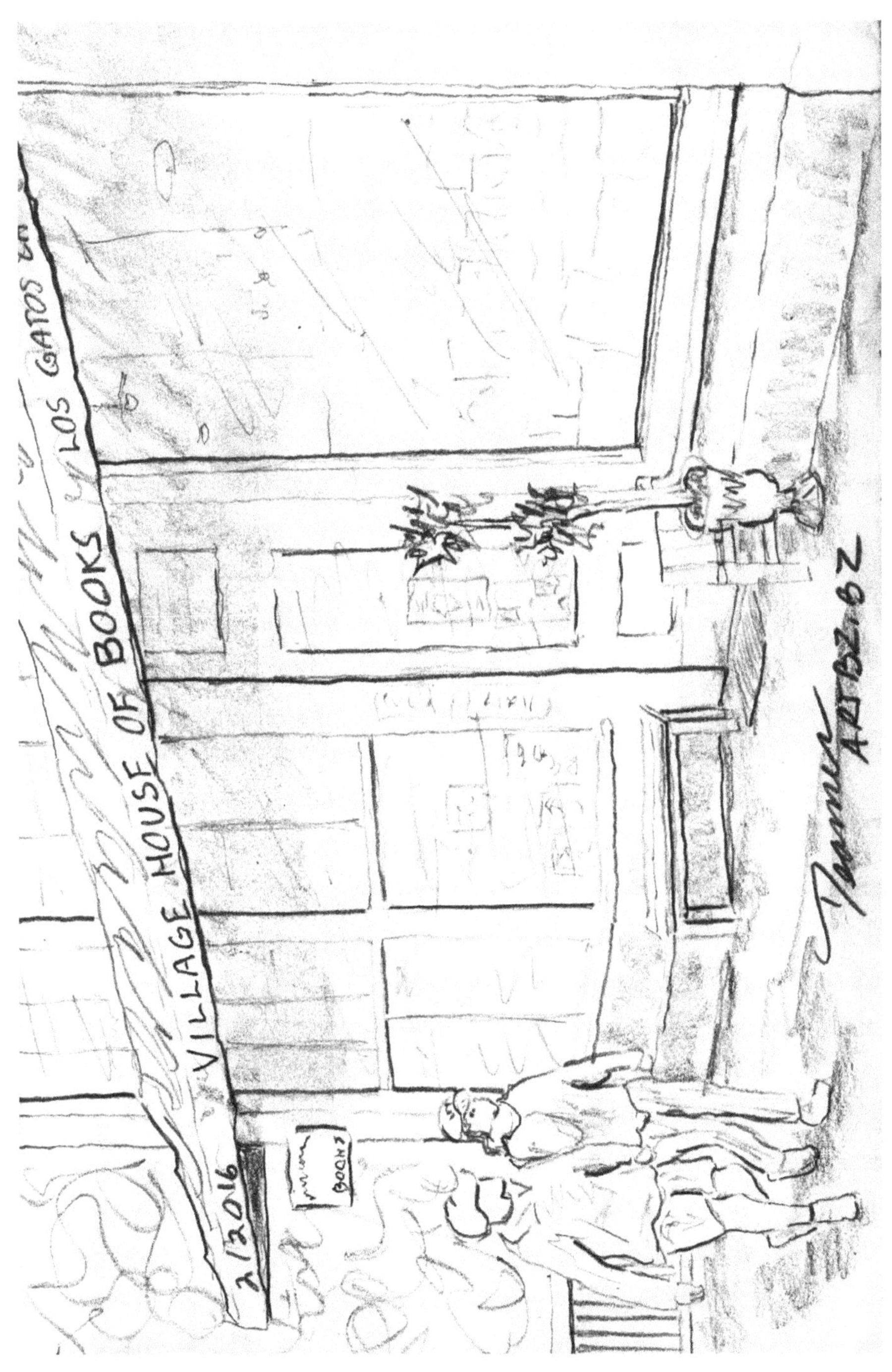
LOS GATOS
VILLAGE HOUSE OF BOOKS
BOOKS
2/30/16

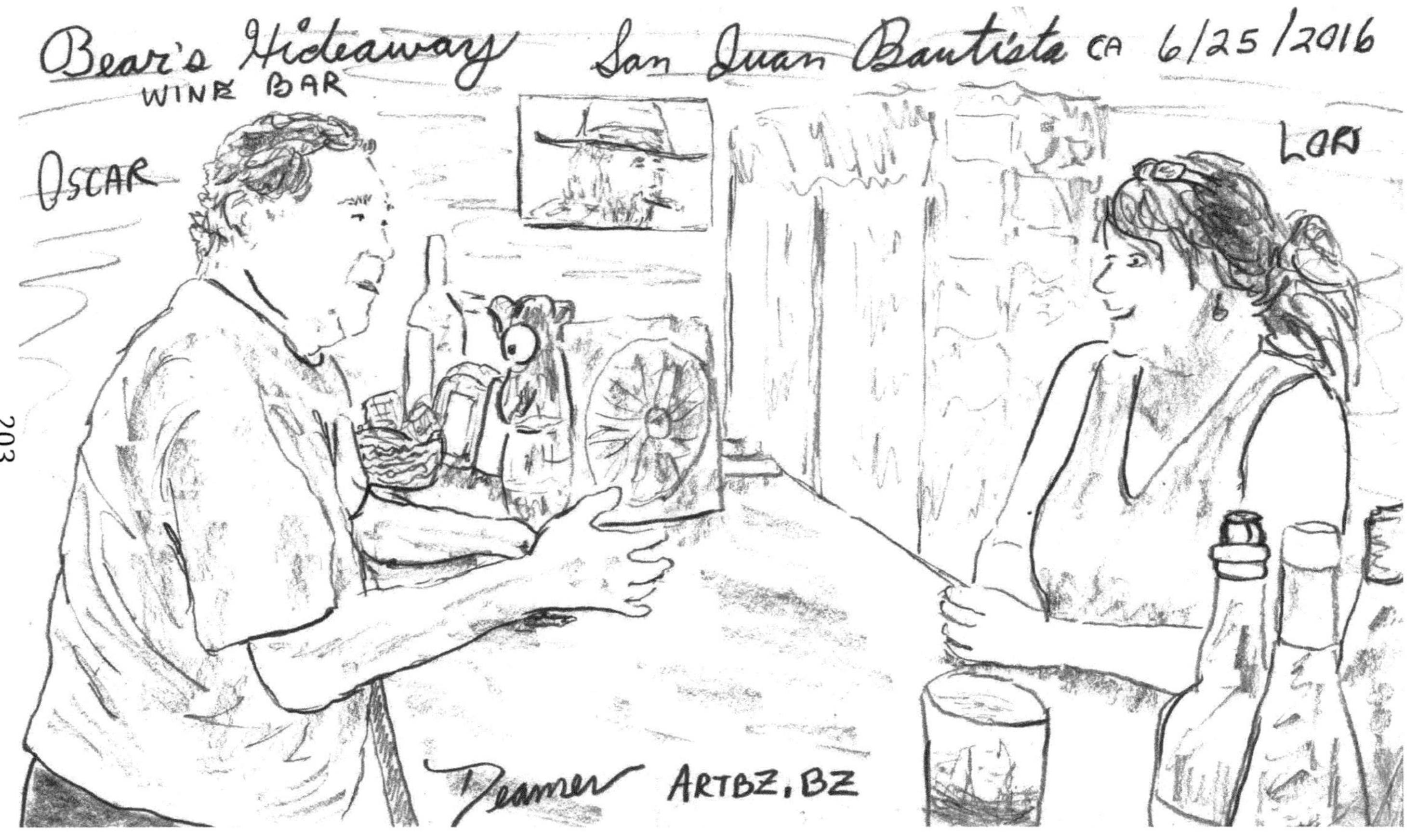

Bear's Hideaway
WINE BAR
San Juan Bautista CA 6/25/2016
OSCAR
LORI
Deamer ARTBZ.BZ

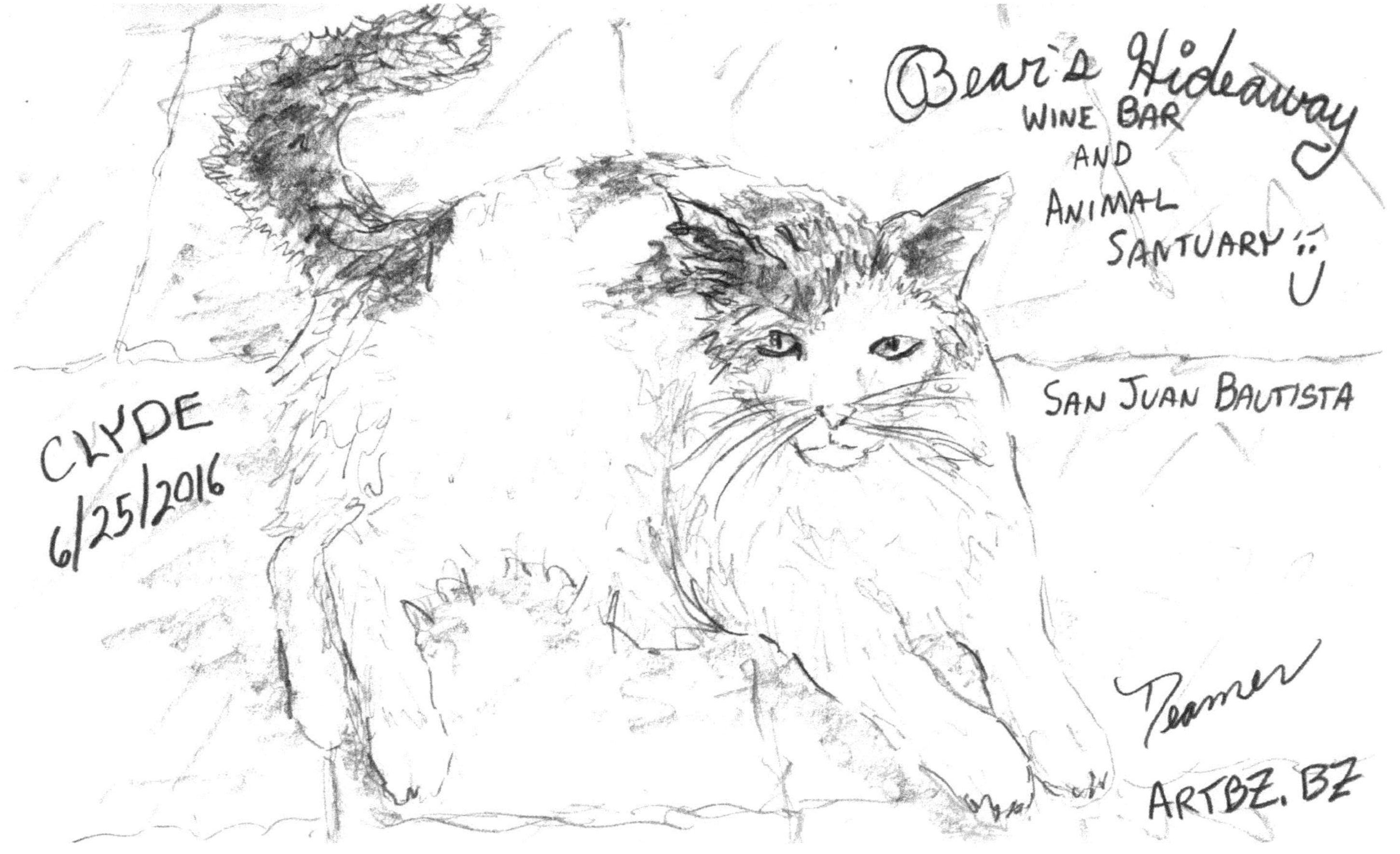
@Bear's Hideaway
WINE BAR
AND
ANIMAL
SANTUARY :)
San Juan Bautista
CLYDE
6/25/2016
Beamer
ARTBZ. BZ

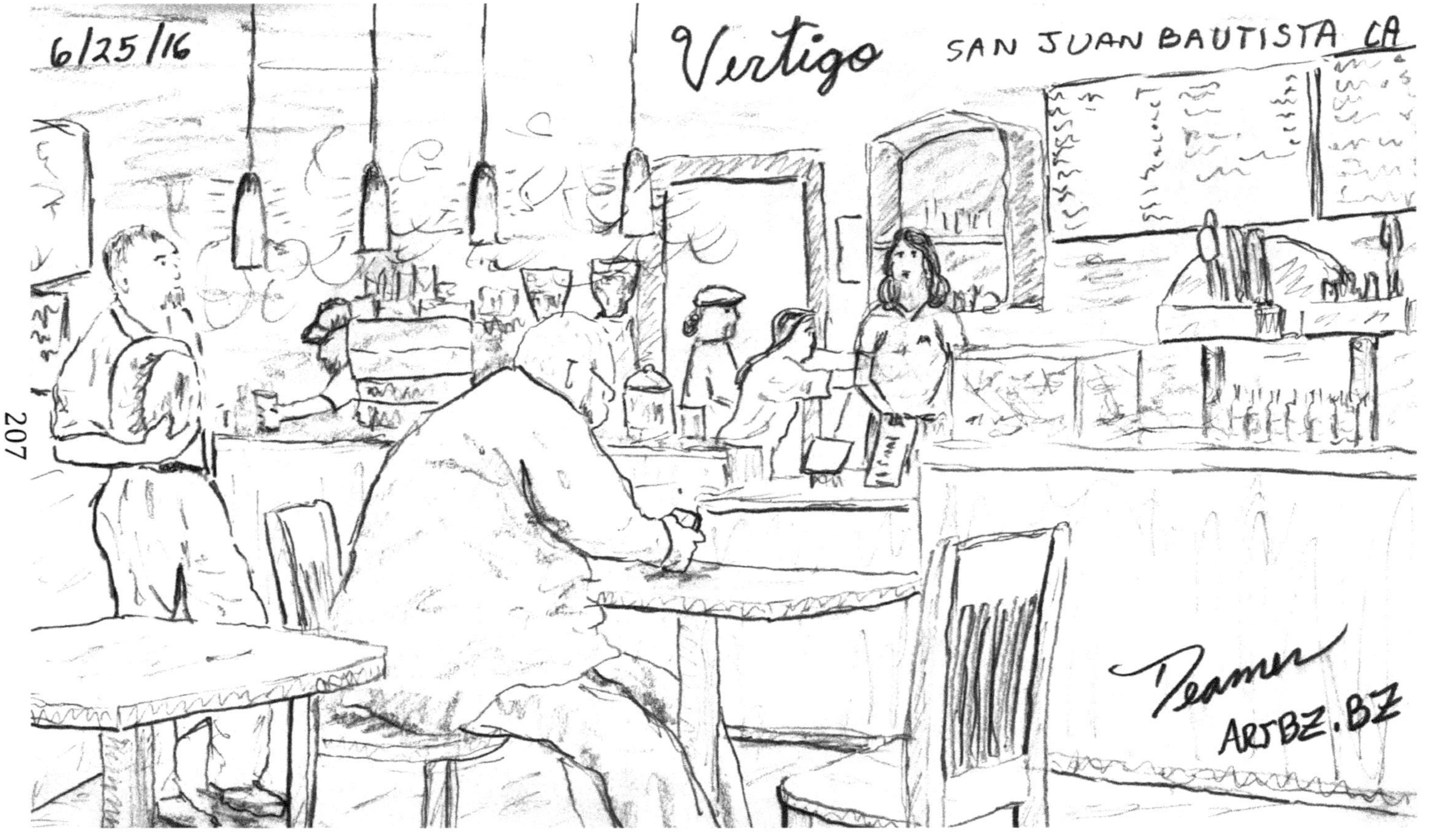
6/25/16
Vertigo   SAN JUAN BAUTISTA CA
Deamer
ARTBZ.BZ

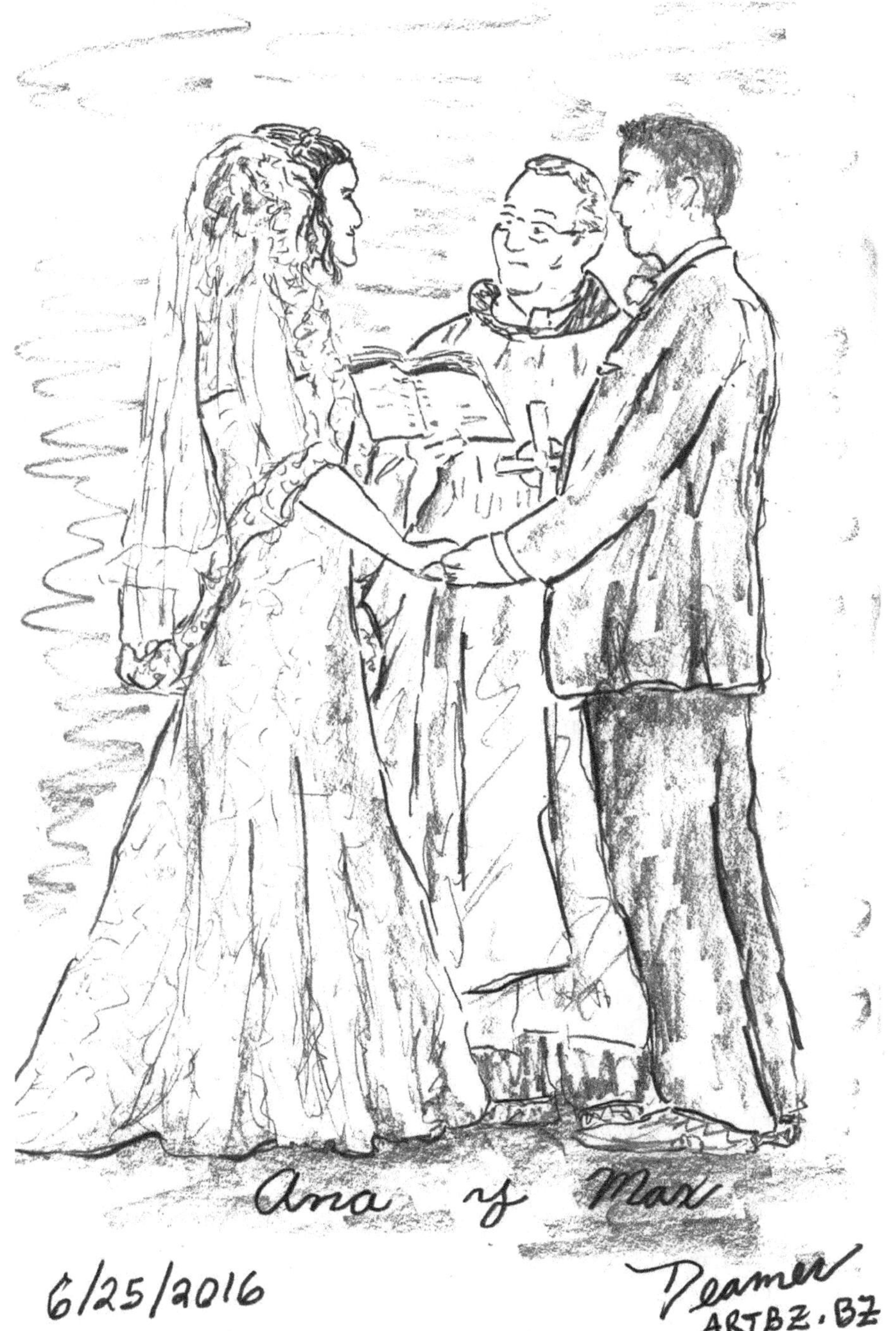

6/25/2016

Mission San Juan Bautista

Deamer Sketchbooks:

Sketches and Stories: Journal/Coloring Books for Adults

In case you haven't heard, coloring books for adults are becoming quite a passion. For many, perhaps a little coloring can still feed a passion for getting into a book and more easily allow the satisfaction of finishing something. Why settle for a computer created coloring book when you can add life to original sketches? Not only is this book designed to be fun as a coloring book, it is also laid out in a journal format. You can add comments and notes for your life or your own artistic doodles. Why settle for a blank book to keep track of life when you can associate your thoughts with an image? The idea is that this is a book that you can make your own. Also enjoy the original short stories included in each Deamer sketchbook.

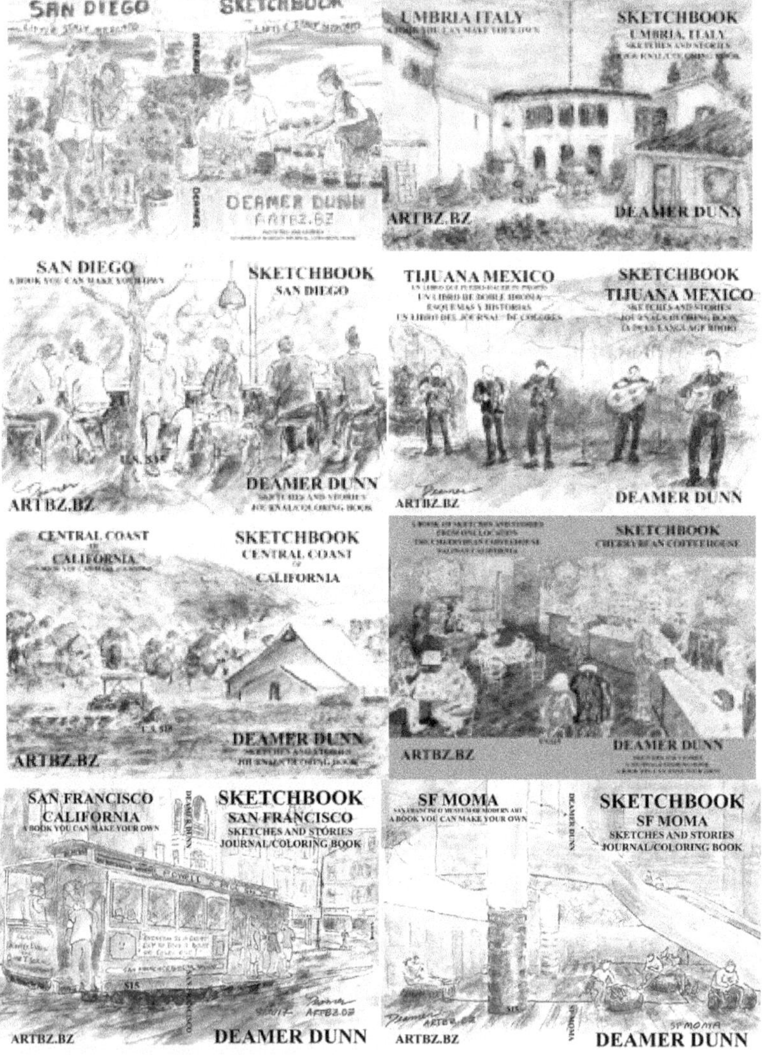

Novels by Deamer:

Pickup a Deamer novel online or from your local bookstore:
https://www.amazon.com/author/deamerdunn

STRENGTH AND GRACE

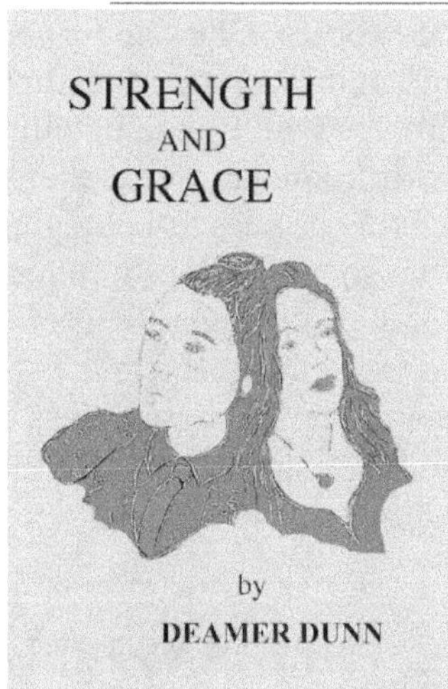

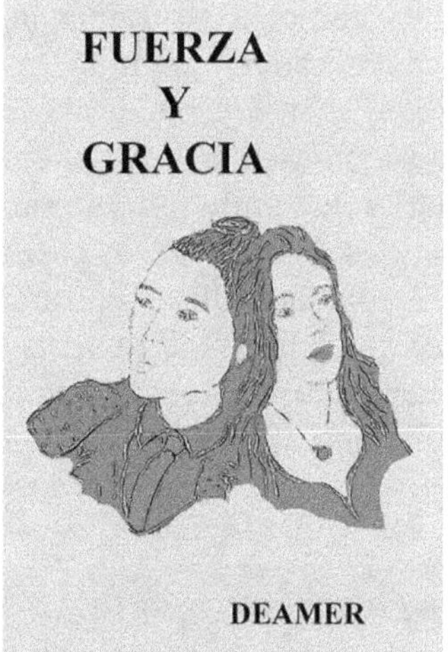

Winner, one of the best fiction novels of 2015,
Southern California Book Festival
Winner, one of the best fiction novels of 2015,
Great Midwest Book Festival

Strength and Grace is the story of a young Mexican woman who stumbles into becoming a bullfighter. She so excels that she becomes a great Matador. The catch is that all but a few think that she is a man. It is a story of female empowerment within the Mexican male culture of the bullfight. There are also coming of age aspects to the story as the reader follows her growth from being a fifteen-year old tomboy to a twenty-five year old woman who spends the majority of her time being a man. This duality creates identity issues that she must face along with all of the dangers of her profession and the tension of her masquerade.

Also available in Spanish:
FUERZA y GRACIA (Español)

MEETANDTELL.COM/ADVENTURE

Winner, one of best romance novels of 2016
Los Angeles Book Festival

What is more adventurous than looking for and starting a romantic relationship? Especially with all the new tools and avenues that the Internet has brought to the tips of our fingers. Clark and Ronda's generation began to date before there was a World Wide Web. As they are drawn inside this new magical world, they bring the perspective of experiencing dating before and after the Internet. Two friends in their forties, Clark and Ronda, take us along on their adventure to meet, start and incorporate relationships into their already mature lives. Clark alternates with Ronda in telling their first person accounts. The story opens with Ronda as a veteran online dater, while Clark reluctantly joins a practice that he sees as belonging to younger generations. What starts as casual fun soon develops into more serious adventure, romance, disappointment and even danger. In a reflection of our time of quick messages, tweets and texts, the chapters are short. They bounce back and forth from the male and female perspectives of Clark and Ronda. This is a story of two people in the timeless pursuit of love during a time of fascinating changes.

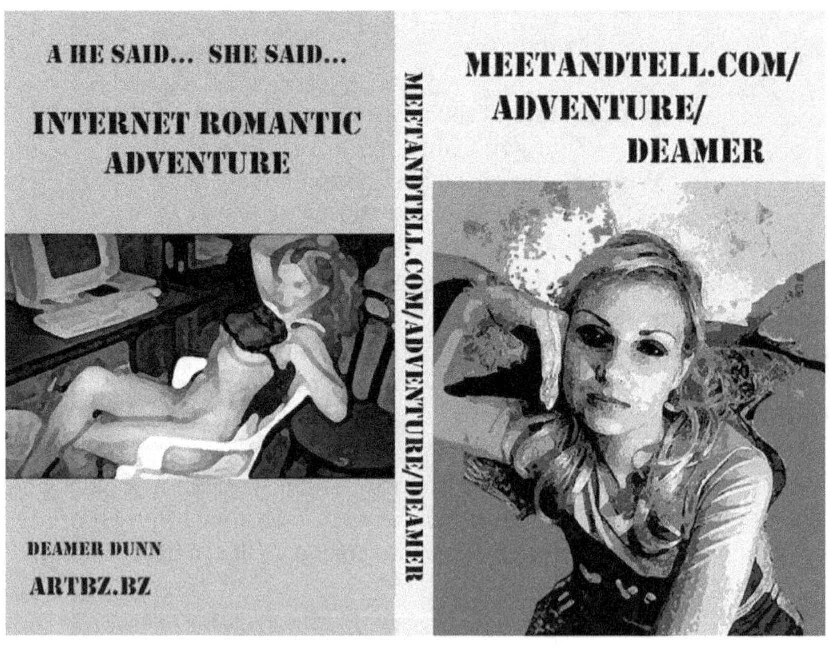

Omar T Series (Mystery "Lite")

In the tradition of a light-hearted contemporary mystery novel, enter the son of a restaurateur and an artist, Mr. Omar T Black. He is a jack-of-all-trades, master-of-none, with passions for women, food, adult beverages, art and adventure. Part travel book, part mystery, part literary reference, these stories are fun and culturally descriptive. Chef Omar enlightens readers to local cuisine with detailed descriptions and recipes. Art and literature aficionado Omar is drawn to the mysteries of creativity and thought. Omar T, the man, falls in love and/or lust, rather easily. Each book is an independent story—you do not need to read them in order. All Omar T novels carry a guarantee of lifting your spirits as well as feeding your appetite for good food and great living! This Mystery "Lite" series concentrates on intriguing instead of violence.

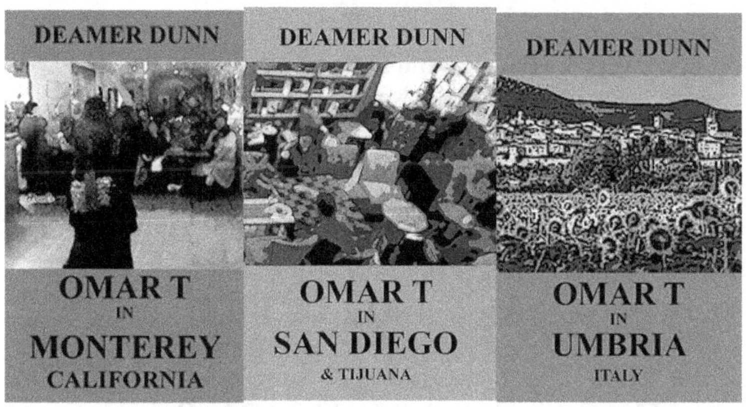

Omar T in Monterey California

Winner, one of the best fiction novels of 2016, San Francisco Book Fair
The first in the series focuses on Monterey California, home to Omar's family restaurant. The riches of Monterey are explored and enhanced with literary ties to Monterey's most acclaimed author, **John Steinbeck**. Omar sets out to find some mysteriously lost Dali drawings from the estate of Bruce Ariss, Dali's assistant for the creation of the 1941 "party of the century."

Omar T in San Diego and Tijuana

Readers are Omar's canvas as he takes us along on his San Diego and Tijuana adventures. They are fed by the insights of Dr. Seuss, the regions craft beer and food culture as well as each of these cities unique history.

Omar T in Umbria Italy

Omar's adventurous spirit is inspired by the revealing of a mysterious fresco as well as by a couple of very different Italian women and an Umbrian winery. Chapters are organized around each Umbria hilltown featured in this book. This allows easy reference as a guidebook for you actual or virtual Umbrian travelers.

OMAR T in SAN FRANCISCO

Omar gets entrenched in the former neighborhood of the "Beat Generation." In this adventure, Omar must deal with ghosts from the past of his life as well as those of the great "Beat" writers.

Coming Soon:

OMAR T in NEW YORK

The Beat writers and Omar continue a relationship as Omar moves to the Big Apple to help with the opening of a new restaurant in the Iconic Chelsea Hotel.

OMAR T in SALT LAKE CITY

Omar finds himself in the middle of a kidnapping as well as some interesting Mormon history and of course some great food.

And then: OMAR is off to PARIS, NEW ORLEANS, HONG KONG, SINGAPORE LAS VEGAS, ISTANBUL AND AFRICA

And then …

Also Coming from Pajaro Street Publishing:

UMBILICAL CORD co-author Tererai Trent African short stories

RM Blake EROTICA:

EROTIC REFLECTIONS

This book of erotica includes twenty-two stories, eleven told by a woman, eleven recalled by a man.

THE SEXUAL EDUCATION OF ZOE

AND

THE SEXUAL EDUCATION OF COLIN

These two companion novels mirror each other. Young Zoe approaches her favorite professor to help her further her education.

Colin, like Zoe is also from a difficult background. In this book, his much older professor of philosophy approaches her promising student with continuing his education in her bedroom.

RM Blake Love Song Journals Poignant stories of loss & love

Stephen and Linda

So many of us face addiction, obsession and a drive of compulsion. These drives can create beauty as well as destroy.

Joseph and Mickey

Love later in life can often be complicated. Relationships and history between each lover's families can put a strain on love.

About the Author/Artist

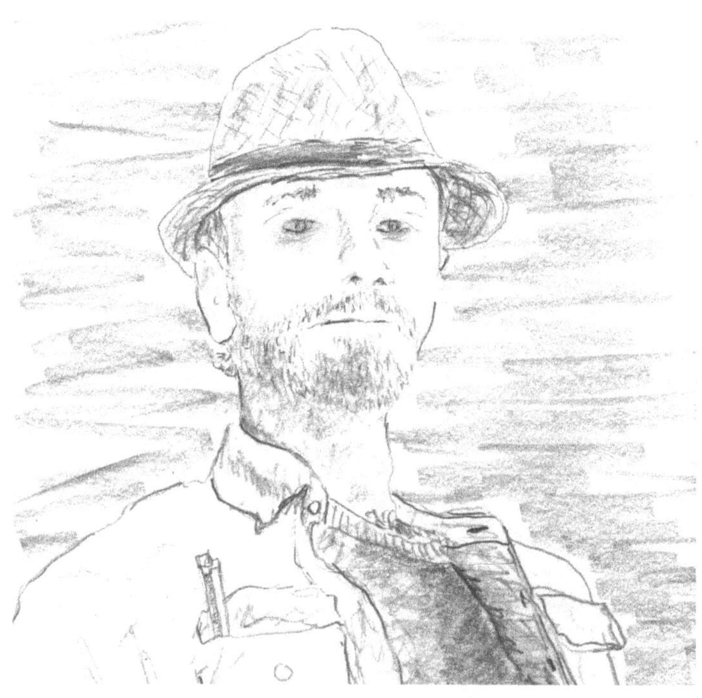

Deamer was born and raised in Salt Lake City, Utah. He lived in Switzerland and the Washington D.C. area before settling in Monterey County California in the early 1980's. He currently resides in the birth city of John Steinbeck, Salinas California, the former home of his dinner only restaurant, Pajaro Street Grill. Deamer now spends much of his time in Tijuana Mexico and traveling the world with his recurring character, Omar T Black. "I have a list of some thirty more locations I hope to write Omar adventures– come join the journey!

http://artbz.bz

"Everyday is a great day to read a book or color one!!!"

Keep in touch with Deamer, as Omar travels the world! deamer@artbz.bz Please pass on your impressions; write a review on Amazon and/or other sites such as Goodreads – your thoughts can really make a difference! Most your local bookstores can also get you Deamer novels at the same price as Amazon ☺
https://www.amazon.com/author/deamerdunn

www.ingramcontent.com/pod-product-compliance
Lightning Source LLC
Chambersburg PA
CBHW051447050726
47593CB00005B/1957